Women's HOME WORKOUT Bible

BRAD SCHOENFELD, CSCS, CPT

Human Kinetics

Library of Congress Cataloging-in-Publication Data

Schoenfeld, Brad, 1962-
 Women's home workout bible / Brad Schoenfeld.
     p. cm.
 Includes index.
 ISBN-13: 978-0-7360-7828-3 (soft cover)
 ISBN-10: 0-7360-7828-2 (soft cover)
 ISBN-13: 978-0-7360-8623-3 (Adobe PDF)
 ISBN-10: 0-7360-8623-3 (Adobe PDF)
 1. Physical fitness for women. 2. Bodybuilding for women. I. Title.
 GV482.S39 22009
 613.7'045--dc22

                                2009016092

ISBN-10: 0-7360-7828-2 (print)   ISBN-10: 0-7360-8623-3 (Adobe PDF)
ISBN-13: 978-0-7360-7828-3 (print)   ISBN-13: 978-0-7360-8623-3 (Adobe PDF)

This publication is written and published to provide accurate and authoritative information relevant to the subject matter presented. It is published and sold with the understanding that the author and publisher are not engaged in rendering legal, medical, or other professional services by reason of their authorship or publication of this work. If medical or other expert assistance is required, the services of a competent professional person should be sought.

Acquisitions Editor: Laurel Plotzke; **Developmental Editor:** Leigh Keylock; **Assistant Editor:** Laura Podeschi; **Copyeditor:** Joy Wotherspoon; **Indexer:** Betty Frizzéll; **Graphic Designer:** Robert Reuther; **Graphic Artist:** Francine Hamerski; **Cover Designer:** Keith Blomberg; **Photographer (cover):** Tetra Images/Corbis; **Photographers (interior):** Neil Bernstein and Jason Allen, unless otherwise noted; **Visual Production Assistant:** Joyce Brumfield; **Photo Production Manager:** Jason Allen; **Art Manager:** Kelly Hendren; **Associate Art Manager:** Alan L. Wilborn; **Illustrator:** Jennifer Gibas; **Printer:** Premier Print Group

Human Kinetics books are available at special discounts for bulk purchase. Special editions or book excerpts can also be created to specification. For details, contact the Special Sales Manager at Human Kinetics.

Printed in the United States of America   10 9 8 7 6 5 4 3 2 1

Human Kinetics
Web site: www.HumanKinetics.com

United States: Human Kinetics
P.O. Box 5076
Champaign, IL 61825-5076
800-747-4457
e-mail: humank@hkusa.com

Canada: Human Kinetics
475 Devonshire Road Unit 100
Windsor, ON N8Y 2L5
800-465-7301 (in Canada only)
e-mail: info@hkcanada.com

Europe: Human Kinetics
107 Bradford Road
Stanningley
Leeds LS28 6AT, United Kingdom
+44 (0) 113 255 5665
e-mail: hk@hkeurope.com

Australia: Human Kinetics
57A Price Avenue
Lower Mitcham, South Australia 5062
08 8372 0999
e-mail: info@hkaustralia.com

New Zealand: Human Kinetics
Division of Sports Distributors NZ Ltd.
P.O. Box 300 226 Albany
North Shore City
Auckland
0064 9 448 1207
e-mail: info@humankinetics.co.nz

E4657

*In loving memory of my father:
my mentor, my inspiration.*

Contents

Exercise Finder

Exercise	Page number	Single-joint exercise	Multijoint exercise	BUDGET			
				$100 US	$500 US	$1000 US	$2500+ US
SHOULDERS							
Arnold press with dumbbells	114		●		●	●	●
Arnold press with resistance band	26		●	●	●	●	●
Bent lateral raise with dumbbells	118	●			●	●	●
Bent lateral raise with resistance band	28	●		●	●	●	●
Front raise with barbell	132	●				●	●
Front raise with dumbbells	116	●			●	●	●
Kneeling bent lateral raise with cable	181	●					●
Lateral raise with dumbbells	117	●			●	●	●
Lateral raise with resistance band	27	●		●	●	●	●
Military press with barbell	129		●			●	●
One-arm lateral raise with cable	180	●					●
Pike press	22		●	●	●	●	●
Prone reverse fly with dumbbells	119	●			●	●	●
Shoulder press with cable	178		●				●
Shoulder press with dumbbells	113		●		●	●	●
Shoulder press with machine	177		●				●
Shoulder press with resistance band	25		●	●	●	●	●
Standing reverse fly with resistance band	29	●		●	●	●	●
Upright row with barbell	130		●			●	●
Upright row with cable	179		●				●
Upright row with dumbbells	115		●		●	●	●
Upright row with resistance band	24		●	●	●	●	●

Exercise	Page number	Single-joint exercise	Multijoint exercise	BUDGET			
				$100 US	$500 US	$1000 US	$2500+ US
ARMS							
21s with barbell	135	●				●	●
Arm curl with barbell	134	●				●	●
Arm curl with dumbbells	120	●			●	●	●
Arm curl with resistance band	30	●		●	●	●	●
Close-grip bench press with barbell	131	●				●	●
Concentration curl with dumbbells	123	●			●	●	●
Concentration curl with resistance band	32	●		●	●	●	●
Drag curl with barbell	137	●				●	●
Hammer curl with cable	182	●					●
Hammer curl with dumbbells	125	●			●	●	●
Hammer curl with resistance band	31	●		●	●	●	●
Incline curl with dumbbells	121	●			●	●	●
Lying triceps extension with dumbbells	127	●			●	●	●
Nose breaker with barbell	136	●				●	●
One-arm curl with cable	183	●					●
Overhead triceps extension with cable	184	●					●
Overhead triceps extension with dumbbells	126	●			●	●	●
Overhead triceps extension with resistance band	34	●		●	●	●	●
Preacher curl with barbell and stability ball	133	●				●	●
Preacher curl with dumbbells	122	●			●	●	●
Press-down with cable	185	●					●
Press-down with resistance band	33	●		●	●	●	●
Prone incline curl with dumbbells	124	●			●	●	●
Triceps dip	23		●	●	●	●	●
Triceps kickback with cable	186	●					●
Triceps kickback with dumbbells	128	●			●	●	●
Triceps kickback with resistance band	35	●		●	●	●	●

(continued)

Exercise	Page number	Single-joint exercise	Multijoint exercise	BUDGET			
				$100 US	$500 US	$1000 US	$2500+ US
CHEST							
Chest press with cable	188		●				●
Crossover fly with cable	189	●					●
Flat chest press with barbell	149		●			●	●
Flat chest press with dumbbells	142		●		●	●	●
Flat fly with dumbbells	143	●			●	●	●
Incline chest press with barbell	148		●			●	●
Incline chest press with dumbbells	141		●		●	●	●
Incline chest press with machine	187		●				●
Incline fly with dumbbells	144	●			●	●	●
Incline push-up	37		●	●	●	●	●
Push-up	36		●	●	●	●	●
Reverse push-up with stability ball	40		●	●	●	●	●
Standing chest press with resistance band	48		●	●	●	●	●
Standing fly with resistance band	50	●		●	●	●	●
Standing incline chest press with resistance band	49		●	●	●	●	●
Standing low fly with resistance band	51	●		●	●	●	●
BACK							
Chin-up	38		●	●	●	●	●
Front lat pull-down with machine	190		●				●
Incline row with barbell	146		●			●	●
Incline row with dumbbells	140		●		●	●	●
Lat pull-down with resistance band	44		●	●	●	●	●
Lying pullover with resistance band	47	●		●	●	●	●
One-arm low row with resistance band	45		●	●	●	●	●
One-arm row with dumbbells	139		●		●	●	●
Pullover with dumbbells	138	●			●	●	●
Pull-up	39		●	●	●	●	●
Prone lat pull with stability ball	41	●		●	●	●	●
Reverse bent row with barbell	147		●			●	●
Reverse low row with cable	193		●				●
Row with resistance band and stability ball	43		●	●	●	●	●
Seated row with cable	191		●				●

Exercise	Page number	Single-joint exercise	Multijoint exercise	BUDGET			
				$100 US	$500 US	$1000 US	$2500+ US
BACK *(continued)*							
Seated row with machine	192		●				●
Seated row with resistance band	42		●	●	●	●	●
Straight-arm pull-down with cable	194	●					●
Straight-arm pull-down with resistance band	46	●		●	●	●	●
T-bar row with barbell	145		●			●	●
CORE							
Bicycle crunch	53	●		●	●	●	●
Bird dog	56	●		●	●	●	●
Crunch	57	●		●	●	●	●
Crunch with stability ball	66	●		●	●	●	●
Hanging knee raise	64		●	●	●	●	●
Helicopter with stability ball	69	●		●	●	●	●
Horizontal woodchop with resistance band	73	●		●	●	●	●
Kneeling and twisting crunch with cable	196	●					●
Kneeling crunch with cable	195	●					●
Kneeling crunch with resistance band	74	●		●	●	●	●
Low-to-high woodchop with cable	198	●					●
Plank	61	●		●	●	●	●
Reverse crunch	58	●		●	●	●	●
Reverse hyperextension with stability ball	65	●		●	●	●	●
Reverse pendulum	60	●		●	●	●	●
Roll-out with barbell	151	●				●	●
Rotating crunch with stability ball	70	●		●	●	●	●
Russian twist with stability ball	71	●		●	●	●	●
Side bend with cable	197	●					●
Side bend with dumbbells	150	●			●	●	●
Side bridge	62	●		●	●	●	●
Side crunch with stability ball	67	●		●	●	●	●
Side jackknife	59	●		●	●	●	●
Superwoman	55		●	●	●	●	●
Toe touch	52	●		●	●	●	●
Twisting crunch	54	●		●	●	●	●

(continued)

Exercise	Page number	Single-joint exercise	Multijoint exercise	BUDGET			
				$100 US	$500 US	$1000 US	$2500+ US
FRONT OF THIGHS							
Back squat with barbell	162		●			●	●
Front squat with barbell	163		●			●	●
Hack squat with barbell	164		●			●	●
Leg extension with machine	200	●					●
Leg extension with resistance band	98	●		●	●	●	●
Leg extension with stability ball	94	●		●	●	●	●
Leg press with machine	199		●				●
Leg press with resistance band	97		●	●	●	●	●
Lunge	80		●	●	●	●	●
Lunge with barbell	166		●			●	●
Lunge with dumbbells	156		●		●	●	●
Lying adductor raise	88	●		●	●	●	●
One-leg squat	76		●	●	●	●	●
One-leg squat with dumbbells	153		●		●	●	●
Reverse lunge	81		●	●	●	●	●
Reverse lunge with barbell	167		●			●	●
Reverse lunge with dumbbells	157		●		●	●	●
Side lunge	82		●	●	●	●	●
Side lunge with dumbbells	158		●		●	●	●
Sissy squat	78	●		●	●	●	●
Split squat lunge	79		●	●	●	●	●
Split squat lunge with barbell	165		●			●	●
Split squat lunge with dumbbells	155		●		●	●	●
Split squat lunge with resistance band	96		●	●	●	●	●
Squat	75		●	●	●	●	●
Squat with dumbbells	152		●		●	●	●
Squat with resistance band	95		●	●	●	●	●
Standing adductor raise with cable	202	●					●
Standing adductor raise with resistance band	101	●		●	●	●	●
Step-up	83		●	●	●	●	●
Step-up with dumbbells	159		●		●	●	●

Exercise	Page number	Single-joint exercise	Multijoint exercise	BUDGET			
				$100 US	$500 US	$1000 US	$2500+ US
FRONT OF THIGHS *(continued)*							
Sumo squat	77		●	●	●	●	●
Sumo squat with dumbbells	154		●		●	●	●
BACK OF THIGHS AND GLUTES							
Bridge	63	●		●	●	●	●
Bridge with stability ball	72	●		●	●	●	●
Floor kick	84	●		●	●	●	●
Glute back kick with cable	204	●					●
Good morning with barbell	168	●				●	●
Hyperextension with stability ball	68	●		●	●	●	●
Leg curl with stability ball	93	●		●	●	●	●
Prone hip extension	85	●		●	●	●	●
Prone leg curl	87	●		●	●	●	●
Prone leg curl with machine	201	●					●
Prone one-leg curl with resistance band	99	●		●	●	●	●
Lying abductor raise	90	●		●	●	●	●
Standing abductor raise	89	●		●	●	●	●
Standing abductor raise with cable	203	●					●
Standing abductor raise with resistance band	100	●		●	●	●	●
Standing leg curl	86	●		●	●	●	●
Stiff-legged deadlift with barbell	169	●				●	●
CALVES							
Bent-knee toe press with resistance band	103	●		●	●	●	●
Seated calf raise	92	●		●	●	●	●
Seated calf raise with dumbbells	161	●			●	●	●
Standing calf raise	91	●		●	●	●	●
Standing calf raise with dumbbells	160	●			●	●	●
Standing calf raise with resistance band	102	●		●	●	●	●
Toe press with machine	205	●					●
Toe press with resistance band	104	●		●	●	●	●

Acknowledgments

To my longtime agent, Bob Silverstein, who found the proper home for this book. It's been a great run!

To Jason Muzinic, who saw the potential in this project and ensured the allocation of resources necessary for success.

To Laurel Plotzke, who worked to bring the book to fruition. Your insights and recommendations throughout the course of production proved invaluable for making this a definitive resource.

To Leigh Keylock, who developed the project and took it to a higher level. It was a true pleasure working with you!

To my mom, who always supported my dreams. You've always been there for me. I love you more than I can express.

To Janet DeRico, Zara Young, Alisha Hale, and Petal Modeste, who always smiled through the grind of long photo sessions. You are the essence of professionalism!

To Fred Hoag at Inspire Fitness. You guys make the best multifunction machines on the market!

To Mark Walsh and BJ Lathan at State of the Art Fitness, who opened up their fine facility for the photo shoot. Your hospitality was greatly appreciated!

To Buddy Lee, the guru of jumping rope. The quality of your jump ropes is unmatched.

Finally, to Human Kinetics, the best publisher of sports and fitness books, hands down!

Introduction

It's 6 p.m. and you've just come home from a hard day's work. You're tired and hungry, and it's raining harder than Noah himself ever could have fathomed. But you've made a commitment to start a new workout program and get into shape once and for all. No two ways about it, you have to haul your butt into the gym . . . now!

So, you throw on some sweats, lug the kids into the car, and endure the 15-minute drive to your neighborhood health club, getting soaked as you make the 100-yard dash from the overcrowded parking lot to the front desk. By the time you finish checking the kids into child care and putting your stuff away in the locker room, it's pushing 7 o'clock. You make your way onto the congested gym floor only to find that all the machines you want to use are taken. You consider entering the free-weight area, but a couple of meatheads are pressing dumbbells the size of ship anchors and grunting like they're giving birth. Scratch that idea.

So, you wait . . . and wait. An hour and a half later, you finally finish your last set of the evening. You grab the kids (who won't stop complaining about how bored they've been), pay the babysitting fee, and again brave the drenching rain on the trek back to your car. When you finally arrive home, your husband is grumbling that he had to make himself a TV dinner. By this point, all you want to do is take an aspirin and hit the sack.

Although this example may seem a bit melodramatic, at some point, everyone who has fitness goals faces the hassles associated with training in a facility. For many women, it's enough of a turnoff to derail their workout programs. But things don't have to be this way.

What if you could simply amble into your basement or den and blast through a quick workout while little Tommy does his homework and Jen practices her violin? You could wear whatever you want, without any obligation to put on makeup or fix your hair, and you could listen to whatever music your heart desires. After you'd finished sweating up a storm, you could shower in the privacy of your own bathroom with your own toiletries and fluffy towels. No driving in inclement weather. No waiting for machines. No worrying about contracting a fungus from unsanitary equipment. No crass pickup lines. No judgments of catty members. Sound good?

Welcome to the wonderful world of home-gym ownership. The benefits of having your very own gym at home can be summarized in one word: freedom. You're free to do what you want, when you want, and how you want. Of course, you're also free from paying those hefty membership dues that can run as high as thousands of dollars per year. One popular facility in New York City charges over $5,000 annually, not including towel service! Considering that a basic home gym can be put together for a fraction of this price, the potential savings are huge, especially over the long term.

If you're convinced that a home gym is right for you, this book is the perfect resource for guiding you through every step of the process. Over the past two decades, I have helped countless women customize home gyms and have shown them how to utilize the equipment to best achieve their fitness goals. In the pages that follow, I'll do the same for you. Whether you're starting from scratch, expanding an existing home gym, or simply looking to make better use of the equipment you have, this book will show you how.

Chapters 1 and 2 take you through the all-important first steps of setting up a home gym; namely, how to purchase equipment that matches your space and budget. You'll gain insight into how to choose an exercise room, how to maximize the use of your space, and how to spruce up your training area for optimum comfort and inspiration. Next, you'll learn the keys to researching equipment vendors, where to go when you're ready to buy, and some tried-and-true tricks for getting the best bang for your buck.

Chapters 3 through 7 cover equipment and exercises for strength training, cardio, and flexibility. Far too many women purchase expensive equipment that doesn't suit their needs. Ultimately, they end up trading it in or selling it for far less than they paid. The information in these chapters will help you avoid this problem. I'll show you what to look for in virtually every imaginable type of fitness product, highlighting the inherent advantages and drawbacks of each, as well as recommending which pieces are necessary and which are optional. Each chapter concludes with detailed descriptions of dozens of home-based exercises that are categorized into muscle groups for easy reference.

Chapter 8 provides the fundamental tools for using your equipment to its fullest potential. You will learn how to set fitness goals that keep you motivated, and you'll explore the Ten Commandments of Fitness. These guidelines are crucial to achieving your goals. This chapter is a must-read if you expect to optimize your training results.

Chapters 9 through 12 explore the subject of training with customized routines that target popular fitness goals by suggesting exercises, sets, repetitions, and intensity levels. Routines are provided for four different budgets, allowing you to enjoy a terrific workout whether you have minimal equipment or a fully stocked home gym. The chapters also provide expert tips for long-term training that will help you sustain results and continue to progress.

In summary, this book provides a complete blueprint for creating the ultimate workout experience at home. Follow the advice outlined herein and you'll have the knowledge and wherewithal to build a personalized gym for years of lasting pleasure, as well as a fit and healthy body. I'll stake my reputation on it.

PART I

Space, Budget, and Setup

Claim Your Workout Space

The fact that you've picked up this book indicates that you're serious about customizing a home gym and starting your workout program. If so, great. Enthusiasm goes a long way toward fitness success. However, before you plunk down your hard-earned money for any equipment, a little homework is in order.

All too often, people create home gyms on impulse. They buy a few dumbbells or purchase a high-tech exercise gizmo from an ad on late-night television, and then expect to sculpt the body of their dreams with a hastily conceived routine. Unfortunately, this scenario is not likely to bring about desired results. To do things right, you need a plan of action. Begin by deciding where to set up shop.

Although space undoubtedly limits the type and quantity of equipment you can buy, it's not a make-or-break consideration. I've helped women turn rooms not much larger than walk-in closets into fully functional home gyms, and I'll show you how to do the same. In the following chapters, you'll learn how to maximize your space by choosing space-saving equipment, such as selectorized dumbbells and folding cardio equipment, and using household items as fitness implements. As you'll see, you can achieve a sufficient workout with even a bare-bones setup in the corner of your den or basement.

That being said, you can reap significant rewards by allocating just a little more space for your gym. Ask yourself the following questions to assess the best use of your space for your needs:

- *How much space are you willing (or able) to devote for a gym?* The fact remains that the more space you have, the greater your options for equipment will be. If you have your mind set on purchasing a particular unit, make sure you have the space necessary to house it. For example, a multistation resistance machine can take up an entire 12-by-12-foot (4-by-4-m) room. If you're unwilling to devote a room of this size to fitness, then you should cross the multistation unit off your wish list. What's more, if you're not able to leave equipment set up, make sure you purchase equipment that can be broken down and stored after each workout.

▪ *What is the flow of traffic?* Your workout time is your own. Try to keep it that way. Choose an area that's free of distractions. Make every effort to avoid setting up your gym in a spot where the kids run around playing hide-and-seek or your hubby kicks back in front of the TV with a cold one. Trust me, these places will both prevent you from getting a good workout and make you stressed-out and on edge—not a good way to finish an exercise session. Safety issues can also arise if children have unfettered access to a room filled with equipment. Make sure to childproof the equipment or restrict access to the area when you're not around. You don't want to tempt fate on this issue.

▪ *Does the room have adequate ventilation and insulation?* Working out in a room that is overly hot or humid saps your strength and energy, impairing the quality of your workout. In extreme cases, you can fall victim to heat stroke or perhaps even pass out. Don't take chances. Make sure the area is ventilated well. At the very least, place a large fan in the room to circulate stagnant air and keep the room somewhat cool. Air-conditioning is a big plus. If you don't have central AC, consider a room unit. Some do not even require window space. Just make sure your power outlets can support the unit's electrical requirements. The room should also be properly heated during frigid winter months; you shouldn't have to wear a parka, gloves, and earmuffs to get through a training session. Extreme cold impairs adequate circulation and exercise performance. If you plan to convert an unfinished basement, attic, or garage, you'll probably need to insulate the ceilings and walls. Baseboard heating is your best bet, but you can also use space heaters. If you choose to set up shop in your basement, make sure the area is free of mold and mildew. Not only is the smell tough to take during an intense workout, but molds sometimes contain toxins that negatively impact your health and well-being.

Bearing in mind your answers to these questions, give some thought to the layout of your house or apartment and decide which area might be best suited for your gym. If you live in a cramped studio loft, you won't have many options, but if you have a condo or house, you very well might have a variety of choices. Be creative. Think outside of the box. If your basement is cluttered with junk you never use, consider having a yard sale to free up some space. Who knows—you might even make enough money from the sale to purchase some of your home-gym equipment! If you park your car in the garage, consider moving it onto the street or driveway. A little ingenuity goes a long way.

Size It Up

Once you've chosen a workout space, get out your trusty tape measure—one that's long enough to span the entire area—and figure out precisely what you have to work with. Start by measuring the length and width of the space. For a good visual aid, draw the area to scale on a sheet of graph paper. If you have any furniture that can't be moved, include its image in the schematic. Factor in any nooks and crannies that influence the amount of usable space. A small alcove that extends a couple extra feet can provide the perfect opportunity for an additional piece of equipment. On the other hand, the presence of a protruding support beam might prevent you from making the same purchase. Account for every aspect of the space and be as exact as possible. Small discrepancies can lead to miscalculations and big headaches.

If you plan to purchase cardio equipment or a multifunction gym, you should also measure the height of the room. Many basements and attics have ceilings that are too low for certain units. Don't forget about doorways and stairwells. The last thing you want to discover after making a significant purchase is that it doesn't fit through your front door or up the spiral staircase to your den.

Got it? Good. Measurements in hand, you're ready to see if your designated space will accommodate the equipment you plan to purchase. Don't try to cram the room with equipment. The general rule is that you should have roughly the same amount of free space as occupied space in the room. Table 1.1 estimates the space requirements for different types of fitness equipment. Use it as a guide, but keep in mind that the dimensions of equipment vary for different brands and models.

When you start deciding where to place your equipment, try to let go of any preconceived notions. Experiment with different scenarios. Sometimes rearranging different pieces allows you to fit more equipment into a space. Just make sure you leave enough room around the perimeter so that you can easily move around and access the equipment.

You must plan how to fit large machines like multifunction units into your space.
Photo courtesy of Body-Solid, Inc.

If you can't seem to make things fit but don't want to scale back your vision, remember my previous tip on getting creative. Consider putting equipment in different rooms. You might, for instance, keep your weights in the den, your treadmill in the basement, and your multistation unit in the garage. Or you could opt to go portable and buy equipment that can be stashed in a closet or under the bed. Where there's a will, there's usually a way.

TABLE 1.1

Estimated Space Requirements for Exercise Equipment

Equipment		Space required
Free weights	Barbells	50-75 sq ft (15-23 sq m)
	Dumbbells	20-50 sq ft (6-15 sq m)
Treadmill		30 sq ft (9 sq m)
Ski machine		20-30 sq ft (6-9 sq m)
Elliptical trainer		20-30 sq ft (6-9 sq m)
Rowing machine		15-20 sq ft (5-6 sq m)
Stationary bike		10 sq ft (3 sq m)
Stair climber		5-10 sq ft (1.5-3 sq m)
Multifunction gym with multiple stations		50-250 sq ft (15-76 sq m)
Multifunction gym with a single station		30 sq ft (9 sq m)

Dress It Up

Okay, things are shaping up. You've picked out the ideal spot—one that is big enough for all your desired equipment, is properly insulated and ventilated, and is located away from disturbances. Fantastic! Now, you need to make the space as comfortable and as aesthetically pleasing as possible. This isn't just for show. A dingy garage or basement won't inspire you to work out. You might not care at first, but you'll probably begin to dread the dungeonlike atmosphere as time goes on. You will enjoy your training less, and both your performance and adherence will likely suffer. In the end, the atmosphere of a fitness space can determine whether or not you stick with your workout regimen.

The good news is that it doesn't take much to create a cozy training environment. It's amazing what a little paint or wallpaper can do to spruce up a drab room. Bright colors are generally best; they've been shown to elevate mood. Place a couple of floor lamps or some track lighting to enhance the ambience. Hang some inspirational photos or prints on the walls, such as photos of women with physiques that you admire or motivational sayings about fitness. Add a plant or two to give the room some life, and you're on your way.

It's time for a few final touches. Consider adding the following accoutrements to improve the functionality of your home gym:

■ *Mirrors.* Mirrors are invaluable tools for monitoring form. Full-length, wall-to-wall mirrors work best. They allow you to view your entire body from every angle and to observe inconsistencies in exercise technique. However, most people find it impractical to mirror all their walls. No problem. One or two strategically placed mirrors will do just fine. Just be careful when training with free weights. Mirrors break easily. Turn the wrong way with a barbell on your back and—*crack!*—seven years of bad luck!

■ *Music.* There is no doubt that music can pump up both your spirits and your workouts. Research has shown that people perform better when listening to their favorite tunes. Music helps stimulate your brain, putting you "in the zone" to train your best. Although some people spend big bucks on music systems, your gym doesn't need professionally installed hi-fi equipment to be inspirational. Stick a portable stereo, radio, or CD player on a shelf, and you're in business. MP3 players are viable options, too, but be careful with the headphones during resistance training. The cord can get in the way of your lifts, hampering your workout and potentially causing an injury.

■ *Video.* Televisions and DVD players are excellent additions to any home gym. When slaving away on the treadmill or an elliptical trainer, the time seems to pass a lot faster if you're watching your favorite movie or TV show. Between sets of resistance training, you can catch up on news items, get updates on the stock market, or perhaps pick up a few cooking tips. Advances in technology have made it easy to fit a TV almost anywhere. Flat panel screens can be positioned on any wall, hung from the ceiling, or even mounted on exercise equipment. Once you've chosen the best angle for viewing, you should have no problem accommodating your needs.

■ *Floor mats.* If you care about the quality of your floors, consider purchasing rubberized mats for areas where you'll be using weights. Dumbbells, barbells, and other weighted implements can wreak havoc on hardwood flooring and tile, no matter how careful you are. Mats are an inexpensive insurance policy against irreparable damage. Better to be safe than sorry.

Exercise Room Checklist

Your ideal workout space should have the following qualities:

- Adequate ventilation
- Proper insulation
- Low humidity
- Room for as much open space as equipment
- Seclusion from disturbances
- An inspirational ambience

The Everywoman Budget and Setup

2

You've picked out the perfect spot for your home gym and have decided exactly how to furnish it. So far, so good. Time to run out to the store and buy some equipment, right? Wrong! In order to purchase equipment intelligently, you must first establish a budget. Start by asking yourself the following two questions: 1) How much money am I willing and able to spend on a home gym? 2) How much money do I need to spend to get a satisfactory workout?

The first question is purely monetary. Evaluate your checking account, credit line, purse, piggy bank, and any other sources of funding you might be able to tap into (now's the time to ring that ultra-rich uncle for a loan!). Add it all up and then decide how much of the total you're prepared to commit to a gym. If your finances are limited, it's a safe bet you can forget about that high-end treadmill or the multifunction apparatus with cable pulleys for now. That's okay. You can build your gym gradually. In fact, advances in technology continue to improve the quality and reduce the prices of equipment. Chances are that you'll be able to buy a better unit for less money in the not-too-distant future.

If you really want a specific piece of equipment, don't settle for a cheap alternative. You'll be unhappy with performance and chances are it'll break down after just a few months of use. Instead, save up for the real thing. Earmark the money you would have otherwise spent on membership dues at the local health club. Forgo that double latte you have every morning at your favorite coffeehouse. You'll be surprised by how quickly these small sacrifices can add up to big savings.

The second question reconciles your fitness goals and your financial resources. Even if you are flush with cash, you shouldn't throw it away on unnecessary equipment that takes up valuable space in your home. For example, if your goal is to improve balance and coordination, you don't need a multifunction gym (see chapter 6 for a full explanation). If you're creating a gym to supplement a health-club membership, you could probably get by with a no-frills setup just to carry you over between workouts. Either way, you've slashed a couple of grand from your budget. When in doubt, start out slow. Buy only the most necessary pieces. You can always add to your collection as you go along.

Budgets for Every Body

First, the good news: You don't need to spend a fortune on a home gym. No matter what your budget is, you can build a gym that suits your needs. Now for the caveat: The less money you have, the more savvy you need to be in making your purchases.

The key to getting the best value for your money is to prioritize. If your financial resources are limited, focus on obtaining equipment for resistance training first. The reason is simple: A good resistance-training workout is more dependent on equipment than a cardio workout. Although you can do resistance training using only your body weight, results will be compromised. Once you've satisfied these requirements, if there's anything left in your budget, you can shift your attention to buying a cardio unit.

To guide you in your efforts, I've designed four categories with exercises and equipment for different budgets. As the budgets increase in each successive category, so does the amount of equipment. Thus, the $500 budget includes exercises from the $100 budget, and the $1,000 budget includes exercises from both the $100 and $500 budgets. To emphasize the importance of first acquiring the necessary tools for resistance training, I have not included cardio equipment in any of the budgets. If your finances allow, add the cardio equipment afterward. Otherwise, see chapter 6 for innovative ways to get a good cardio workout with little or no equipment. Note: All amounts for budgets and equipment in this book are given in U.S. dollars.

- *Budget of up to $100.* Don't have a lot of disposable income? No problem. You can perform a myriad of exercises by using your body weight, a stability ball, a chinning bar, leg weights, and a set of resistance bands. Total cost: less than a hundred bucks. Further offset your expenditures by using ordinary household items to supplement your routine. See chapter 3 for a complete discussion.

- *Budget of up to $500.* By increasing your budget to around $500, you can add a high-quality bench and some dumbbells to the mix. The additional expense comes out to less than a year of membership at most health clubs. If you can possibly commit the funds, it's an investment worth making. Chapter 4 delves into this topic in detail.

- *Budget of up to $1,000.* An expenditure of approximately one grand gets you a fairly well-stocked home gym. In addition to the equipment in the previous budget, the extra cash allows you to add barbells and an upgraded bench with a power rack. You'll have a nice little setup with lots of possibilities for varying your routine. The second half of chapter 4 covers all the specifics.

- *Budget of $2,500 or more.* When you invest $2,500 or more, you're into the big time as far as home gyms are concerned. The major purchase here is a multifunction resistance unit with a cable apparatus. This piece, when combined with the other home equipment, comes closest to simulating the health-club experience. All that's missing is the masseuse and the personal trainer. Chapter 5 provides a complete overview of what's important when considering machines.

From Budgeting to Buying

Once you've figured out your budget, turn your attention to equipment specifics. Part II of this book covers everything you need to know to make an informed decision, including the advantages and disadvantages of each modality and what to look for in a unit.

The one thing I can't do is to tell you which brand to buy. There are dozens upon dozens of companies that manufacture fitness equipment. You are the only one who can evaluate the personal factors that come into play. You can make the selection process easier, however, by taking a systematic approach.

The first step in the process is to power up your computer and activate your Web browser. If you don't own a computer, use the one at your local library. Although you might not end up purchasing equipment on the Internet, you should start your search online. Begin by looking for sites that provide unbiased information on the type of equipment you're looking for. For example, my Web site has a wealth of information on this topic. Check out the offerings in your price range and examine the differences between products. You can find the same information online that you would learn in a store, including specifics and reviews. Research with diligence, comparing as many brands and models as possible.

Keep in mind that you generally get what you pay for. Common sense should dictate that you're not going to find a high-end treadmill or cable apparatus for $200. Quality equipment cannot be produced for such an insanely low price. That said, the most expensive products don't always provide the best value for your money. Manufacturers that spend big bucks on advertising and celebrity endorsements usually pass these costs on to the consumer. You can often find cheaper units of comparable or even better quality from companies that maintain a lower profile. Shop around and you're bound to come up with competitive alternatives.

Once you've honed in on a product that fits your needs, you must then decide whether to purchase it from a Web site or from your local sporting-goods store. Although each supplier has its merits, here are some things to consider.

Internet

Perhaps the best thing about purchasing on the Internet is that it's quick and easy. No high-pressured sales tactics, no waiting in lines, no lugging heavy boxes to and from your car. Just sit back in your chair, pick out the unit you want, make a few clicks with the mouse, and you're done; the equipment shows up at your door several days later.

You often can save money purchasing on the Net—a result of low overhead. Internet sites don't have to pay rent for a storefront or employ salespeople. Theoretically, this allows them to pass these savings on to you, the consumer, in the form of lower prices. In some cases, you might not even have to pay a sales tax. This can be a significant amount, depending on where you live and what you purchase. However, not all e-tailers offer savings to the consumer; some simply pocket the difference. It pays to be an educated consumer, literally.

Smart Internet Shopping

The Internet can be an invaluable shopping tool if you understand how to use it properly. For a hassle-free experience, heed the following recommendations:

- *Buy only from reputable Web sites.* Anyone can become an e-tailer for 10 bucks or less—that's the going rate for a domain name these days. Unscrupulous rip-off artists take advantage of cheap domain names to perpetrate an array of devious scams. Horror stories abound about merchandise that never arrives or defective products that don't work. Don't let this happen to you. Whenever possible, buy from known Web sites or those recommended by people you trust. Check for a phone number and call to make sure the Web site is legitimate. Consult a watchdog site to find store ratings for thousands of e-tail establishments and gain valuable insight into the business practices of a particular site.

- *Factor in shipping costs.* Some sites charge for shipping, and others don't. Make sure you take these fees into account. A savings of $100 on a particular unit can be obliterated if it costs twice that amount to ship it. It's the total price that counts, not the unit price.

- *Buy securely.* When you buy online, you give sensitive personal information to someone you don't know. To make sure this information stays private, look for sites that have encrypted shopping carts (usually designated by a padlock at the bottom of the payment screen). If possible, pay by credit card rather than debit card. This practice limits your liability if anything goes wrong.

- *Make sure the site has a consumer-friendly return policy.* If the equipment you receive is different from what was advertised or is damaged in any way, you should be able to return it for a full refund within a given period of time. Check out your obligations for return shipping—often, the merchant will not cover this cost. Also, make sure there isn't a restocking fee. Some sites tack on a hefty surcharge for returns, but it shouldn't be your burden. Print out a copy of the company's policies for your records; it may come in handy in the future should any disputes arise.

The biggest downside to buying fitness equipment from a Web site is that you can't try a product out before you buy it. This generally isn't much of an issue for products that don't rely on mechanics or electronics. You can usually buy dumbbells, barbells, resistance bands, stability balls, and other similar products sight unseen if you've done your research.

Cardio equipment and multistation gyms are another matter. Just as you wouldn't buy a dress without trying it on, you shouldn't buy any product that has mechanical or electronic components without testing it in person. Exercise machines are often designed to fit certain body types. If you're tall, short, heavy, thin, big-boned, or small-boned, the unit might not accommodate your individual shape. The feel of the equipment is also very important. A unit that feels smooth and steady to one person may feel clumsy to another. The only way you can know for sure whether a unit works for you is to check it out yourself.

Retail Stores

Your local sporting-goods store should be happy to let you try out any product in stock. Although you could simply test out a product in the store and then purchase it on the Internet, this decision might not be in your best interest. One advantage of buying in person is that employees from a local store are more likely to set up your equipment so that it runs properly. This is no small issue. Many units come unassembled, which may cost you hours of time and aggravation.

Smart Brick-and-Mortar Shopping

Purchasing fitness equipment from a retail store requires some know-how. The following tips will help you to be an informed consumer:

■ *Be prepared to negotiate.* You should conduct preliminary research on the Internet even if you intend to purchase from a retail outlet. Enter the product you're interested in on Google or a similar online search engine, search for the lowest price you can find, and print a copy from the Web site. Bring the copy to the store and show it to the salesperson. Often, salespeople match the price you found online or at least lower their listed price. You can sometimes get a package deal if you're purchasing multiple pieces. It can't hurt to ask.

■ *Watch out for bait-and-switch tactics.* Retail sales is no different than most professions: There are honest salespeople and sleazy salespeople. The problem is that you generally can't differentiate one from the other at the time of purchase. An unprincipled salesperson may steer you toward a product not because it's best for you, but rather because it has a higher profit margin or because it includes a better employee commission. Don't be swayed at the time of purchase. If a salesperson tells you a product is better than the one you intended to buy, thank him and do your own research. A little time on the Internet should give you a good idea whether you're being scammed.

■ *Beware of clearance sales.* While an item marked down for final clearance might seem like a great buy, it may spell trouble in the future. Products are sometimes discontinued because they have inherent design problems or have received bad feedback. If sales for a unit were unsuccessful, manufacturers might not stock its parts in the future. This makes repairs difficult or impossible. Weigh the savings against the potential disadvantages and compare the risks and rewards. Make a purchase only when you're confident that the upside outweighs the downside.

■ *Get it in writing.* Salespeople can promise you the world at the time of purchase, but what happens if you run into a problem down the road? Those same people could deny they ever promised you a lifetime warranty or that they would take back the product if you didn't like it. Then what? Don't risk anything of consequence on verbal assurances. No matter what they tell you, make sure all sales promises are included in the contract. This leaves no chance for miscommunication.

What's more, retail outlets usually provide better help if you have problems or questions in the future. Neighborhood businesspeople who make their living in the community don't want bad publicity from dissatisfied customers. If worse comes to worst, you can go to the store and speak to the manager or owner in person. It's pretty hard to do that for a Web-based purchase, where the e-tailer likely resides hundreds, if not thousands, of miles away (and good luck trying to resolve your issue with a faceless online technician).

Used Equipment

Want to acquire fitness equipment on the cheap? Consider purchasing it second-hand. Fortunately for you, numerous would-be exercisers build home gyms but find they lack the motivation and knowledge to stick with a program. This means you can often get terrific deals from people looking to unload that weight set they never use or the rowing machine that's been collecting dust in their basement.

You can find used equipment in a variety of places. Peruse your local classified ads for garage sales. Check Internet resale sites such as eBay and Craigslist. With diligence, you can usually find what you're looking for.

As Seen on TV

Picture this scenario: It's late at night and you're watching television. While changing channels, you see a fitness show that grabs your interest. Some B-list celebrity you remember from a 1980s sitcom is on a set that's glitzier than a Las Vegas variety show, hocking a device called the Ab Buster. She is accompanied by a buff woman with six-pack abs. "If you buy this unit today," the show's announcer proclaims, "you can lose 2 inches from your waist by next week. It's so easy to use that you'll barely have to exert any effort to get results."

Every day, slickly produced infomercials like this hit the airwaves, reaching millions of people worldwide. They use musical interludes, fancy pyrotechnics, and laser light shows to feature high-tech pieces of equipment that supposedly trim fat from your abs, butt, thighs, arms, and any other body part imaginable. With more than a billion dollars a year in sales, these products are, without question, a big hit with consumers. For many, the prospect of an easy way to physique heaven is an irresistible premise.

However, the majority of these products don't deliver on their promises. Infomercials rely on consumers who make impulse purchases during a vulnerable moment in which they somehow believe the hype. That gut-blasting abdominal gizmo or fat-zapping thigh reducer likely isn't a revolutionary new concept but rather some entrepreneur's scheme to get rich quick.

My advice is to stay away. More often than not, you'll receive a poorly constructed piece of junk that you'll never use. If you're sufficiently intrigued by a particular product, take a moment to do an Internet search before you pick up the phone. Seek out unbiased reviews from consumers who've purchased the product (but don't trust reviews on the company's Web site!). You'll usually find enough comments to make an informed decision.

The problem with purchasing previously owned equipment is that you're almost always buying on an "as is" basis. The equipment may have underlying problems, which is a significant issue for mechanical or electronic equipment, such as treadmills, bikes, and resistance machines. It's pot luck whether you'll end up with a perfectly functioning gem or someone else's headache. Intermittent problems often don't arise until you've taken the unit home, making it difficult or impossible to know what you're getting at the time of purchase. Heed the adage of "Buyer beware."

PART II

Equipment and Exercise Selection

3

Choose From Body Weight, Balls, and Bands

Don't have a lot of money to spend on a home gym? Strapped for room to store weights and machines? No problem. You can create a pretty decent gym without spending much money or taking up much space. You just have to know how to make effective use of a few key pieces of equipment.

Body Weight

You might be surprised to learn that you already possess all the equipment you need for a butt-kicking workout at home. What equipment could I possibly be referring to? Your own body, of course!

Resistance training is simply the act of lifting a weighted object in a way that taxes your muscles. Any object that has mass qualifies as a form of resistance, whether it's a barbell, a dumbbell, a paint can, a sandbag, or even your body. As long as you place your body in a position to directly oppose gravity, you can work all of the major muscle groups in a variety of different ways.

However, body-weight exercises do have an inherent limitation. Namely, the degree of difficulty depends heavily on body type. For example, take the crunch (page 57). Because you must lift your shoulders off the floor, you will find this move to be significantly harder if you store the majority of your weight in your torso. The reverse crunch (page 58), on the other hand, will be more difficult if you are bottom-heavy, since you must initiate the lift from your pelvis.

Even if your body type isn't suited for a particular body-weight movement, all is not lost. Although you can't change your body weight from one set to the next, you can do several things to alter an exercise's degree of difficulty, including varying the training angle, increasing or decreasing leverage, and introducing unstable surfaces into the mix. For example, performing a push-up against a wall is much easier than doing a modified push-up (page 36), which, in turn, is easier than doing a standard push-up (page 36). These simple adjustments in positioning make a big difference in the exercise's degree of difficulty.

You can further enhance your body-weight training experience by using ordinary implements found around your home. For instance, make calf raises more challenging by placing your toes on a staircase. This practice increases the range of motion during the move's descent. Elevating your feet on a chair or sofa during push-ups both heightens the degree of difficulty and shifts the emphasis to the upper portion of your chest. You can use tables to perform step-ups, door jambs to secure resistance bands, and things like paint cans, plastic jugs, and even Tupperware containers filled with water or sand to serve as free weights. Be creative! A little ingenuity goes a long way.

The one body-weight training accessory I do recommend that you purchase is a chinning bar (see figure 3.1). This handy device allows you to both work your back from multiple angles and perform hanging abdominal exercises. Go with a doorway unit that can be easily installed and removed when you're not using it. These units, which cost about $30, are preferable to wall-mounted units because they don't mar your interior. Make sure it's an adjustable unit made of reinforced steel with a heavy gauge. You can also purchase arm straps (see figure 3.2) to assist in the performance of abdominal movements, which alleviate stress to your hands and wrists.

You should also get a good exercise mat for floor-based body-weight movements. Nothing fancy needed here; any cushioned material that increases your comfort level will do just fine. If you're exercising on a hard surface such as wood or concrete, opt for a mat with extra padding so that your knees and back won't get sore.

Finally, you'll definitely need a set of leg weights. These nifty little devices strap around your ankles, making many nonweighted lower-body exercises more challenging. Some of these can even be strapped around your wrists for an extra challenge in upper-body movements. Go with an adjustable 10-pound (4-kg) set; the cost is only a few dollars more than that of a 5-pound (2-kg) set, and the extra weights come in very handy as you get stronger.

FIGURE 3.1   Chinning bar.
Photo courtesy of Title Boxing/Everlast.

FIGURE 3.2   Hanging arm straps.

Stability Balls

In a recent poll of fitness professionals, the stability ball (see figure 3.3) was cited as one of the most indispensable items in a personal trainer's tool kit. Although this may be debatable, no one doubts the value of stability balls as a training resource—one that you should certainly make use of in your home gym.

Elegant in their simplicity, stability balls are nothing more than large, inflatable rubber balls that can be used to perform a wide array of seated and prone exercises. Pretty much any exercise that can be done on a bench can also be done on a ball. Better yet, its air-filled structure conforms to the unique shape of your body, providing a comfortable base to work out on.

In addition to injecting some fun into your routine, ball training is unique in that it places your body in an unstable environment. Your core is thereby forced into a stabilizing role, stimulating your body's natural motor reflexes to maintain proper posture and alignment. Studies show that core activity is substantially higher when exercises are performed on unstable surfaces. The evidence is pretty compelling. Training on a ball is extremely effective for developing the muscles of your abdomen and lower back.

FIGURE 3.3 **Stability ball.**

The stability ball is particularly useful for direct abdominal training. It elicits higher abdominal muscle recruitment and allows a greater range of motion during performance. Since your torso is not grounded, you can achieve an increased degree of extension at the onset of the movement. Range of motion is an extremely important component of training; the better the range, the more muscle fibers are activated during the exercise. And the more fibers that are activated, the better your results will be.

Now, before you start thinking that perhaps every exercise should be performed on a ball, understand that training on an unstable surface comes at the expense of force output. Specifically, the amount of weight you can lift is reduced in stability-ball movements. In certain lifts, it is limited by as much as 60 percent. Since muscular development is a direct product of the amount of tension placed on muscles, training on a ball rather than on a stable surface results in suboptimal development of all muscles other than those of the core.

Your best strategy is to use a combination of stable and unstable surfaces for training. The exact mix depends on your fitness goals. For example, if you want to maximize core activation, ball exercises should play a prominent role in your routine. But if your aim is to tone and sculpt, you should use the ball selectively, primarily as a way to keep your muscles off guard. You'll see how this concept plays out in the routines provided in part III.

Stability balls come in different sizes. Table 3.1 shows which ball sizes are appropriate for different heights. Body type is another important factor to consider, especially with respect to your leg length. A simple test is to sit on the ball. Your thighs should be parallel with the ground. If your thighs slope down, the ball is too big; if your thighs slope up, the ball is too small.

TABLE 3.1

Size Recommendations for Stability Balls

Height	Ball diameter
<4 ft 7 in (140 cm)	30 cm
4 ft 7 in to 5 ft 0 in (140-150 cm)	45 cm
5 ft 1 in to 5 ft 6 in (155-168 cm)	55 cm
5 ft 7 in to 5 ft 11 in (170-180 cm)	65 cm
≥6 ft 0 in (183 cm)	75 cm

Although you can find stability balls for as little as $10, cheap equipment isn't necessarily preferable. Low-priced models tend to be made of thin material, causing them to lose air quickly. Don't underestimate the nuisance of filling up your ball several times a week—trust me, it's a tedious chore, especially if you're using a manual pump. Worse, low-quality balls are prone to bursting, which could cause serious injury if it occurs during an intense set. Bottom line: It's worth spending an extra couple of bucks to get a heavy-duty ball. Look for one that can hold at least 600 pounds (272 kg). It should run you no more than about $30, including the pump.

The popularity of stability balls has led to the marketing of many other types of unstable surfaces, including BOSU trainers, wobble boards, foam rollers, and balance discs. Although these props are not essential, they can add diversity to your workout, especially for exercises performed in the standing position. At less than $100, they are worthy of your consideration, depending on your training objectives.

Resistance Bands

Resistance bands are a must for any home gym. Lightweight and versatile, they allow you to simulate cable-pulley movements (see chapter 5 for more detail) at a fraction of the cost. Using them couldn't be easier: Simply attach one end of the band to a stationary object (or stand on it) and pull to create resistance at the opposite end. The less slack in the band, the greater the tension will be, and thus the more challenging the exercise will be.

One of the best things about resistance bands is that they can adapt to a wide range of exercises, many of which are difficult or impossible to approximate with free weights or machines. You can use resistance bands for movement in any direction, affording huge latitude to vary the training angle and maximize muscle involvement.

A nice side benefit of bands is their portability. Whether you're on vacation or on a business trip, just pack them in your suitcase for instant access to a workout, even when the nearest gym is miles away.

Bands do have a downside, though. The resistance tends to start off easily, but then becomes progressively more difficult as you move through a range of motion. This is contrary to the way your muscles are designed work. In real life, the force placed on a muscle usually drops substantially toward the end of a lift, as does the muscle's leverage. In order to ensure optimal functionality, it's best to integrate band training with other exercise modalities. Combine them with body-weight movements for a low-cost workout that you can perform anywhere. Add weighted implements to the mix, and you have the makings to work your muscles to their fullest potential.

Bands are available in five levels of graded resistance; thicker bands offer more tension than thinner ones. Most manufacturers adhere to a standardized color-coding system in which each colored band corresponds to a unique level of tension (see table 3.2). Since different exercises require different levels of resistance, it's best to buy one band in each color. You'll need thicker bands for multijoint exercises like rows and presses, and thinner ones for single-joint moves like arm curls and lateral raises. If you have an assortment of bands, you'll be able to perform exercises in every possible range of repetitions.

TABLE 3.2

Color Coding for Resistance Bands

Color	Resistance
Yellow	Low
Red	Moderate
Green	Heavy
Blue	Extra heavy
Black	Super heavy

For less than $50, you can find complete kits that include a set of five colored tube-style bands. Stick with bands that are made of circular tubing rather than the flat latex models. Latex bands are flimsy and don't hold up well under consistent use. Consider them only for physical-therapy applications.

Make sure the bands come with a detachable ankle strap, loop handles, and door-anchor attachments (see figure 3.4). The ankle strap and loop handles allow you to perform a full range of upper- and lower-body movements, and the door anchor facilitates execution of numerous exercises, especially overhead moves like lat pull-downs and triceps press-downs.

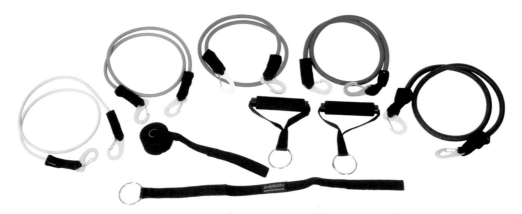

FIGURE 3.4 **Resistance bands with detachable ankle strap, loop handles, and door-anchor attachment.**

A quality band can endure about 20,000 stretches before it begins to lose elasticity. Under normal workout conditions, this corresponds to a year or two of moderate use. To prolong life expectancy, keep your bands in a temperature-controlled environment, away from direct sunlight. The elements tend to degrade the rubber tubing, impairing performance and increasing the possibility of breakage.

Performance Tips for Resistance Bands

- Make sure bands are securely attached when training. Otherwise, they can snap back at an inopportune time, potentially causing injury.
- Before beginning an exercise, make sure the band is slightly stretched in the start position. There shouldn't be any slack in the band. Don't stretch it too far, though. The rubber is only made to stretch about three times its original length. If you stretch the band beyond that, it may snap.

Pike Press

This move targets the shoulder muscles.

Equipment needed: None

Start: Place your palms and toes on the floor, keep your arms straight and rigid (as in a push-up), and walk your hands backward by lifting the hips straight up until your upper body is almost perpendicular to the floor. Your knees and back should be straight, and your core should be tight.

Movement: Bend your elbows and slowly lower your head toward the floor. Contract your shoulder muscles and then reverse your direction, returning along the same path to the starting position.

Expert tips:

- Try to keep your torso in a position as close to perpendicular to the ground as possible. This maintains maximum tension on the shoulders rather than on the chest muscles.
- You can increase difficulty of the move by elevating your feet onto a bench or chair.

Triceps Dip

This move targets the triceps.

Equipment needed: Bench or chair

Start: Place your heels on the floor and your palms on the edge of a flat bench. Keep your arms straight and your knees slightly bent.

Movement: Slowly bend your elbows as far as possible without discomfort, allowing your butt to descend below the level of the bench. Make sure to keep your elbows close to your body throughout the move. Reverse your direction by straightening your arms and return to the starting position.

Expert tips:

- You can make the move easier by bending more at the knees, or you can make it harder by reducing the bend of your knees and further extending your feet. The further your feet reach out, the more difficult the move will be.
- Keep your back close to the bench at all times. If your body gravitates forward, the stress on the shoulder joints increases.

A   B

Upright Row

This move targets the shoulders.

Equipment needed: Resistance band

Start: Attach loop handles to the ends of a resistance band. Grasp the loop handles and stand on the band with your feet shoulder-width apart, your torso erect, your knees slightly bent, and your core held tightly. Allow your arms to hang down from your shoulders in front of your body with your palms facing your thighs. Extend your arms but don't lock your elbows.

Movement: Pull the handles up along the line of your body until your upper arms approach shoulder level. Contract your deltoids, and then slowly lower the band along the same path back to the starting position.

Expert tips:

- Make sure there is no slack in the band at the beginning of the move.
- Be careful not to lift your elbows beyond a position that is parallel with the ground. Doing so can lead to shoulder impingement, which injures the rotator cuff.
- Keep your hands as close to your body as possible throughout the move.
- Keep your elbows higher than your wrists at all times—otherwise, you're lifting from the arms rather than the shoulders.

A

B

Shoulder Press

This move targets the deltoids, with an emphasis on the front delts. Secondary emphasis is placed on the upper trapezius and triceps.

Equipment needed: Resistance band

Start: Attach loop handles to the ends of a resistance band. Grasp the loop handles and stand on the band with your feet shoulder-width apart, your torso erect, your knees slightly bent, and your core held tightly. Bring your hands to shoulder level, with your palms facing away from your body.

Movement: Press the handles directly up and in, allowing them to come together directly over your head. Contract your deltoids, and then slowly reverse your direction, returning the handles along the same path back to the starting position.

Expert tips:

- Make sure there is no slack in the band at the beginning of the move.
- Don't arc your hands outward as you press—this increases stress on the connective tissue in the shoulder joint.
- Don't lock your elbows at the top of the move—doing so reduces tension on the target muscles.

A

B

Arnold Press

This move targets the deltoids and places secondary emphasis on the upper trapezius and triceps. The addition of the rotating movement activates the shoulder rotators to a greater degree than the shoulder press.

Equipment needed: Resistance band

Start: Attach loop handles to the ends of a resistance band. Grasp the loop handles and stand on the band with your feet shoulder-width apart, your torso erect, your knees slightly bent, and your core held tightly. Bring your hands to shoulder level, with your palms facing your body.

Movement: Press the handles directly up, simultaneously rotating your hands so that your palms face forward during the last portion of the movement. Contract your delts, and then slowly return the handles along the same arc, rotating your hands back to the starting position.

Expert tips:

- Make sure there is no slack in the band at the beginning of the move.
- This shouldn't be a mechanical movement—rotate your hands smoothly as you press.
- Don't lock your elbows at the top of the move—doing so reduces tension on the target muscles.

A   B

Lateral Raise

This move targets the medial (middle) deltoids.

Equipment needed: Resistance band

Start: Attach loop handles to a resistance band. Grasp the loop handles and stand on the band with your feet shoulder-width apart, your torso erect, your knees slightly bent, your core held tightly, and your palms facing your sides.

Movement: Maintaining a slight bend to your elbows, raise the handles up and out to the sides until they reach shoulder level. Contract your delts at the top of the movement, and then slowly return the handles to the starting position.

Expert tips:

- Make sure there is no slack in the band at the beginning of the move.
- Think of pouring a cup of milk as you lift. Your pinky should be higher than your thumb at the top of the move. This keeps maximum tension on your middle delts.

A
B

VARIATION

One-Arm Lateral Raise

Grasp the loop handle with your right hand and perform the move as previously described. After performing the desired number of repetitions, repeat on the left.

Bent Lateral Raise

This move targets the posterior (rear) deltoids.

Equipment needed: Resistance band

Start: Attach loop handles to the ends of a resistance band. Grasp the handles and stand on the middle of the band with your feet shoulder-width apart, your torso erect, and your knees slightly bent. Bend your torso forward so that it is roughly parallel with the ground and allow your arms to hang down in front of your body, palms facing each other. Keep your core tight and your back slightly hyperextended.

Movement: With a slight bend to your elbows, raise your arms up and out to the sides until they are parallel with the ground. Contract your delts at the top of the movement, and then slowly return the handles back to the starting position.

Expert tips:

- Make sure there is no slack in the band at the beginning of the move.
- Don't swing your body to complete a rep—this takes work away from the target muscles.
- Avoid the tendency to bring your elbows in toward your body during the lift. The elbows should remain out and away from the body throughout the move to keep tension on the rear delts.

A

B

Standing Reverse Fly

This move targets the posterior (rear) delts.

Equipment needed: Resistance band

Start: Attach loop handles to the ends of a resistance band and secure the center of the band to a stationary object (such as a door jamb) so it is at chest height. Grasp the loop handles and stand facing the stationary object with a shoulder-width stance, erect torso, and a slight bend to your knees. Bring your arms up until they are parallel with the ground. Maintain a slight bend to your elbows.

Movement: Keeping your core tight, open your arms out to the sides and move them backward as far as possible without discomfort. Contract your rear delts, and then return the handles along the same path back to the starting position.

Expert tips:

- Make sure there is no slack in the band at the beginning of the move.
- Your arms should remain parallel with the floor—don't allow the band to sag or elevate at any time.
- Keep your elbows fixed in place throughout the move—your shoulder joints should be the only points of movement.

A

B

Arm Curl

This move targets the biceps.

Equipment needed: Resistance band

Start: Attach loop handles to a resistance band. Grasp the loop handles and stand on the band with your feet shoulder-width apart, your torso erect, your knees slightly bent, and your core held tightly. Press your elbows in toward your sides, with your palms facing forward and your elbows slightly bent.

Movement: Keeping your upper arms immobile throughout the move, curl the handles up toward your shoulders. Contract your biceps, slowly reverse the direction, and return the handles to the starting position.

Expert tips:

- Make sure there is no slack in the band at the beginning of the move.
- If you desire, you can begin by holding your palms facing your sides, and then actively turn your palms forward and up (called supination) as you lift.
- Keep your wrists straight as you lift—don't roll your wrists!
- Don't allow your upper arms to move forward as you lift—this involves your shoulders at the expense of your arm muscles.

A

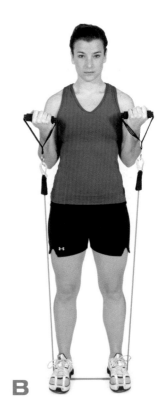
B

VARIATION

One-Arm Curl

Grasp the loop handle with your right hand and perform the move as previously described. After performing the desired number of repetitions, repeat on the left side.

Hammer Curl

This move targets the upper arms, with an emphasis on the brachialis.

Equipment needed: Resistance band

Start: Grasp a resistance band and stand on it with your feet shoulder-width apart, your torso erect, your knees slightly bent, and your core held tightly. Press your elbows in toward your sides, with your palms facing in.

Movement: Keeping your upper arms immobile, curl the band up toward your shoulders and contract your biceps at the top of the move. Then, slowly reverse the direction and return the band to the starting position.

Expert tips:

- Make sure there is no slack in the band at the beginning of the move.
- Don't allow your upper arms to move forward as you lift—this involves your shoulders at the expense of your arm muscles.
- Keep your wrists straight as you lift—don't roll them to complete the move.

A

B

VARIATION

One-Arm Hammer Curl
Grasp the loop handle with your right hand and perform the move as previously described. After performing the desired number of repetitions, repeat on the left side.

Concentration Curl

This move targets the biceps, with an emphasis on the short head of the muscle.

Equipment needed: Resistance band

Start: Attach a loop handle to a resistance band. Grasp the loop handle with your right hand and assume a wide stance. Bend forward at the hips and knees until you reach a semisquat position. Stand on the band and brace your right elbow on the inside of your right thigh. Straighten your arm toward the floor until your elbow is almost locked.

Movement: Keeping your core tight and your back slightly hyperextended, curl your arm up toward your right shoulder, contracting your biceps at the top of the move. Reverse the direction and slowly return your arm to the starting position. After completing the desired number of reps, repeat the process on your left side.

Expert tips:
- Make sure there is no slack in the band at the beginning of the move.
- Keep your exercising arm braced against your inner thigh at all times. If you are struggling to complete a rep, use the opposite hand to assist the move rather than swinging your exercising arm.
- Keep your wrist straight as you lift—don't roll it to complete the move.

A   B

Press-Down

This move targets the triceps.

Equipment needed: Resistance band

Start: Attach loop handles to the ends of a resistance band and secure the middle of the band at the top of a door with a door-anchor attachment. You could also loop the band around a stationary object like a chinning bar. Grasp the handles with an overhand grip and keep your arms shoulder-width apart, your posture erect, your knees slightly bent, and your core tight. Bend your arms until your elbows form an angle of 90 degrees or slightly greater.

Movement: Keeping your elbows by your sides, straighten your arms as far as possible without discomfort. Contract your triceps, reverse your direction, and return your arms to the starting position.

Expert tips:

- Make sure there is no slack in the band at the beginning of the move.
- Don't allow your arms to move out as you lift—this brings the chest muscles into play at the expense of your triceps.
- For an added contraction, turn your palms out so they face away from each other at the end of the move.

A   **B**

VARIATION

One-Arm Press-Down
Grasp the loop handle with your right hand and perform the move as previously described. After performing the desired number of repetitions, repeat on the left side.

Overhead Triceps Extension

This move targets the triceps.

Equipment needed: Resistance band

Start: Attach loop handles to the ends of a resistance band. Grasp the loop handles and stand on the band with your feet shoulder-width apart, your torso erect, your knees slightly bent, and your core held tightly. Keeping your upper arms close to your ears, bend your elbows and allow your hands to hang down behind your head as far as comfortably possible, with your palms facing forward.

Movement: Straighten your arms, holding your elbows still throughout the move. Contract your triceps, and then slowly lower your hands along the same path back toward the starting position.

Expert tips:

- Make sure there is no slack in the band at the beginning of the move.
- Keep your upper arms pinned to your ears as you lift—if your elbows flare, you'll reduce stress on the triceps.

A

B

VARIATION

One-Arm Overhead Triceps Extension

Grasp the loop handle with your right hand and perform the move as previously described. After performing the desired number of repetitions, repeat on the left side.

Triceps Kickback

This move targets the triceps.

Equipment needed: Resistance band

Start: Attach loop handles to the ends of a resistance band. Grasp one of the loop handles with your right hand and stand on the band with your feet shoulder-width apart, your torso erect, and your knees slightly bent. Bend your torso forward until it is roughly parallel with the ground. Press your right arm against your side with your right elbow bent at a 90-degree angle and your palm facing backward.

Movement: Keeping your upper arm stable, raise the handle by straightening your arm until it is near parallel with the floor. Then, reverse the direction and return the weight to the starting position. After finishing the desired number of repetitions, repeat the process on your left side.

Expert tips:

- Make sure there is no slack in the band at the beginning of the move.
- Don't flick your wrist at the top of movement—this is a common performance error that fatigues the forearm muscles before the triceps tire and reduces the effectiveness of the move.
- Keep your back slightly arched and your torso parallel with the floor throughout the movement.
- Never round your spine—this places undue stress on the lumbar area and could lead to injury.

A

B

Push-Up

This move targets the pectorals, with secondary emphasis placed on the shoulders and triceps.

Equipment needed: None

Start: Place your palms and toes on the floor, and hold your arms straight and rigid. Your hands should be approximately shoulder-width apart, your elbows flared out to the sides, and your core held tightly.

Movement: Keeping your back perfectly straight, slowly bend your arms and lower your body down, stopping just before your chest touches the ground. Feel a stretch in your chest muscles and then reverse the direction, pushing your body up along the same path back to the starting position.

Expert tips:

- Your torso and legs should remain in a straight line at all times. Don't wriggle like a caterpillar to complete a rep.
- When you straighten your arms, stop just before your elbows lock. This practice maintains constant tension on your chest muscles.
- Bringing your elbows close to your body shifts the emphasis to the triceps and reduces stimulation of the pectoral muscles.

A

B

VARIATION

Modified Push-Up
Place your knees on the floor and perform the movement as previously described.

Incline Push-Up

This move targets the pectorals, with particular emphasis on the upper portion of the chest. Secondary emphasis is placed on the shoulders and triceps.

Equipment needed: Bench or chair

Start: Place your toes on top of a bench or chair, with your palms flat on the floor and your arms held straight and rigid. Your hands should be approximately shoulder-width apart, your elbows flared out to the sides, and your core held tightly.

Movement: Bend your arms and lower your body down, stopping just before your chest touches the ground. Feel a stretch in your chest muscles and then reverse the direction, pushing your body up along the same path back to the starting position.

Expert tips:

- Your torso and legs should remain in a straight line at all times. Don't wriggle like a caterpillar to complete a rep.
- When you straighten your arms, stop before your elbows lock. This practice maintains constant tension on your chest muscles.

A

B

Chin-Up

This move targets the back muscles and places secondary emphasis on the biceps. It's a bit easier to perform than the pull-up.

Equipment needed: Chinning bar

Start: Grasp a chinning bar with an underhand, shoulder-width grip (palms facing your body). Straighten your arms, bend your knees, and cross one foot over the other.

Movement: Keeping your upper body stable and your core held tightly, pull your body up until your chin reaches the bar. Contract your lats and then release along the same path back to the starting position.

Expert tips:

- Don't allow your body to swing or kick your feet—this introduces momentum into the movement, reducing tension to the target muscles.
- This can be a very difficult move to execute, especially for those who carry more weight in the lower body. If you can't reach your target-rep range, place your feet on a chair and push up until your chin reaches the bar, and then lift your feet from the chair and slowly lower yourself down. Performing slow negatives in this fashion helps develop strength for the move.

A

B

Pull-Up

This move targets the back muscles.

Equipment needed: Chinning bar

Start: Grasp a chinning bar with an overhand grip (palms facing away from your body). Straighten your arms, bend your knees, and cross one foot over the other.

Movement: Keeping your torso stable and your core held tightly, pull your body up until your chin reaches the bar. Contract your lats and then release along the same path back to the starting position.

Expert tips:

- Don't allow your body to swing or kick your feet—this introduces momentum into the movement, reducing tension to the target muscles.
- This can be a very difficult move to execute, especially for those who carry more weight in the lower body. If you can't reach your target-rep range, place your feet on a chair and push up until your chin reaches the bar, and then lift your feet from the chair and slowly lower yourself down. Performing slow negatives in this fashion helps develop strength for the move.

A

B

Reverse Push-Up

This move targets the pectorals, with particular emphasis on the upper portion of the chest. Secondary emphasis is placed on the shoulders and triceps.

Equipment needed: Stability ball

Start: Place your toes on top of a stability ball, with your palms flat on the floor, your core held tightly, and your arms straight and rigid. Your hands should be approximately shoulder-width apart and your elbows should be flared out to the sides.

Movement: Bend your arms and lower your body down, stopping just before your chest touches the ground. Feel a stretch in your chest muscles and then reverse the direction, pushing your body up along the same path back to the starting position.

Expert tips:

- Your torso and legs should remain in a straight line at all times. Don't wriggle like a caterpillar to complete a rep.
- When you straighten your arms, stop just before your elbows lock. This practice maintains constant tension on your chest muscles.
- If the move is too difficult, place your thighs on the ball instead of your toes. The further up you position your thighs on the ball, the easier the move will be.

A

B

Prone Lat Pull

This move targets the back muscles.

Equipment needed: Stability ball

Start: Roll on a ball so that your midsection rests on top of the ball, with your palms on the floor. Stretch your arms straight out in front of the shoulders as far as is comfortably possible. Your legs should be suspended in the air off the back of the ball, with your feet held together.

Movement: Keeping your hands in place, pull your body forward until your arms are perpendicular to the floor. Contract your back muscles and then reverse the direction, slowly returning to the starting position.

Expert tip: To make the exercise easier, start with your body resting further up on the ball. To make it harder, begin with your lower body resting on the ball.

A

B

Seated Row

This move targets the back muscles, particularly the inner musculature of the rhomboids and the middle traps.

Equipment needed: Resistance band

Start: Attach loop handles to the ends of a resistance band and secure the middle of the band to a stationary object at ankle height. You can use the soles of your feet if you desire. Sit on the floor and grasp the handles, with your core held tightly, your palms facing each other, and your knees slightly bent. Fully straighten your arms so that you feel a complete stretch in your lats.

Movement: Keeping your posture erect and your lower back slightly arched, pull the handles toward your lower abdomen, keeping your elbows close to your sides and your lower back slightly arched. As the handles touch your body, squeeze your shoulder blades together and then reverse the direction, slowly returning the handles to the starting position.

Expert tips:
- Make sure there is no slack in the band at the beginning of the move.
- Don't let your body lean forward on the return. This interjects momentum into the move's concentric action, reducing tension on the target muscles.
- Never round your spine—this places the spinal discs in a precarious position and can lead to serious injury.

A

B

Row

This move targets the back muscles.

Equipment needed: Stability ball, resistance band

Start: Attach loop handles to the ends of a resistance band and secure the middle of the band to a stationary object (such as a door jamb) at knee height. Sit on a stability ball and grasp the handles, with your core held tightly, your palms facing each other, and your feet on the floor. Fully straighten your arms so that you feel a complete stretch in your lats.

Movement: Keeping your posture erect, your lower back slightly arched, and your elbows close to your sides, pull the handles toward your lower abdomen. When the handles touch your body, squeeze your shoulder blades together and then reverse the direction, slowly returning the handles to the starting position.

Expert tips:
- Make sure there is no slack in the band at the beginning of the move.
- Avoid allowing your body to lean forward on the return. This interjects momentum into the move's concentric action, reducing tension on the target muscles.
- Never round your spine—this places the discs in a precarious position and can lead to serious injury.

A   B

Lat Pull-Down

This move targets the back muscles, particularly the lats.

Equipment needed: Resistance band

Start: Attach loop handles to the ends of a resistance band and secure the middle of the band to the top of a door (or another stationary object, such as a chinning bar). Grasp the handles with an overhand, shoulder-width grip (palms facing away from your body) and kneel on the floor. Your arms should be held straight and overhead. Maintain a tight core and a slight backward tilt to your body as you arch your lower back.

Movement: Pull the handles down toward your shoulders, bringing your elbows back slightly as you pull. Contract your lats and then slowly reverse the direction, returning the handles to the starting position.

Expert tip: Make sure there is no slack in the band at the beginning of the move.

A

B

VARIATIONS

◀ Neutral-Grip Lat Pull-Down
Grasp the loop handles with a neutral grip (palms facing each other) and perform the move as previously described.

Reverse-Grip Lat Pull-Down ▶
Grasp the loop handles with a reverse grip (palms facing your body) and perform the move as previously described.

One-Arm Low Row

This move targets the back muscles.

Equipment needed: Resistance band

Start: Attach loop handles to the ends of a resistance band and secure the band to a stationary object (such as a door jamb) at ankle height. Grasp one of the handles in your right hand with a neutral grip (palm facing in). Step back and straighten your right arm so you feel a stretch in your right lat. Keeping your right leg back, bend your left leg so your weight is placed forward. Place your left hand on your left knee for balance and keep your core tight.

Movement: Pull the loop handle toward your right side, keeping your elbow close to your body. Contract your right lat and then reverse the direction, slowly returning the handle to the starting position. After finishing the desired reps with your right arm, repeat on your left side.

Expert tip: Make sure there is no slack in the band at the beginning of the move.

A

B

Straight-Arm Pull-Down

This move targets the back muscles, particularly the lats.

Equipment needed: Resistance band

Start: Attach loop handles to the ends of a resistance band and secure the middle of the band to the top of a door (or another stationary object, such as a chinning bar). Grasp the handles and assume a shoulder-width stance, with erect posture and slightly bent knees. Slightly bend your elbows and, with a shoulder-width grip, bring the handles to eye level.

Movement: Pull the handles down in a semicircle until they approach your upper thighs. Contract your back muscles and then reverse the direction, slowly returning the handles to the starting position.

Expert tips:

- Make sure there is no slack in the band at the beginning of the move.
- Your entire body should remain immobile throughout the exercise—only the arms should move. Any other movement removes tension from the target muscles.

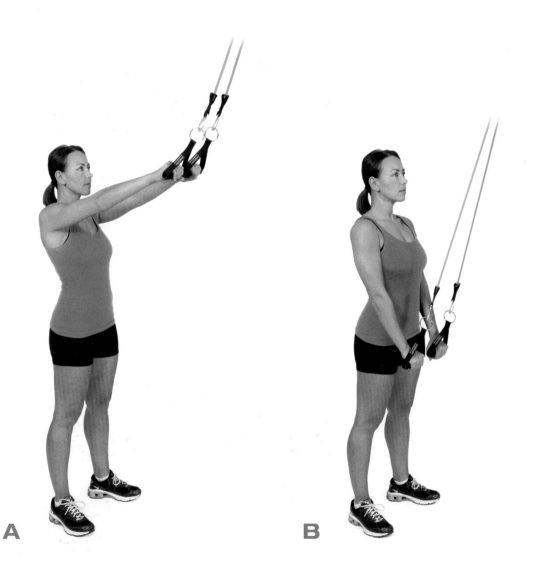

A   B

Lying Pullover

This move targets the back muscles, particularly the lats.

Equipment needed: Resistance band, bench

Start: Attach loop handles to the ends of a resistance band and secure the middle of the band to a stationary object (such as a door jamb) at knee height. Lie on your back on a flat bench, a sofa, a table, or even the floor. Grasp the handles and extend your arms toward your ears so that the band attachment is behind your head.

Movement: Keeping your elbows slightly bent, pull the handles up in a semicircle until they are directly over your head. Contract your lats and then reverse the direction, slowly returning the handles to the starting position.

Expert tips:

- Make sure there is no slack in the band at the beginning of the move.
- Stretch only in a comfortable range—overstretching can lead to shoulder injury.
- Your elbows should maintain a slight bend throughout the movement. Do not straighten as you lift. This error increases triceps activation at the expense of your target muscles.

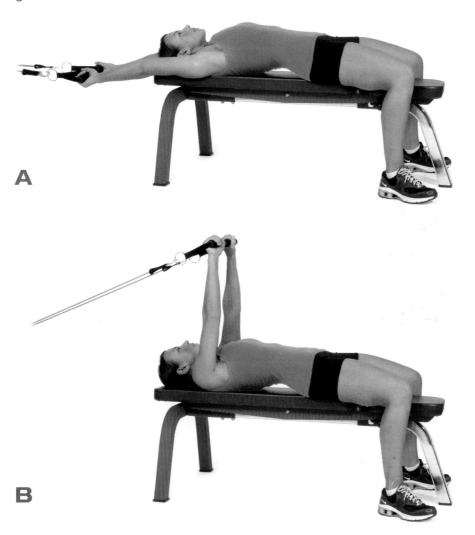

A

B

Standing Chest Press

This move targets the pectorals, particularly the upper portion.

Equipment needed: Resistance band

Start: Attach loop handles to the ends of a resistance band and secure the center of the band to a stationary object (such as a door jamb) so it is at chest height. Grasp the loop handles and stand facing away from the object with a staggered stance (one foot in front of the other), your knees slightly bent, and your core held tightly. Bring your arms up and out to the sides until they are parallel with the ground, with your palms down and your elbows bent at a 90-degree angle.

Movement: Keeping your upper body motionless, press your hands forward and in. Your hands should remain parallel with the floor at all times. Gently touch your hands together at the end of the move as you contract your chest muscles, and then slowly return them along the same path back to the starting position.

Expert tips:

- Make sure there is no slack in the band at the beginning of the move.
- Keep your elbows flared throughout the move to maintain maximal activation of the pectoral muscles.
- As you press, think of moving your hands in an inverted V-pattern to increase range of motion.
- To maintain continuous muscular tension, do not lock your elbows at the end of the move.

A   **B**

Standing Incline Chest Press

This move targets the pectorals, particularly the middle portion.

Equipment needed: Resistance band

Start: Attach loop handles to the ends of a resistance band and secure the center of the band to a stationary object (such as a door jamb) so it is at chest height. Grasp the loop handles and stand facing away from the object with a staggered stance (one foot in front of the other), your knees slightly bent, and your core held tightly. Bring your arms up and out to the sides until they are parallel with the ground, with your palms down and your elbows bent at a 90-degree angle.

Movement: Keeping your upper body motionless, press your hands up and in at a 120-degree angle to the floor (midway between parallel with the floor and straight up in the air). Gently touch your hands together at the end of the move as you contract your chest muscles, and then slowly return your hands along the same path back to the starting position.

Expert tips:

- Make sure there is no slack in the band at the beginning of the move.
- Keep your elbows flared throughout the move to maintain maximal activation of the pectoral muscles.
- As you press, think of moving your hands in an inverted V-pattern to increase range of motion.
- To maintain continuous muscular tension, do not lock your elbows at the end of the move.

A

B

Standing Fly

This move targets the pectorals, particularly the middle portion.

Equipment needed: Resistance band

Start: Attach loop handles to the ends of a resistance band and secure the center of the band to a stationary object (such as a door jamb) so it is at chest height. Grasp the loop handles and stand facing away from the object with a staggered stance (one foot in front of the other), your knees slightly bent, and your core held tightly. Bring your arms up and out to the sides until they are parallel with the ground, maintaining a slight bend in your elbows.

Movement: Keeping your upper body motionless, pull your hands across your body in a semi-circular motion, gently touching them together at the end of the move. Contract your chest muscles and then slowly return your hands along the same path back to the starting position.

Expert tips:

- Make sure there is no slack in the band at the beginning of the move.
- Your arms should remain horizontal to the ground at all times.
- Your elbows should remain slightly bent and fixed throughout the move—don't flex or extend them at any time. This error effectively makes the exercise a pressing movement rather than a fly.

A   B

Standing Low Fly

This move targets the pectorals, particularly the upper portion.

Equipment needed: Resistance band

Start: Attach loop handles to the ends of a resistance band and secure the center of the band to a stationary object (such as a door jamb) so it is at ankle height. Grasp the loop handles and stand facing away from the object with a staggered stance (one foot in front of the other), your knees slightly bent, and your core held tightly. Bring your arms up until they are parallel with the ground, maintaining a slight bend in your elbows.

Movement: Keeping your upper body stable, pull your hands up and across your body in a semicircular motion, gently touching them together at the end of the move. Contract your chest muscles and then slowly return your hands along the same path back to the starting position.

Expert tips:

- Make sure there is no slack in the band at the beginning of the move.
- Your arms should remain horizontal to the ground at all times.
- Your elbows should remain slightly bent and fixed throughout the move—don't flex or extend them at any time. This error effectively makes the exercise a pressing movement rather than a fly.

A   **B**

Toe Touch

This move targets the abs, with a focus on the upper abdominal region.

Equipment needed: None

Start: Lie on the floor on your back with your arms and legs held straight in the air and perpendicular to your body. You should hold your upper back slightly off the ground to maintain constant tension on the target muscles and should press your lower back into the floor.

Movement: Keeping your lower back pressed to the floor, curl your torso up and forward, raising your hands as close to your toes as possible. Contract your abs and then reverse the direction, returning your body to the starting position.

Expert tips:

- Your lumbar region should remain fixed throughout the move—only your upper back should rise off the floor.
- Keep your head stable at all times—any unwanted movement can potentially injure the cervical spine.
- For added intensity, hold a weighted object (such as a filled paint can or a plastic jug) in your hands.

A

B

Bicycle Crunch

This move targets the abs, with a focus on the obliques.

Equipment needed: None

Start: Lie on the floor on your back and bend your legs at a 90-degree angle. Ball your hands into fists and place them at your ears. Your upper back should be held slightly off the ground to maintain constant tension on the target muscles.

Movement: Bring your right knee up toward your left elbow and try to touch them together. As you return your right leg and left elbow to the starting position, bring your left knee toward your right elbow in the same manner. Continue this movement, alternating between right and left sides as if you were pedaling a bike.

Expert tips:

- Never place your hands behind your head—this pulls on the neck muscles and can potentially lead to injury.
- Avoid the temptation to speed up on this move. Perform this exercise in a smooth, controlled manner for optimal results.

A

B

Twisting Crunch

This move targets the abs, with a focus on the obliques.

Equipment needed: None

Start: Lie on the floor on your back with your knees bent and your feet on the floor. Press your lower back into the floor and fold your hands across your chest. Your upper back should be held slightly off the ground to maintain constant tension on the target muscles.

Movement: Lift your shoulders up and forward toward your chest, twisting your body to the right. Feel a contraction in your abdominal muscles and then slowly reverse the direction, returning to the starting position. Perform the move to the left and then alternate from side to side for the desired number of repetitions.

Expert tips:

- Never place your hands behind your head—this pulls on the neck muscles and can potentially lead to injury.
- If the move becomes easy, hold a weighted object (such as a filled paint can or a plastic jug) against your chest.

A

B

Superwoman

This move targets the lower back muscles, glutes, and hamstrings.

Equipment needed: None

Start: Lie facedown on the floor, holding your legs together, your arms straight and extended forward, and your head and neck in a neutral position.

Movement: Keeping your midsection stationary, simultaneously lift your arms and thighs up toward the ceiling to form a soft curve with your body. Contract your glutes, slowly reverse the direction, and return to the starting position.

Expert tips:

- Don't bob your head as you perform the move. This error can cause injury to the neck muscles and the cervical spine.
- Avoid the alternating version of this move (where one upper limb is lifted with the opposite lower limb). Since the legs are much heavier than the arms, you may tend to twist your torso when you lift opposing limbs. This places undue torsion on the spine.

A

B

Bird Dog

This move targets the entire core.

Equipment needed: None

Start: Kneel on your hands and knees, holding your chin up and your spine in a neutral position.

Movement: Simultaneously extend your left leg and right arm until they are parallel with the floor. Hold this position for as long as possible, and then repeat with the opposite arm and leg.

Expert tips:

- This is a static hold move—your body should remain motionless throughout the exercise.
- Avoid hiking up your hip, which places undue stress on the spine.
- Use your core strength to keep your body rigid—don't allow any part of your body to sag at any time.
- Aim to work up to a hold of at least 60 seconds.

Crunch

This move targets the abs, with a focus on the upper abdominal region.

Equipment needed: None

Start: Lie on the floor on your back with your knees bent and your feet planted on the floor. Press your lower back into the floor and fold your hands across your chest. Your upper back should be held slightly off the ground to maintain constant tension on the target muscles.

Movement: Keeping your lower back fixed to the floor, move your shoulders up and forward toward your chest. Feel a contraction in your abdominal muscles and then slowly reverse the direction, returning to the starting position.

Expert tips:

- To facilitate performance, visualize bringing your shoulders down toward your pelvis.
- Don't allow your upper back to touch the floor when lowering your shoulders—doing so reduces tension to the abs.
- If the move becomes easy, hold a weighted object (such as a filled paint can or a plastic jug) against your chest.
- Never place your hands behind your head—this pulls on the neck muscles and can potentially lead to injury.

A

B

Reverse Crunch

This move targets the abs, with a focus on the lower abdominal region.

Equipment needed: None

Start: Lie supine on the floor with your hands at your sides. Curl your knees up toward your belly until your butt is lifted slightly off the ground.

Movement: Keeping your upper back pressed into the floor, raise your butt as high as possible so that your pelvis tilts toward your chest. Contract your abs and then reverse the direction, returning your butt to the starting position.

Expert tips:

- Keep your upper torso completely stable—your hips should be the only moving part of your body.
- Don't just push your butt up in the air. Rather, focus on pulling your pelvis backward so that it approaches your belly button. This forces the lower portion of the abs to do more of the work. When done properly, this short range of motion really hits the target muscle.
- Don't allow your butt to touch the floor as you lower it—doing so reduces tension on the abs.
- If the move becomes easy, place a medicine ball between your thighs.

A

B

Side Jackknife

This move targets the obliques.

Equipment needed: None

Start: Lie on your left side with your feet held together. Make a fist with your right hand and press it to your right ear. Hold your left forearm flat on the floor for support.

Movement: Simultaneously raise your right leg and torso into the air so they come as close together as possible without discomfort. Contract your oblique muscles, slowly reverse the direction, and return to the starting position. After performing the prescribed number of repetitions, repeat the process on the left side.

Expert tips:

- Visualize holding your entire body against a wall as you perform the movement. This prevents twisting of the torso, which can cause spinal injury.
- Your torso flexibility will dictate your range of motion. Don't try to move further than your body allows. This error can overstrain the core musculature.

A

B

Reverse Pendulum

This move targets the obliques.

Equipment needed: None

Start: Lie on your back with your arms held out to the sides and your palms held flat on the floor. Keeping your legs straight and your feet together, raise your thighs until they are perpendicular with the ground.

Movement: Keeping your upper back pressed to the floor, slowly lower your legs to the right. Raise your legs back to the starting position and repeat the process on your left. Alternate from side to side for the desired number of repetitions.

Expert tips:

- Initiate the action from your waist, not your hips. This practice keeps the focus on the oblique muscles.
- If the movement becomes easy, attach leg weights to your ankles.

A **B**

VARIATION

Twister
Bend your knees and perform the movement as previously described. If the movement becomes easy, place a medicine ball between your thighs.

Plank

This move targets the entire core.

Equipment needed: None

Start: Lie on your stomach with your palms on the floor, your feet together, and your spine in a neutral position.

Movement: Lift your body up on your palms and toes, keeping your head, torso, and legs in a straight line. Maintain this position for as long as possible. Challenge yourself to maintain the plank position longer each time you perform it.

Expert tips:

- This is a static hold—your body should remain motionless throughout the exercise.
- Use your core strength to keep your body rigid—don't allow any part of your body to sag at any time.
- Aim to work up to a hold of at least 60 seconds.

VARIATION

Modified Plank
Place your forearms on the floor and perform the move as previously described. Use this variation if you have difficulty with the straight-armed version.

Side Bridge

This move targets the entire core.

Equipment needed: None

Start: Lie on your right side with your legs straight, your right palm on the floor, and your feet stacked on top of each other.

Movement: Straighten your right arm, keeping it in line with your shoulder, and then place your free hand on or near your opposite shoulder. Hold this position for as long as possible, and then repeat on the opposite side.

Expert tips:

- This is a static hold—your body should remain motionless throughout the exercise.
- Use your core strength to keep your body rigid—don't allow any part of your body to sag at any time.
- Balance on the sides of your feet, not the soles.
- Aim to work up to a hold of at least 60 seconds.

VARIATION

Modified Side Bridge
Place your forearm on the floor and perform the movement as described.

Bridge

This move targets the glutes.

Equipment needed: None

Start: Lie on the floor on your back with your knees bent at a 90-degree angle and your hands palms-down at your sides.

Movement: Keeping your back straight, lift your hips off the floor. Contract your glutes and then return along the same path back to the starting position.

Expert tip: Your back and thighs should form a straight line at the top of the move. Don't hyperextend your back, since this can cause injury to the lumbar region.

A

B

VARIATION

One-Leg Bridge
Keep your left leg straight and your right leg bent. Push up with your right leg to lift your hips and perform the move as previously described, with your left leg rising off the floor. After completing the desired number of reps, repeat on the opposite side.

Hanging Knee Raise

This move targets the abdominals.

Equipment needed: Chinning bar

Start: Grasp a chinning bar with a shoulder-width grip, bend your knees, and stabilize your torso.

Movement: Keeping your knees bent, raise your thighs upward, lifting your butt so that your pelvis tilts toward your stomach. Contract your abs and then slowly reverse the direction, returning your legs back to the starting position.

Expert tips:

- Focus on pulling your pelvis up and back so that it approaches your belly button. This forces the lower portion of the abs to do more of the work.
- If you have trouble holding your body weight, consider using hanging arm straps (shown below).
- Keep your upper torso motionless throughout the move—don't swing to complete a repetition.
- For increased intensity, straighten your legs while performing the move.

A

B

Reverse Hyperextension

This move targets the lower back, glutes, and hamstrings.

Equipment needed: Stability ball

Start: Lie prone on a stability ball so that the ball rests under the front of your hips. Place your palms on the floor in front of the ball. Extend your legs behind you so that they rise an inch or so off the floor. Your feet should be hip-distance apart.

Movement: Keeping your arms fixed, slowly lift your legs off the floor until your ankles and the back of your head are in a straight line. Contract your glutes and return along the same path back to the starting position.

Expert tips:
- Your knees should remain straight throughout the move—don't use momentum by flexing and whipping the lower legs.
- Don't hyperextend your back. This error can cause lumbar injury.
- If the move becomes easy, attach leg weights to your ankles.

A

B

Crunch

This move targets the abdominals.

Equipment needed: Stability ball

Start: Sit on top of a stability ball with your feet shoulder-width apart. Walk your feet forward until your lower back is firmly supported. Place your hands on your chest and lower your upper back onto the ball.

Movement: Lift your upper back off the ball as far as possible without discomfort. Contract your abs and return along the same path back to the starting position.

Expert tips:

- Sitting higher on the ball (butt on top of the ball) makes the exercise more difficult. Sitting lower on the ball makes it easier.
- Your lower back should remain on the ball at all times. Lifting your lower back engages the hip flexors, reducing the stress on the target muscles. It also increases shear force to the lumbar region, potentially leading to injury.
- Keep your hips anchored so you move over the ball. The ball should not roll under you.
- If the move becomes easy, hold a weighted object (such as a filled paint can or a plastic jug) against your chest.

A

B

Side Crunch

This move targets the obliques.

Equipment needed: Stability ball

Start: Lie sideways on the top of a stability ball, with your feet planted firmly on the floor. Place your fingertips by your temple with your elbow held out to the side. Lower your ball-side elbow as far down as possible without discomfort.

Movement: Keeping your fingertips pressed to your temple, raise your top elbow so your trunk flexes laterally as far as possible. Contract your obliques and then return along the same path back to the starting position. After performing the desired number of reps, repeat on the opposite side.

Expert tip: If you have trouble maintaining stability, position your feet against the bottom of a wall for support.

A

B

Hyperextension

This move targets the glutes, hamstrings, and lower back.

Equipment needed: Stability ball

Start: Lie facedown with your hips on a stability ball. Hold your feet a little wider than shoulder-width apart with your toes on the floor. Place your hands by your thighs and hold your head in line with your torso.

Movement: Keeping your lower body stable, lift your chest and shoulders off the ball as far as possible without discomfort. Contract your glutes and then return along the same path to the starting position.

Expert tips:

- To increase the level of difficulty, hold your arms straight out in front of your head (as in the superwoman exercises on page 55).
- If you have trouble balancing, place your feet against the base of a wall.
- Your center of gravity should be slightly behind the center of the ball.
- Don't move your head during the exercise—doing so can injure your neck.
- Don't hyperextend your lower back—this can cause lumbar injury.

Helicopter

This move targets the obliques.

Equipment needed: Stability ball

Start: Lie face up with your hips placed on a stability ball. Brace your feet against the base of a wall, held shoulder-width apart. Place your arms straight out to your sides.

Movement: Keeping your butt on the ball, rotate your body as far to one side as possible without discomfort. Contract your oblique muscles and then rotate to the other side, repeating the progression until you have performed the desired number of repetitions.

Expert tips:
- Don't turn your head as you rotate.
- If the move becomes easy, hold weighted objects (such as filled paint cans or plastic jugs) in your hands.

A

B

Rotating Crunch

This move targets the abs, with an emphasis on the obliques.

Equipment needed: Stability ball

Start: Sit on top of a stability ball with your feet shoulder-width apart. Walk your feet forward until your lower back is firmly supported. Place your hands on your chest and lower your upper back onto the ball.

Movement: Lift your upper back off the ball as far as possible without discomfort. As you do, turn your torso to the left and then lower yourself down. Contract your abs and return along the same path back to the starting position. Alternate from one side to the other for the desired number of repetitions.

Expert tips:

- Sitting higher on the ball (butt on top of the ball) makes the exercise more difficult. Sitting lower on the ball makes it easier.
- Your lower back should remain on the ball at all times. Lifting your lower back engages the hip flexors, reducing stress to the target muscles. It also increases shear forces on the lumbar region, potentially leading to injury.
- Keep your hips anchored so you move over the ball. The ball should not roll under you.
- If the move becomes easy, hold a weighted object (such as a filled paint can or a plastic jug) against your chest.

A

B

Russian Twist

This move targets the obliques.

Equipment needed: Stability ball

Start: Lie on a stability ball so that your lower back rests on the ball. Your body should be held at approximately a 40-degree angle to the floor. Bend your knees at a 90-degree angle and hold your neck in alignment with your torso. Place your arms straight over your head with your palms facing in. Your core should be parallel with the floor.

Movement: Keeping your lower body stable, turn your shoulders to one side until you are balancing on one shoulder on the ball. Your feet should remain on the floor. Rotate back to center and repeat on the other side.

Expert tips:
- Move only at the core, not at your shoulders or hips.
- If the movement becomes too easy, hold a weighted object (such as a filled paint can or a plastic jug) in your hands.
- Keep your eyes on your hands at all times to enhance core rotation.

A   **B**

Bridge

This move targets the glutes.

Equipment needed: Stability ball

Start: Lie on the floor on your back with your feet resting on top of a stability ball. Your feet should be hip-distance apart and your arms should rest at your sides.

Movement: Keeping your back straight, lift your hips off the floor as high as possible without discomfort. Contract your glutes and then return along the same path back to the starting position.

Expert tip: Your back and thighs should form a straight line at the top of the move. Don't hyperextend your back. This error can injure the lumbar region.

A

B

Horizontal Woodchop

This move targets the obliques.

Equipment needed: Resistance band

Start: Secure a resistance band to a sturdy object at chest height and grasp one end of the band with both hands. Position your body so that your side faces the band attachment and extend your arms as far across your body as possible without discomfort.

Movement: Keeping your lower body stable, pull the band across your torso as if you were chopping wood. Contract your obliques and then return along the same path back to the starting position. After finishing the desired number of reps, repeat on the opposite side.

Expert tips:

- Make sure there is no slack in the band at the beginning of the move.
- To keep constant tension on the obliques, make sure the action takes place at your waist, not your hips.
- If you would like to transfer the skills to a sport that involves hip action, combine motions of the hips and waist.

A   B

Kneeling Crunch

This move targets the abdominals, with a focus on the upper portion.

Equipment needed: Resistance band

Start: Attach loop handles to the ends of a resistance band. Secure the band at the top of a door (or other stationary object such as a chinning bar) and grasp the handles. Kneel down so that your body faces the door. Keep your torso upright and your forearms pinned to your ears.

Movement: Curl your shoulders down, bringing your elbows toward your knees. Contract your abs and then slowly uncurl your body, returning to the starting position.

Expert tips:

- Make sure there is no slack in the band at the beginning of the move.
- Curl only from your upper torso—your hips should remain fixed throughout the move. This maintains tension on the abs.

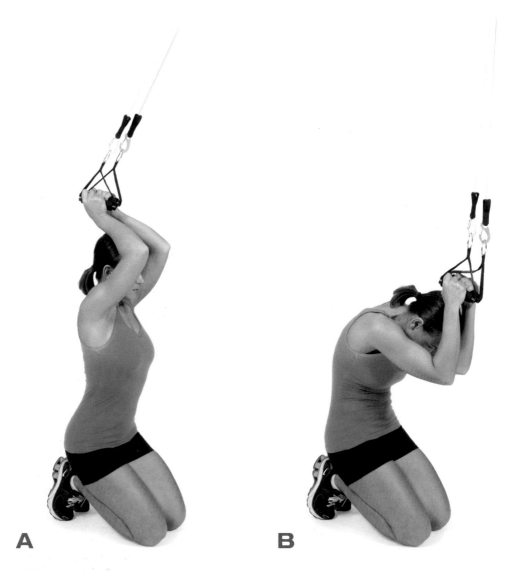

A   B

Squat

This move targets the quads and glutes. Secondary emphasis is on the hamstrings.

Equipment needed: None

Start: Place your hands on your hips or allow your arms to hang down by your sides—whichever is more comfortable. Assume a shoulder-width stance with your toes pointed slightly outward.

Movement: Keeping your core tight, slowly lower your body until your thighs are approximately parallel with the ground. When you reach a seated position, reverse the direction by straightening your legs, and return to the starting position.

Expert tips:

- Your knees should travel in the same plane as your toes at all times.
- Your lower back should be slightly arched and your heels should stay in contact with the floor at all times.
- Look up as you perform the move—this prevents rounding at the upper spine.
- To increase intensity, hold a weighted household object (such as a filled paint can or plastic jug) as you perform the move.

A

B

VARIATION

Wall Squat With Stability Ball

Place a stability ball against the wall, position your body so that the ball sits in the small of your back, and perform the move as described for the standing version. This variation is particularly beneficial for targeting the quadriceps, since it allows you to place your feet farther away from the body.

One-Leg Squat

This move targets the quads and glutes. Secondary emphasis is placed on the hamstrings. This is an excellent move for promoting dynamic balance and core stability.

Equipment needed: Bench or chair

Start: Place your right instep on a bench or chair and take a moderate step out with your left foot so that it is about 2 feet (.6 m) in front of the bench. Place your hands on your hips or allow your arms to hang down by your sides—whichever is more comfortable.

Movement: Keeping your core tight, slowly lower your body until your left thigh is approximately parallel with the ground. Your lower back should be slightly arched and your left heel should stay in contact with the floor at all times. When you reach a seated position, reverse the direction by straightening your left leg and return to the starting position. After performing the desired number of repetitions, repeat on the opposite side.

Expert tips:

- Make sure your knee travels in line with the plane of your toes.
- Look up as you perform the move—this prevents rounding at the upper spine.
- Do not allow your knee to travel beyond your big toe. This error increases stress to the joint capsule. If you can't keep your knee from going past your toes, assume a wider stance.
- To increase intensity, hold a weighted household object (such as a filled paint can or plastic jug) as you perform the move.

A

B

Sumo Squat

This move targets the quads and glutes. The wide stance creates a significant activation of the inner thigh muscles (adductors). The hamstrings receive secondary stimulation.

Equipment needed: None

Start: Place your hands on your hips or allow your arms to hang down by your sides—whichever is more comfortable. Move your feet approximately 12 inches (30 cm) or more wider than your shoulders to assume a stance similar to the sumo wrestlers in Japan.

Movement: Keeping your core tight, slowly lower your body until your thighs are approximately parallel with the ground. Your lower back should be slightly arched and your heels should stay in contact with the floor at all times. When you reach a seated position, reverse the direction by straightening your legs and return to the starting position.

Expert tips:

- Your knees should travel in the same plane as your toes. This is especially important in this move because of the extra-wide stance and the associated potential for increased shear force.
- Look up as you perform the move—this prevents rounding at the upper spine.
- To increase intensity, hold a weighted household object (such as a filled paint can or plastic jug) as you perform the move.

A

B

Sissy Squat

This move targets the quadriceps. It's one of the best exercises for the frontal thighs, especially for targeting the rectus femoris.

Equipment needed: None

Start: Assume a shoulder-width stance. Grasp a stationary object with one hand and rise up on your toes with your core held tightly.

Movement: With one motion, slowly slant your torso back, bend your knees, and lower your body down. Push your knees forward as you descend, and lean back until your torso is almost parallel with the floor. Reverse the direction and rise up until you reach the starting position.

Expert tips:

- Make sure you stay on your toes throughout the move. Keeping your feet planted can result in knee injury.
- If the exercise becomes too easy, you can hold a weighted object (such as a filled paint can or plastic jug) to your chest for added intensity.
- Your upper body should remain in a straight line with your thighs—don't allow your butt to sag during the movement.
- This move is contraindicated for those with existing knee injuries.

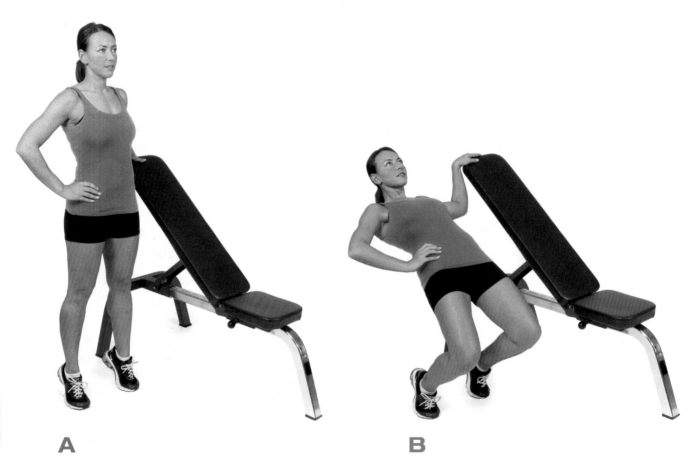

A   B

Split Squat Lunge

This move targets the thighs and glutes. It's a good exercise for developing balance.

Equipment needed: None

Start: Place your hands on your hips or allow your arms to hang down by your sides—whichever is more comfortable. Take a long stride forward with your left leg and raise your right heel so that only the toes of your right foot touch the ground.

Movement: Holding your shoulders back, your core tight, and your chin up, slowly lower your body by flexing your left knee and hip. Continue your descent until your right knee is almost touching the floor. Reverse the direction by forcibly extending your left hip and knee until you return to the starting position. After performing the desired number of reps, repeat the process on the opposite side.

Expert tips:

- Make sure your front knee travels in line with the plane of your toes.
- Focus on dropping down on your rear leg. This keeps the front knee from pushing too far forward, which can place undue stress on the joint capsule.
- Look up as you perform the move—this prevents rounding at the upper spine.
- To increase intensity, hold a weighted household object (such as a filled paint can or plastic jug) as you perform the move.

A

B

Lunge

This move targets the thighs and glutes. It's a good exercise for developing dynamic balance.

Equipment needed: None

Start: Place your hands on your hips or allow your arms to hang down by your sides—whichever is more comfortable. Assume a shoulder-width stance, holding your shoulders back and your chin up.

Movement: Keeping your core tight, take a long step forward with your left leg and slowly lower your body by flexing your left knee and hip. Continue your descent until your right knee is almost touching the floor. Reverse the direction by forcibly extending your left hip and knee, bringing the leg backward until you return to the starting position. Perform the move the same way on your right, then alternate between legs until you have reached the desired number of repetitions.

Expert tips:
- Make sure your front knee travels in line with the plane of your toes.
- Focus on dropping down on your rear leg. This keeps the front knee from pushing too far forward, which can place undue stress on the joint capsule.
- Look up as you perform the move—this prevents rounding at the upper spine.
- To increase intensity, hold a weighted household object (such as a filled paint can or plastic jug) as you perform the move.

A   B

Reverse Lunge

This move targets most of the lower-body muscles, with particular emphasis on the quads and glutes. It's an excellent exercise for improving dynamic balance.

Equipment needed: None

Start: Place your hands on your hips or allow your arms to hang down by your sides—whichever is more comfortable. Assume a shoulder-width stance, holding your shoulders back and your chin up.

Movement: Keeping your core tight, take a long step backward with your right leg and slowly lower your body by flexing your right knee and hip. Continue your descent until your right knee is almost touching the floor. Reverse the direction by forcibly extending the right hip and knee, bringing the leg forward until you return to the starting position. Perform the move the same way on your left side, and then alternate between legs until you have reached the desired number of repetitions.

Expert tips:

- A longer stride works the glutes; a shorter stride targets the quads.
- Look up as you perform the move—this prevents rounding at the upper spine.
- To increase intensity, hold a weighted household object (such as a filled paint can or plastic jug) as you perform the move.

B

A

Side Lunge

This move targets the muscles of the lower body, with a particular emphasis on the adductors of the inner thigh. It's a good exercise for promoting lateral balance. It can also be beneficial for sports such as tennis and soccer.

Equipment needed: None

Start: Assume a wide stance, extending your feet at least a foot (30 cm) beyond your shoulders so that your left foot is perpendicular to your right foot. Place your hands on your hips or allow your arms to hang down by your sides—whichever is more comfortable.

Movement: Keeping your right leg straight and your core held tightly, slowly bend your left knee out to the side until your left thigh is parallel with the floor. Reverse the direction by forcibly extending your left hip and knee, straightening the leg until you reach the starting position. When you have reached the desired number of repetitions, repeat the process on the opposite side.

Expert tips:

- Make sure your front knee travels in line with the plane of your toes.
- Focus on dropping your straight leg down. This keeps the flexing knee from pushing too far forward, which can place undue stress on the joint capsule.
- Look up as you perform the move—this prevents rounding at the upper spine.
- To increase intensity, hold a weighted household object (such as a filled paint can or plastic jug) as you perform the move.

A

B

Step-Up

This move targets the thighs and glutes. It also provides quite a cardiorespiratory workout—you'll be gasping hard by the end of your set!

Equipment needed: Bench, chair, or table

Start: Stand facing the side of a flat bench, chair, or table. Hold your feet shoulder-width apart and core tight. Place your hands on your hips or allow your arms to hang down by your sides—whichever is more comfortable. Step up onto the bench with your right foot.

Movement: Immediately, follow with your left foot so that both feet are flat on the bench. Step back down in the same order (right foot, left foot), returning to the starting position. Continue to step up and down for the desired number of repetitions.

Expert tips:

- A higher step increases stimulation of the glutes.
- Look up as you perform the move—this prevents rounding at the upper spine.
- To increase intensity, hold a weighted household object as you perform the move.

A   B

Floor Kick

This move targets the glutes.

Equipment needed: None

Start: Kneel on the ground on your hands and knees. Bend your left leg at a 90-degree angle and raise your left knee a couple of inches off the floor.

Movement: Holding the sole of your shoe about parallel with the ceiling and your core tight, raise your leg up as far as possible without discomfort. Contract your glutes and then reverse the direction, slowly returning to the starting position. After finishing the desired number of repetitions, repeat the process on your right side.

Expert tips:
- For added intensity, attach leg weights to your ankles.
- If you have trouble supporting your body weight, place a stability ball underneath your torso.

A

B

Prone Hip Extension

This move targets the glutes.

Equipment needed: Bench or table

Start: Lie facedown on a raised flat object (such as a bench, table, or bed) with your lower torso hanging off the end of the bench and your feet almost touching the floor. Grasp the sides of the bench with both hands to support your body.

Movement: Slowly raise your feet up until they are almost parallel with the ground, contracting your glutes at the top of the move. Then, reverse the direction and return your legs to the starting position.

Expert tip: For added intensity, attach leg weights to your ankles.

A

B

Standing Leg Curl

This move targets the hamstrings.

Equipment needed: Leg weights

Start: Attach a weight to your right ankle and stand with your feet shoulder-width apart. Grasp a stationary object for support and bend your torso slightly forward at the hips until you feel a stretch in your hamstrings.

Movement: Holding your back straight and core tight, curl your right foot up, stopping just before it touches your butt (or as far as possible without discomfort). Contract your right hamstrings and then reverse the direction, slowly returning to the starting position. After finishing the desired number of repetitions, repeat the process on your left side.

Expert tip: Only the lower leg should move—keep your thigh stable throughout the exercise.

A

B

Prone Leg Curl

This move targets the hamstrings.

Equipment needed: Leg weights

Start: Attach ankle weights to both ankles and lie facedown on a flat bench or on the floor, holding your toes slightly off the floor.

Movement: Keeping your thighs pressed against the flat surface, curl your feet up, stopping just before your feet touch your butt (or going as far as possible without discomfort). Contract your hamstrings and then reverse the direction, slowly returning to the starting position.

Expert tip: Don't allow your toes to touch the floor at the start of the move—doing so takes tension off the hamstrings.

A

B

Lying Adductor Raise

This move targets the inner thigh muscles.

Equipment needed: None

Start: Lie on your right side. Bring your left leg over your right leg and plant your left foot firmly on the floor. Your left leg should remain bent at a 90-degree angle.

Movement: Keeping your right leg straight, raise it as high as possible. Contract your inner thigh and slowly return to the starting position. After finishing the desired number of repetitions, turn over and repeat the process on your left side.

Expert tips:

- Don't allow your working leg to touch the floor at the start of the move—this reduces tension to the target muscles.
- For added intensity, attach leg weights to your ankles.

A

B

Standing Abductor Raise

This move targets the glutes, particularly the gluteus medius and minimus, as well as the outer thigh muscles.

Equipment needed: Leg weights

Start: Attach a leg weight to your right ankle and grasp a stationary object for support.

Movement: Lift your right leg directly out to the side as high as possible without discomfort. Contract your glutes and slowly return along the same path back to the starting position. After finishing the desired number of repetitions, reverse the process and repeat on the left side.

Expert tip: To shift tension to the external rotator muscles (piriformis, gemellus, and obturators), rotate your little toe out as you perform the move.

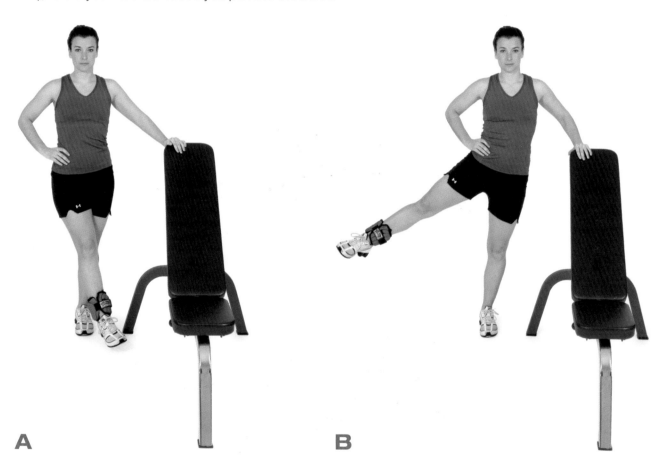

A

B

Lying Abductor Raise

This move targets the glutes, particularly the gluteus medius and minimus, as well as the outer thigh muscles.

Equipment needed: None

Start: Lie on your right side. Bend your right leg at a 90-degree angle and bring your right foot to rest underneath your left knee.

Movement: Keeping your left leg straight, raise it as high as possible without discomfort. Contract your glutes and slowly return to the starting position. After finishing the desired number of repetitions, turn over and repeat the process on your left side.

Expert tips:

- To shift tension to the external rotator muscles (piriformis, gemellus, and obturators), rotate your little toe out as you perform the move.
- Don't allow your working leg to touch the floor at the start of the move—this reduces tension to the target muscles.
- For added intensity, attach leg weights to your ankles.

A

B

Standing Calf Raise

This move targets the calves.

Equipment needed: Wood block or staircase

Start: Stand on a step, such as a block of wood or a staircase, and allow your heels to drop below your toes. Hold onto a stationary object with one hand to maintain balance.

Movement: Keeping your core tight, rise as high as you can on your toes until your calves are fully extended. Contract your calves and then slowly reverse the direction, returning to the starting position.

Expert tips:

- Never bounce during the stretched position of the move—this can cause severe injury to the Achilles tendon.
- Keep your toes pointed straight ahead—significant outward or inward rotation places the knee in a position of poor tracking, which can lead to injury. Contrary to popular belief, this shift will not work the calf muscles any differently.
- To increase intensity, hold a weighted household object (such as a filled paint can or plastic jug) as you perform the move.

A

B

VARIATION

One-Leg Standing Calf Raise
Keeping your left leg behind your body, hold onto a stationary object with one hand. Perform the move with your right leg just as you would for the two-leg version. After completing the desired number of repetitions, repeat with the opposite leg.

Seated Calf Raise

This move targets the calves, with an emphasis on the soleus muscle.

Equipment needed: Bench or chair, wood block

Start: Sit at the edge of a flat bench or chair with the balls of your feet on a block of wood or step. Drop your heels as far below your toes as possible.

Movement: Rise as high as you can on your toes until your calves are fully extended. Contract your calves and then slowly reverse the direction, returning to the starting position.

Expert tips:

- Never bounce during the stretched position of the move—this can cause severe injury to the Achilles tendon.
- Keep your toes pointed straight ahead—significant outward or inward rotation places the knee in a position of poor tracking that can lead to injury. Contrary to popular belief, the shift will not work the calf muscles any differently.
- To increase intensity, place a weighted household object (such as a filled paint can or plastic jug) on your thighs as you perform the move.

A   **B**

VARIATION

One-Leg Seated Calf Raise
Keeping only your right foot on the step, perform the move as you did in the two-leg version. After completing the desired number of repetitions, repeat with your left leg.

Leg Curl

This move targets the hamstrings. It's an excellent move for isolating the hamstrings without allowing the more powerful glutes to dominate.

Equipment needed: Stability ball

Start: Lie on your back on the floor and place your heels on top of a stability ball. Your arms should rest by your sides and your head should be in line with your body.

Movement: Keeping your torso and thighs in a straight line, use your feet to pull the ball as close to you as possible by raising your hips off the floor. Contract your hamstrings and return along the same path back to the starting position.

Expert tips:

- At the top of the move, the soles of your feet should be flat on the ball.
- Use a larger ball to increase range of motion.

A

B

Leg Extension

This move targets the quadriceps.

Equipment needed: Stability ball, leg weights

Start: Sit on a stability ball and attach a leg weight to your right ankle. Keep your left foot planted firmly on the floor and grasp the sides of the ball for support. With your right knee bent at a 90-degree angle, lift your right foot so that it is a couple inches from the floor.

Movement: Maintaining an erect torso, lift your right foot up until your lower leg is almost parallel with the ground. Contract your right quad and then reverse the direction, slowly returning to the starting position. After performing the desired number of reps, repeat the process on your left side.

Expert tips:

- If you have trouble maintaining balance, brace the ball against a wall.
- Don't lift your thigh at any point during the move—this allows the hip flexors to dominate over the quads.

A

B

Squat

This move targets the quads and glutes. Secondary emphasis is placed on the hamstrings.

Equipment needed: Resistance band

Start: Attach a loop handle to each end of a resistance band, grip a handle with each hand, and stand on the center of the band with both feet. Assume a shoulder-width stance, pointing your toes slightly outward. Lower your body until your thighs are approximately parallel with the ground, and then raise the handles to shoulder level, creating tension in the band.

Movement: Keeping your core tight and your hands pinned to your shoulders, stand up against the resistance until your legs are almost completely straight.

Expert tips:

- Your knees should travel in the same plane as your toes at all times.
- Your lower back should be slightly arched and your heels should stay in contact with the floor at all times.
- Look up as you perform the move—this prevents rounding at the upper spine.
- Don't lock your knees—this error keeps constant tension on the target muscles.

A

B

VARIATION

Wall Squat With Resistance Band and Stability Ball
Place a stability ball against the wall, position your body so that the ball sits in the small of your back, and perform the move as described for the standing version. This variation is particularly beneficial for targeting the quadriceps, since it allows you to place your feet farther away from the body.

Split Squat Lunge

This move targets the thighs and glutes. It's a good move for developing balance.

Equipment needed: Resistance band

Start: Attach a loop handle to each end of a resistance band, grip a handle with each hand, and stand on the center of the band with your left foot. Take a long stride backward with your right leg and raise your right heel until only the toes of your right foot are touching the ground. Lower your body until your left thigh is approximately parallel with the ground and then raise the handles to shoulder level, creating tension in the band.

Movement: Keeping your core tight and your hands pinned to your shoulders, rise up against the resistance until your legs are almost completely straight.

Expert tips:

- Make sure your front knee travels in line with the plane of your toes.
- Focus on dropping down on your rear leg. This keeps the front knee from pushing too far forward, which can place undue stress on the joint capsule.
- Look up as you perform the move—this prevents rounding at the upper spine.

A   **B**

Leg Press

This move targets the glutes and quads, with secondary emphasis on the hamstrings.

Equipment needed: Resistance band

Start: Lie on your back on the floor and bring your knees toward your chest. Wrap loop attachments on the ends of a resistance band around the middle of both feet and hold the middle of the band.

Movement: Keeping your torso stable, forcefully extend your hips and knees until they are almost locked. Contract your quads, and then slowly return along the same path back to the starting position.

Expert tip: Make sure there is no slack in the band at the beginning of the move.

A

B

Leg Extension

This move targets the quadriceps.

Equipment needed: Resistance band

Start: Secure the center of a resistance band to a stationary object (such as a door jamb) at approximately knee height and attach the ends of the band to your ankles with leg cuffs. Lie facedown on the floor with your head facing the stationary object. Your knees should be bent at about a 90-degree angle, and there should not be any slack in the band.

Movement: Keeping your thighs pressed to the floor, push your feet down until they reach the floor. Contract your quads and then reverse the direction, returning back to the starting position.

Expert tip: Make sure there is no slack in the band at the beginning of the move.

A

B

VARIATION

One-Leg Extension
Secure the center of a resistance band to a stationary object (such as a door jamb) at approximately knee height, attach one end of the band to your right ankle with a leg cuff, and perform the move as described. After completing the desired number of repetitions, repeat on the opposite leg.

Prone One-Leg Curl

This move targets the hamstrings.

Equipment needed: Resistance band

Start: Secure the center of a resistance band to a stationary object (such as a door jamb) at approximately ankle height and attach the end of the band to your left ankle with a leg cuff. Lie facedown on the floor, holding your head away from the stationary object and your legs straight.

Movement: Keeping your thighs pressed to the floor, curl your left foot up, stopping just before your foot touches your butt (or going as far as possible without discomfort). Contract your left hamstrings and then reverse the direction, returning back to the starting position. After finishing the desired number of repetitions, repeat on your right leg.

Expert tip: Make sure there is no slack in the band at the beginning of the move.

A

B

Standing Abductor Raise

This move targets the glutes, particularly the gluteus medius and minimus, as well as the outer thigh muscles.

Equipment needed: Resistance band

Start: Attach a resistance band to a stationary object (such as a door jamb), and then fasten the other end to your right ankle with a leg cuff. Position yourself so that your left side faces the stationary object and grasp something sturdy for support.

Movement: Keeping your core tight, pull your right leg across your body and directly out to the side. Contract your glutes and then slowly return the weight along the same path back to the starting position. After finishing the desired number of repetitions, invert the process and repeat it on the opposite side.

Expert tips:

- Make sure there is no slack in the band at the beginning of the move.
- Don't lean to complete the move—this introduces momentum into the lift, decreasing stimulation of the target muscles.
- To shift tension to the external rotator muscles (piriformis, gemellus, and obturators), rotate your little toe out as you perform the move.

A

B

Standing Adductor Raise

This move targets the inner thigh muscles.

Equipment needed: Resistance band

Start: Attach a resistance band to a stationary object (such as a door jamb) and then fasten the other end to your left ankle with a leg cuff. Position yourself so that your left side faces the stationary object and grasp something sturdy for support.

Movement: Keeping your core tight, pull your left leg toward and across the midline of your body, moving it as far to the right as possible. Contract your inner thigh muscles and then reverse the direction, returning your leg back to the starting position. After performing the desired number of reps, repeat the process on your right side.

Expert tips:

- Make sure there is no slack in the band at the beginning of the move.
- Don't lean to complete the move—this introduces momentum into the lift, decreasing stimulation of the target muscles.

A

B

Standing Calf Raise

This move targets the calves.

Equipment needed: Resistance band

Start: Secure the center of a resistance band to a stationary object (such as a door jamb) at approximately ankle height and attach loop handles to both ends of the band. Grasp a handle in each hand and face away from the door. Bring your arms to shoulder level and step away from the door until there is significant tension in the band.

Movement: Keeping your back straight, your core tight, and your hands pinned to your shoulders, rise up on your toes as high as you can until your calves are fully extended.

Expert tip: Keep your toes pointed straight ahead—significant outward or inward rotation places the knee in a position of poor tracking that can lead to injury. Contrary to popular belief, this shift will not work the calf muscles any differently.

A   B

Bent-Knee Toe Press

This move targets the calves.

Equipment needed: Resistance band

Start: Lie on your back on the floor and bring your knees in toward your chest. Wrap loop attachments attached to a resistance band around the balls of both feet and hold the middle of the band. Flex your ankles so your toes point backward as far as possible without discomfort.

Movement: Keeping your legs stable and motionless, push down with your toes until they are extended as far as possible (as if you were rising high onto your toes). Contract your calves and then slowly return along the same path back to the starting position.

Expert tips:
- Make sure there is no slack in the band at the beginning of the move.
- There is no benefit to turning the toes in or out—just keep them pointed straight ahead.

A

B

VARIATION

One-Leg Bent-Knee Toe Press
Wrap a loop attachment around the ball of your right foot and perform the move as previously described. After completing the desired number of repetitions, repeat with the opposite leg.

Toe Press

This move targets the calves.

Equipment needed: Resistance band

Start: Sit upright on the floor, with your back straight, your core tight, and your feet extended out in front of you. Wrap loop attachments attached to a resistance band around the balls of both feet and hold the middle of the band. Flex your ankles so your toes point backward as far as possible without discomfort.

Movement: Keeping your torso motionless, push down with your toes until they are extended as far as possible (as if you were rising high onto your toes). Contract your calves and then slowly return along the same path back to the starting position.

Expert tips:

- Make sure there is no slack in the band at the beginning of the move.
- There is no benefit to turning the toes in or out—just keep them pointed straight ahead.

A   B

VARIATION

One-Leg Toe Press
Wrap a loop attachment around the ball of your right foot and perform the move as previously described. After completing the desired number of repetitions, repeat with the opposite leg.

Do It With Dumbbells and Barbells

4

No piece of home-gym equipment is as versatile as a set of free weights. Free weights, or dumbbells and barbells, are named as such because they aren't attached to a machine. They give you the ability to perform hundreds of exercise variations for every muscle group imaginable. Better yet, they are adaptable to every body type. Heavy or thin, short or tall, big-boned or petite—no problem. With free weights, you'll never have trouble getting a great workout.

Perhaps the biggest benefit of free weights is that they allow you to work your muscles in three-dimensional space. When lifting a dumbbell or barbell, the weight moves not only up and down, but also forward and backward, right and left, and any direction in between. Most machines cannot deliver this unrestricted freedom of movement.

Why is freedom of movement so important during exercise? Well, for one, it mimics real-life activities. Consider that in order to pick up a package, move furniture, or perform pretty much any physical chore, you must balance and stabilize the object in all planes. Life doesn't provide cams, rods, or other mechanisms to help your cause. Since training with dumbbells and barbells requires the same balance and stability as activities of daily living do, free-weight training improves your ability to perform these tasks in a way that machines simply can't replicate.

Perhaps you're more concerned about toning up than improving functional capacity. Well, freedom of movement also has important implications for body sculpting. Since lifts require greater stabilization, they bring many supporting muscles into play. This gives your physique a polished look with better muscle detail. Bottom line: If you want to optimize shape and symmetry, free weights aren't an option, they're a necessity.

Dumbbells

Dumbbells are the heart of any home gym. In addition to the benefits previously mentioned, they confer several other advantages that can't be derived from other exercise modalities, including the following qualities:

- *Improved muscular balance.* After nearly two decades as a fitness professional, one thing that stands out to me is the number of women who have strength deficits between muscle groups. For some women, it's a function of right or left dominance; for others, it's an adaptation to previous injury; and for others still, it's an imbalance that comes from using one side more than the other in the course of everyday activities (a woman often will be stronger on the side where she holds her purse). These imbalances can't be corrected with machine training (or barbells, to a lesser extent), because your stronger side forces up the weight at the expense of the weaker counterpart. In fact, imbalances can actually be exacerbated by the exclusive use of machines. Dumbbells, on the other hand, require that all of your muscles work equally. Over time, this brings about uniform muscle development, making both sides of your body equivalent in terms of strength and proportions. If the weaker side doesn't do its fair share, you won't be able to complete the lift.

- *Increased range of motion.* With machines and barbells, your range of motion is limited by a fixed hand position on the bar—you can only move the weight as far as your grip will allow. Not so with dumbbells. Because your hands function independently of one another, you can lift through a greater range of motion. For example, during a chest press with dumbbells, you can press the weights both up and inward. This extra range recruits more muscle fibers, leading to greater muscular development and better flexibility.

- *Reduced joint strain.* Dumbbells are better suited to move in line with the natural action of your body than exercises performed on a bar. The reason: You aren't locked into a preset pattern of movement. If necessary, your joints can adopt a more circular pattern of motion, which places less strain on soft-tissue structures and diminishes the chance of injury.

Dumbbells can be classified into two basic categories: fixed and adjustable. You're undoubtedly familiar with the fixed variety (sometimes called stand-alone dumbbells). You can find them in practically every commercial gym in America, lined up in racks against walls or mirrors. The simple design includes a small bar with weighted plates attached at each end; no mess, no fuss.

The primary benefit to fixed dumbbells is that you don't have to spend time adjusting weights. Simply pick them up and you're ready to go. The downside is that they can clutter up your workout area. A complete set of dumbbells up to 25 pounds (11 kg) includes 16 separate weights. If space is an issue, dumbbells can be cumbersome.

Fixed dumbbells (see figure 4.1a) are usually made of cast iron or solid steel and sometimes covered in neoprene, chrome, vinyl, or rubber. I'd advise you to stay clear of plain cast-iron dumbbells. The paint tends to chip off with frequent use, and they are prone to rust. Also, avoid the old, bulky style of dumbbells that are filled with sand. You'll wind up with a big mess if the outer covering breaks. Trust me; it's not much fun trying to vacuum grains of sand out of your carpet or off your hardwood floor!

Adjustable dumbbells are similar to miniature barbells in that you add plates to the ends of a steel bar. The weights are then secured with clips or collars to prevent slipping. Although this style of dumbbell is generally less expensive than the fixed variety, it is inefficient. You'll waste valuable training time while adding and subtracting weights. Housing the plates becomes unruly when you progress to heavier poundages. I don't recommend them.

However, a special type of adjustable weight called a selectorized dumbbell (see figure 4.1b) warrants consideration. Although the exact shape and structure varies from one model to the next, the basic design consists of a handle attached to a series of nested weight plates. You choose the weight by either turning a knob or inserting a pin into the nested plates. This engages the desired amount of weights to the handle.

A **B**

FIGURE 4.1 **Dumbbells:** *(a)* fixed and *(b)* selectorized.

The primary advantage of selectorized dumbbells is their space efficiency. A pair of selectorized 'bells can take the place of a dozen or more pairs of the fixed variety. Just stick them in a closet or tuck them away in a corner, and they're out of harm's way—a big plus if you have a small workout area. The trade-off is that changing from one set of weights to another can take 30 seconds or more. At first, this might not seem like a big deal, but the additional time can be detrimental to circuit training or time-sensitive techniques such as drop sets, supersets, and giant sets.

Medicine Balls

Medicine balls (see figure 4.2) can be an effective training tool. They differ from stability balls in that they're weighted, ranging from 2 to 15 pounds (1-7 kg) or more. You don't train on a medicine ball; rather, you use it to increase the resistance of an exercise. Its main benefit is for plyometric exercises (speed and power training), in which you release the ball after a fast concentric repetition. If you plan to perform plyometric moves, purchasing a variety of medicine balls is a must. You can use them as substitutes for dumbbells or hold them comfortably against your torso or between your legs for abdominal exercises.

FIGURE 4.2 **Medicine ball.**

The choice between fixed or selectorized dumbbells basically boils down to the choice between space and convenience. If you have room to store at least half a dozen sets of dumbbells, you should opt for the fixed variety. The ability to switch from one set of 'bells to another at will is a nice convenience. At the very least, you should probably purchase a set with weights that include 3-, 5-, 8-, 10-, 12-, and 15-pound dumbbells (approximately 1, 2, 4, 5, 6, and 7 kg). Chances are you'll need to purchase heavier weights not long after beginning serious training. Depending on the coating, expect to pay around $1 per pound for quality dumbbells.

If you don't have mats covering your floors, consider buying dumbbells with rubberized ends. Dumbbells made solely of iron or steel can damage flooring if dropped, but their rubberized counterparts tend to be more forgiving of hard surfaces. I'd suggest going with hexagon-shaped dumbbells, which don't roll around on the floor like round dumbbells do.

To reduce clutter, you'll probably want to purchase a rack for storing your fixed dumbbells. The tree-style rack (see figure 4.3*a*) takes up a bit less space than horizontal models (see figure 4.3*b*), but its construction tends to make it more difficult to remove and rack the 'bells. Whatever style you choose, make sure to test its sturdiness. You don't want the rack to give out when holding 100 pounds (45 kg) or more. A high-quality unit should have little or no give when you shake it.

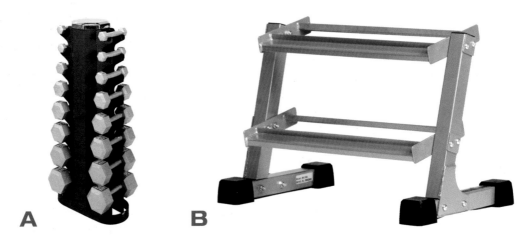

A **B**

FIGURE 4.3 **Dumbbell racks: *(a)* tree and *(b)* horizontal.**
(a) Photo courtesy of Sport Supply Group, Inc., dba BSN Sports/Champion Barbell.
(b) Photo courtesy of Star Trac Fitness.

If you are strapped for space, selectorized dumbbells are the way to go. They range in price from $150 for a set of two 25-pound (11 kg) weights to as much as $450 for a set with a weight capacity of 75 pounds (34 kg). Although you might be tempted to purchase a unit that satisfies current strength levels, I recommend buying a heavier set than you need. Here's why: Let's say that a year from now, you've gained a significant amount of strength from your training efforts. Suddenly, the weights that used to be fine are too light. If you have selectorized dumbbells, you'll need to purchase an entirely new set; there's no way to add to what you've got. That's a big additional expense. Consider 25 pounds as a minimum, but it's probably better to go for a model with a capacity of 45 or 50 pounds (20-22 kg).

A product called PlateMates is a cool accessory for your free-weight collection. PlateMates are small weighted implements that attach to the ends of dumbbells or

barbells with powerful magnets, allowing you to add weight in tiny increments (see figure 4.4). They are particularly useful when training with lighter weights. Consider that the difference between 25- and 30-pound (11-14 kg) dumbbells is only 17 percent, while the difference between 3- and 5-pound (1-2 kg) weights is a whopping 40 percent! PlateMates are currently available in pound increments of 5/8, 1 1/4, 1 7/8, and 2 1/2 (.3, .6, .9, and 1.1 kg). Their limitation is that they only work on free weights with metal exteriors. Weights coated in rubber, neoprene, and other nonmetallic substances won't hold a magnetic charge.

FIGURE 4.4 **PlateMates.**

Barbells

If dumbbells are the heart of a home gym, barbells are the pacemaker. Although they are not quite as versatile, barbells have a couple of advantages over dumbbells. First, they allow you to lift more weight with each repetition. Since the collective force of two limbs is greater than that of a single limb, you can better tax the upper limits of your strength. What's more, certain exercises, such as good mornings and front squats, are just easier to perform with a barbell. In other exercises, such as back squats and lunges, barbells alleviate the hassle and strain of holding onto weights.

Barbells come in two basic categories: Olympic and standard (see figure 4.5, a-b, on page 110). Most fitness pros consider Olympic barbells to be the top of the line. The customary Olympic bar spans 7 feet (2 m), weighs approximately 44 pounds (20 kg), and handles loads of more than a thousand pounds (455 kg). Because of its durability and weight capacity, you'll find this barbell in virtually every gym. Shorter Olympic bars, which are available in 5- and 6-foot (1.5-2 m) lengths, might be more appropriate if your workout space is limited.

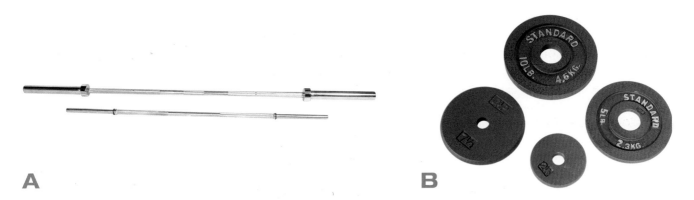

FIGURE 4.5 Olympic and standard *(a)* barbells and *(b)* plates.

A standard barbell has the same length as an Olympic bar, but weighs in at a mere 20 pounds (9 kg). With a load capacity of more than 400 pounds (181 kg), it isn't quite as sturdy as the Olympic model, but should nevertheless accommodate the fitness needs of most women. Standard barbells also come as stand-alone units, with the weights fixed to the bar. Although this configuration provides a modicum of convenience, the added cost and space requirements renders them impractical for the majority of home gyms.

A useful variation of the barbell is called the E-Z curl bar—so named because its S-shaped curves permit a grip that is easier on the joints (see figure 4.6). An Olympic E-Z curl bar spans 4 feet (1.2 m) and weighs 18 pounds (8 kg); its standard counterpart weighs 12 pounds (5 kg). The primary benefit of the E-Z curl bar is in the performance of arm exercises; it helps you perform lifts that are more in line with your natural carrying angle. The curvature reduces stress to your wrists and elbows, making workouts more comfortable and safer. However, the E-Z curl bar is not ideal for squats, lunges, good mornings, or any other exercise where the bar is placed on your upper back; in such movements its irregular conformation is more of a hindrance than a help.

FIGURE 4.6 E-Z curl bar.

The most economical way to purchase barbells is in a set. For example, a standard barbell set costs about $50. This includes a 7-foot (2 m) straight bar, 85 pounds (39 kg) of weighted plates, and collars. If you were to purchase them separately, these same items would cost well over a hundred bucks. A set like this is sufficient for most women at beginning and intermediate levels. You can purchase additional weights as you progress to more advanced levels of training.

Want to go for the top of the line? If you shop around, you can find a complete Olympic set on sale for around $100. This set includes a 7-foot bar, 300 pounds (136 kg) of weighted plates, and collars. This is a real deal, considering the bar alone generally goes for at least $75. Now you're probably thinking, "Why would I ever need 300 pounds of weights?" Fair point. Unless you have aspirations of becoming a powerlifter, you'll likely never need so much weight. However, if you have the space, it's better to have a little more equipment than you need, if for nothing other than the resale value. And here's a potential side benefit: If you convince your husband or boyfriend to work out with you, the extra plates could very well come in handy.

If you purchase plates separately, make sure you match the style of plates to the type of bar you own. Standard plates have holes slightly more than an inch (2.5 cm) in diameter while Olympic plates have 2-inch (5 cm) holes. These plates are not interchangeable. Plates cost approximately 50 cents per pound regardless of the style. Iron is definitely best. Those made of plastic are prone to breakage and don't hold up well over time.

Unless you don't care about plates littering your workout area, consider buying a weight tree (see figure 4.7). These nifty little units, which cost about $80, help you efficiently organize your weights so they're at your disposal whenever you need them.

FIGURE 4.7   Weight tree.
Photo courtesy of CAP Barbell.

Benches

If you're serious about training, I highly recommend that you purchase a high-quality bench. Is a bench an absolute necessity? No. You can certainly get a good workout without one. But owning a bench substantially increases the breadth of exercises you can perform, and also eliminates the need to use household furniture for unintended purposes. This ultimately translates into better results. Prices for high-quality benches begin at $200. Unless you're really strapped for finances or space, make the purchase of a bench a priority.

Your best bet is to go with a bench that's adjustable. This allows you to alter the training angle, thereby enhancing your ability to interject variety into your routine. At the very least, an adjustable bench should have four levels: flat, low incline, high incline, and upright. Some benches have a dozen levels or more, including varying levels of decline. Generally speaking, the more levels you can get, the better.

Safety Tip

Make sure to use collars when working out with a barbell. Collars are rounded fasteners that attach to the ends of a barbell, securing the plates to the bar (see figure 4.8). From a safety perspective, they're a must. If you tilt the wrong way with unsecured plates, you risk serious injury. Look for collars that are spring-loaded. They are easier to operate than the screw-on variety; just squeeze the handles, and they slip on and off in an instant.

FIGURE 4.8   **Collar.**

The most important consideration when selecting a bench is whether or not it is sturdy. Pull back and forth on the padded top. There should be little or no sway and no extraneous movement. Remember, a bench must support both your own body weight and the weights you'll be training with. You certainly don't want to end up in a hospital because you purchased a flimsy piece of junk that gave out in the middle of a set of dumbbell presses.

Comfort is secondary to a bench's sturdiness but still an important consideration. Press the heel of your palm into the center of the bench. The padding should be firm yet supple. If your hand sinks down to the wooden base, look elsewhere.

Many benches expand to include a wide array of attachments, including chinning bars and equipment for leg extensions, leg curls, and dips. If there's any possibility that you might want one or more of these options in the future, look for a bench that's expandable.

If you're purchasing barbells, consider choosing a bench with a power rack (see figure 4.9). Power racks have adjustable uprights flanking each side of the bench. These implements facilitate the performance of various exercises that are difficult to execute on a standard bench, such as barbell squats and bench presses. You'll pay a bit more—good ones go for around $400 to $500—but the range of additional barbell exercises you'll be able to do is definitely worth the extra expense. Opt for one that adjusts to a minimum of 5 feet (1.5 m) so you can rack the bar when performing squats, lunges, and other lower-body exercises. Be sure to take space into account. A 6-foot (2 m) bench with 4-foot (1.2 m) wide uprights requires a workout area of at least 8 square feet (2.4 sq m).

FIGURE 4.9 Bench with power rack.
Photo courtesy of York Barbell Company.

Shoulder Press

This move targets the deltoids, with an emphasis on the front delts. Secondary emphasis is placed on the upper trapezius and triceps.

Equipment needed: Dumbbells, bench

Start: Sit at the edge of a flat bench or chair, with your feet planted firmly on the floor and your core held tight. Grasp two dumbbells and bring the weights to shoulder level, with your palms facing forward.

Movement: Press the dumbbells directly up and in, allowing them to gently touch together directly over your head. Contract your deltoids and then slowly return the dumbbells along the same arc back to the starting position.

Expert tips:

- Don't arc the weights outward as you press them up—this increases stress to the connective tissue in the shoulder joint.
- Don't lock your elbows at the top of the move—doing so reduces tension to the target muscles.

A   B

VARIATIONS

Shoulder Press With Stability Ball
Sit upright on a stability ball and perform the move as previously described.

Standing Shoulder Press
Assume a shoulder-width stance and perform the move as previously described.

Arnold Press

The Arnold Press was named after the one-and-only Governator, Arnold Schwarzenegger, who supposedly considers it his favorite shoulder exercise. The move targets the deltoids, with secondary emphasis on the upper trapezius and triceps. Due to the rotation during movement, it's a good alternative to the traditional shoulder press.

Equipment needed: Dumbbells, bench

Start: Sit at the edge of a flat bench, with your feet planted firmly on the floor and your core held tight. Grasp two dumbbells and bring the weights to shoulder level, with your palms facing your body.

Movement: As you press the dumbbells directly upward, simultaneously rotate your hands so that your palms face forward during the last portion of the movement. Touch the weights together over your head and then slowly return them along the same arc, rotating your hands back to the starting position.

Expert tips:

- This shouldn't be a mechanical movement—rotate your hands smoothly as you press.
- Don't lock your elbows at the top of the move—doing so reduces tension to the target muscles.

A

B

VARIATIONS

Arnold Press With Stability Ball
Sit upright on a stability ball and perform the move as previously described.

Standing Arnold Press
Assume a shoulder-width stance and perform the move as previously described.

Upright Row

This move targets the medial (middle) delts, with secondary emphasis on the biceps.

Equipment needed: Dumbbells

Start: Grasp two dumbbells and allow your arms to hang down from your shoulders in front of your body, with your palms facing in toward your body and your core held tight. Assume a comfortable stance and keep your knees slightly bent.

Movement: Keeping your elbows higher than your wrists at all times, raise the dumbbells up along the line of your body until your upper arms approach shoulder level. Contract your delts and then slowly lower the dumbbells along the same path back to the starting position.

Expert tips:

- Initiate the action by lifting the elbows—not the wrists—to ensure optimal stimulation of the target muscles.
- Be careful not to lift your elbows beyond a position parallel with the ground. Doing so can lead to shoulder impingement, which can injure the rotator cuff.
- Keep the weights as close to your body as possible.

A

B

Front Raise

This move targets the anterior (front) deltoids.

Equipment needed: Dumbbells

Start: Grasp two dumbbells and allow them to hang by your hips. Stand upright with a tight core and a slight bend to your knees.

Movement: With a slight bend to your elbows, raise the dumbbells directly in front of your body until they reach the level of your shoulders (or a little higher). Contract your deltoids and then slowly return the weights along the same path back to the starting position.

Expert tips:

- Keep your arms fixed throughout the exercise. All movement should take place at the shoulder joint—there should be no movement at the elbow joint.
- Since the front delts receive significant work in many compound movements, use this move selectively unless this muscle is underdeveloped with respect to the medial and posterior heads.

A

B

Lateral Raise

This move targets the medial (middle) deltoids.

Equipment needed: Dumbbells, bench

Start: Sit at the edge of a flat bench or chair, with your feet planted firmly on the floor and your core held tight. Grasp two dumbbells and allow them to hang by your hips. Hold your palms to face your sides.

Movement: With a slight bend to your elbows, raise the dumbbells up and out to the sides until they reach shoulder level. At the top of the movement, the rear of the dumbbells should be slightly higher than the front. Contract your deltoids and then slowly return the weights along the same path back to the starting position.

Expert tips:

- Imagine pouring a cup of milk as you lift. Your pinky should be higher than your thumb at the top of the move—this keeps maximum tension on the medial deltoids.
- Keep your upper arms directly out to the sides at all times. Allowing them to gravitate inward switches the emphasis to the front delts at the expense of the medial delts.

A   B

VARIATIONS

Lateral Raise With Stability Ball
Sit upright on a stability ball and perform the move as previously described.

Standing Lateral Raise
Assume a shoulder-width stance and perform the move as previously described.

Bent Lateral Raise

This move targets the posterior (rear) deltoids. I prefer this to the standing version, since it decreases stress on the lower back.

Equipment needed: Dumbbells, bench

Start: Grasp two dumbbells and sit at the edge of a bench or chair with your feet planted firmly on the floor. Bend your torso forward until it is almost parallel with the ground. Allow the dumbbells to hang down in front of your body. Hold your palms facing in.

Movement: With a slight bend to your elbows, raise the dumbbells up and out to the sides until they are parallel with the ground. Contract your delts at the top of the movement and then slowly return the dumbbells back to the starting position.

Expert tips:

- Don't swing your body to complete a rep—this takes work away from the target muscles.
- Avoid the tendency to bring the elbows in toward your sides as you lift. The elbows should remain out and away from the body throughout the move to keep maximal tension on your rear delts.

A

B

VARIATION

Bent Lateral Raise With Stability Ball

Sit on a stability ball, lean as far forward as possible, and perform the move as previously described.

Prone Reverse Fly

This move targets the posterior (rear) delts. It has the advantage of stabilizing your body so that ancillary muscle actions are minimized.

Equipment needed: Dumbbells, adjustable bench

Start: Lie facedown on an adjustable bench that is set at an incline of approximately 30 degrees. Grasp two dumbbells and allow them to hang down in front of your body, with your palms facing in.

Movement: With a slight bend to your elbows, raise the dumbbells up and out to the sides until they are parallel with the ground. Contract your delts at the top of the movement and then slowly return the dumbbells back to the starting position.

Expert tips:

- Don't allow any part of your body to move from the bench as you lift.
- Externally rotate each shoulder as you lift so that your thumb is higher than your pinky at the top of the move.
- Avoid the tendency to bring your elbows in toward your sides as you lift. The elbows should remain out and away from the body throughout the move to keep maximal tension on your rear delts.

A

B

VARIATION

Prone Reverse Fly With Stability Ball
Lie facedown on a stability ball and perform the move as previously described.

Arm Curl

This move targets the biceps.

Equipment needed: Dumbbells, bench

Start: Sit at the edge of a flat bench, with your feet planted firmly on the floor and your core held tightly. Grasp a pair of dumbbells and allow them to hang at your sides. Your elbows should be straight but not locked, and the palms of your hands should face forward. Press your elbows into your sides and keep them stable throughout the move.

Movement: Curl the dumbbells up toward your shoulders and contract your biceps at the top of the move. Then, slowly reverse the direction and return to the starting position.

Expert tips:
- If you desire, you can begin with your palms facing your sides and actively turn your palms up (called supination) as you lift.
- Keep your wrists straight as you lift—don't roll or bend them to complete the move.

A   B

VARIATIONS

Arm Curl With Stability Ball
Sit upright on a stability ball and perform the move as previously described.

Standing Arm Curl
Assume a shoulder-width stance and perform the move as previously described.

Incline Curl

This move targets the biceps. Because the arms are held backward, it's especially effective for targeting the long head of the muscle.

Equipment needed: Dumbbells, adjustable bench

Start: Lie on your back on an adjustable bench that is set at an angle of approximately 40 degrees. Plant your feet firmly on the floor. Grasp two dumbbells and allow the weights to hang behind your body with your palms facing forward. Your elbows should be straight but not locked.

Movement: Keeping your upper arms immobile, curl the dumbbells up toward your shoulders. Contract your biceps, and then slowly return the weights back to the starting position.

Expert tips:
- Make sure your elbows stay back throughout the movement. This keeps maximal tension on the biceps, especially the long head.
- Keep your wrists straight as you lift—don't roll them to complete the move.

A

B

VARIATION

Incline Curl With Stability Ball
Sit with your upper back resting on a stability ball and your body inclined at about a 40-degree angle, and perform the move as previously described.

Preacher Curl

This move targets the biceps, with an emphasis on the short head of the muscle.

Equipment needed: Dumbbells, adjustable bench

Start: Grasp a dumbbell with your left hand. Place the upper portion of your left arm on an incline bench and extend your left forearm until the elbow is almost locked.

Movement: Keeping your upper arm pressed to the bench, curl the dumbbell up toward your shoulders. Contract your biceps and then slowly return the weight back to the starting position. After completing the desired number of reps, repeat on your right side.

Expert tips:
- Your upper arm should be fully braced against the bench—there should be no space between your arm and the bench.
- Keep your wrist straight as you lift—don't roll it to complete the move.

A   B

Concentration Curl

This move targets the biceps, with an emphasis on the short head of the muscle.

Equipment needed: Dumbbells, bench

Start: Sit at the edge of a flat bench with your legs spread wide apart and your feet planted firmly on the floor. Grasp a dumbbell in your left hand and brace your left elbow against the inside of your left thigh. Straighten your arm so that it hangs down near the floor. Your elbow should be straight but not locked.

Movement: Curl the weight up toward your left shoulder, contracting your biceps at the top of the move. Reverse the direction and slowly return to the starting position. After completing the desired number of reps, repeat the process on your right side.

Expert tips:

- Keep your exercising arm braced against your inner thigh at all times. If you are struggling to complete a rep, assist the move with your other hand. Don't swing your exercising arm.
- Keep your wrist straight as you lift—don't roll it to complete the move.

A   B

VARIATION

Concentration Curl With Stability Ball
Sit upright on a stability ball and perform the move as previously described.

Prone Incline Curl

This move targets the biceps. Since the arms are held in front of the body, it's especially effective for targeting the short head of the muscle.

Equipment needed: Dumbbells, adjustable bench

Start: Lie facedown on an incline bench set at 30 degrees. Grasp two dumbbells and allow your arms to hang straight down from your shoulders in front of the bench. Your palms should face away from your body.

Movement: Curl the dumbbells up toward your shoulders, keeping your upper arms stable throughout the movement. Contract your biceps and then slowly return the weights back to the starting position.

Expert tips:
- Don't swing your arms as you lift—this introduces momentum into the movement and reduces stress to the target muscles.
- Keep your wrists straight as you lift—don't roll them to complete the move.

A

B

Hammer Curl

This move targets the upper arms, with an emphasis on the brachialis.

Equipment needed: Dumbbells, bench

Start: Sit at the edge of a flat bench, with your feet planted firmly on the floor and your core held tightly. Grasp a pair of dumbbells and allow your arms to hang at your sides with your palms facing each other.

Movement: Keeping your elbows pressed into your sides, curl the dumbbells up toward your shoulders and contract your biceps at the top of the move. Then, slowly reverse the direction and return to the starting position.

Expert tips:

- Keep your wrists straight as you lift—don't roll them to complete the move.
- Don't allow your upper arms to move forward as you lift—this brings your shoulders into the movement at the expense of your arm muscles.

A   B

VARIATIONS

Hammer Curl With Stability Ball
Sit upright on a stability ball and perform the move as previously described.

Standing Hammer Curl
Assume a shoulder-width stance and perform the move as previously described.

Overhead Triceps Extension

This move targets the triceps, particularly the long head of the muscle.

Equipment needed: Dumbbells, bench

Start: Grasp the stem of a dumbbell with both hands. Sit at the edge of a flat bench or chair, with your feet planted firmly on the floor and your core held tightly. Bring the dumbbell overhead, bend your elbows, and allow the weight to hang down behind your head as far as possible without discomfort.

Movement: Straighten your arms, pointing your elbows toward the ceiling throughout the move. Contract your triceps and then slowly lower the weight along the same path back to the starting position.

Expert tips:

- Keep your elbows pinned to your ears as you lift—if your elbows flare, you'll reduce stress to the triceps.
- If you have difficulty maintaining erect posture, place the bench in the upright position and brace your back against the pad.
- If you desire, you can perform this exercise one arm at a time. This may help you alleviate stress on your elbows and focus on each arm individually.

A   B

VARIATIONS

Overhead Triceps Extension With Stability Ball
Sit upright on a stability ball and perform the move as previously described.

Standing Overhead Triceps Extension
Assume a shoulder-width stance and perform the move as previously described.

Lying Triceps Extension

This move targets the triceps.

Equipment needed: Dumbbells, bench

Start: Lie on your back on a flat bench with your feet planted firmly on the floor. Grasp a dumbbell in each hand, palms facing one another, and straighten your arms until the dumbbells are directly over you (your arms should be perpendicular to your body).

Movement: Keeping your elbows pointed in and toward the ceiling, slowly bend your elbows to lower the dumbbells until they reach a point just above your forehead. Press the dumbbells back up until they reach the starting position, contracting your triceps at the top of the move.

Expert tips:

- Keep your elbows perpendicular to your body as you lift—if your elbows flare, you'll reduce stress to the triceps.
- Your upper arms should remain motionless throughout the move—only your forearms should carry out the lift.
- This exercise can also be performed one arm at a time, which lets you focus on each arm individually.

A

B

Triceps Kickback

This move targets the triceps, particularly the medial and lateral heads.

Equipment needed: Dumbbells

Start: Stand and bend your body forward until it is almost parallel with the ground. Hold your core tight. Grasp a dumbbell with your right hand and press the upper portion of your right arm against your side. Bend your elbow to a 90-degree angle and move your palm so it faces your body.

Movement: Raise the weight by straightening your arm until it is parallel with the floor. Reverse the direction and return the weight back to the starting position. After finishing the desired number of repetitions, repeat on your left side.

Expert tips:
- Don't let your upper arm sag down as you lift—this reduces the effects of gravity and thus diminishes tension to the target muscle.
- Don't flick your wrist at the top of movement—this common performance error fatigues the forearm muscles before the triceps and reduces the effectiveness of the move.
- Keep your back slightly arched and your torso approximately parallel with the floor throughout the movement. Never round your spine—this places undue stress on the lumbar area and could lead to injury.

 A

 B

Military Press

This move targets the shoulders, particularly the front delts. Secondary emphasis is placed on the upper trapezius and the triceps.

Equipment needed: Barbell, bench

Start: Sit at the edge of a flat bench, with your feet planted firmly on the floor and your core held tightly. Grasp a barbell and bring it to the level of your upper chest. Your palms should face away from your body.

Movement: Press the barbell directly up and over your head, contracting your deltoids at the top of the move. Slowly return the bar along the same path back to the starting position.

Expert tips:

- Your elbows should remain forward, not flared, throughout the move to maintain movement in the proper plane.
- Don't lock your elbows at the top of the move—doing so reduces tension to the target muscles.
- It's wise to have a spotter on this movement to ensure safety.

A   B

Upright Row

This move targets the middle delts, with secondary emphasis on the biceps.

Equipment needed: Barbell

Start: Allow your arms to hang down from your shoulders with your palms facing in toward your body. Grasp a barbell with a shoulder-width grip. Assume a shoulder-width stance, with your core tight and your knees slightly bent.

Movement: Keeping your elbows higher than your wrists at all times, raise the bar up along the line of your body until your upper arms approach shoulder level. Contract your delts and then slowly lower the bar along the same path back to the starting position.

Expert tips:

- Initiate the action by lifting the elbows—not the wrists—to ensure optimal stimulation of the target muscles.
- Be careful not to lift your elbows beyond a point that is parallel with the ground. Doing so can lead to shoulder impingement, which injures the rotator cuff.
- Keep the bar as close to your body as possible.

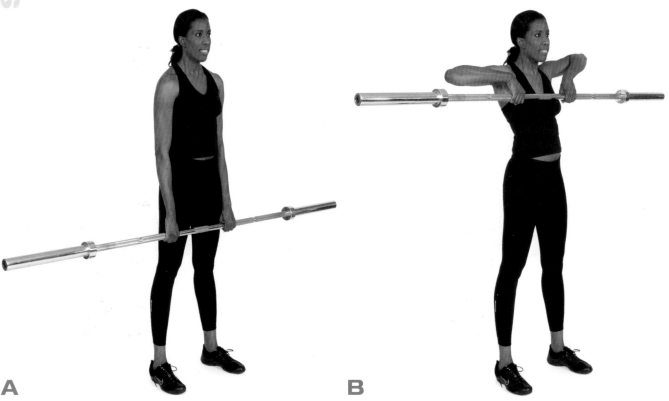

A   B

Close-Grip Bench Press

This move targets the triceps. The pecs also are worked to a significant degree.

Equipment needed: Barbell, bench

Start: Lie on your back on a flat bench with your feet planted firmly on the floor. Grasp an E-Z curl bar with your hands approximately 1 foot (30 cm) apart. Bring the bar directly under your breasts.

Movement: Keeping your elbows close to your sides, press the weight straight up over your chest toward the ceiling. Contract your triceps and slowly return the bar along the same path to the starting position.

Expert tips:

- Don't grip the bar with your hands too close together—this actually causes the elbows to flare, reducing stress to the triceps. The goal is to keep the elbows close to your sides at all times.
- You can also use a straight bar for this move, although it tends to place greater stress on the wrists.
- It's wise to have a spotter for this movement to ensure safety.

A

B

Front Raise

This move targets the anterior (front) deltoids.

Equipment needed: Barbell

Start: Stand with your palms facing your body, grasp a barbell with a shoulder-width grip, and allow it to hang in front of your body by your hips. Stand upright with your core held tightly and your knees slightly bent.

Movement: With a slight bend to your elbows, raise the bar directly in front of your body to just above shoulder level. Contract your deltoids and then slowly return the bar along the same path back to the starting position.

Expert tips:

- Keep your arms fixed throughout the exercise. All movement should take place at the shoulder joint—there should be no movement at the elbow joint.
- Since the front delts receive significant work in many compound movements, use this move sparingly.

A

B

Preacher Curl

This move targets the biceps, especially the short head.

Equipment needed: Barbell, stability ball

Start: Grasp a barbell with a shoulder-width grip and your palms facing away from your body. Kneel on the floor, lean on top of the stability ball, and drape your upper arms over the other side of the ball. Allow your forearms to fully extend, but don't lock your elbows.

Movement: Keeping your upper arms pressed against the ball, curl the bar up toward your shoulders. Contract your biceps and then slowly return the bar back to the starting position.

Expert tip: Keep your wrists straight as you lift—don't roll them to complete the move.

A

B

Arm Curl

This move targets the biceps.

Equipment needed: Barbell

Start: Assume a comfortable stance, about shoulder-width, with your core held tightly and your knees slightly bent. Grasp an E-Z curl bar with a palms-up, shoulder-width grip.

Movement: Keeping your upper arms pressed to your sides, curl the bar up toward your shoulders and contract your biceps at the top of the move. Slowly reverse the direction and return to the starting position.

Expert tips:

- Keep your upper arms motionless throughout the move—all activity takes place at the elbow.
- This move can also be performed with a straight bar.

A

B

21s

This move targets the biceps. It's a great way to improve strength in your weak points of the curl.

Equipment needed: Barbell

Start: Assume a comfortable stance with a slight bend to your knees. Grasp an E-Z curl bar with your hands shoulder-width apart, your palms up, and your elbows pinned to your sides.

Movement: Curl the bar until your elbows are at a 90-degree angle. Return to the starting position. After performing seven reps, curl the bar to a 90-degree angle, and then curl the weight to your shoulders. Return to the 90-degree angle and perform seven reps. Finally, lower the bar fully and perform seven complete reps, bringing the weight to shoulder level and returning to a fully stretched position.

Expert tips:

- Keep your upper arms motionless throughout the move—all activity should take place at the elbow.
- This move can also be performed with a straight bar.

A

B

C

Nose Breaker

This move is also called a skull crusher; don't worry though, as long as you utilize proper form, you won't break any bones! The target muscles are the triceps.

Equipment needed: Barbell, bench

Start: Lie on your back on a flat bench with your feet planted firmly on the floor. Grasp an E-Z curl bar with your palms facing away from your body. Straighten your arms so that the bar is directly over your chest (your arms should be perpendicular to your body).

Movement: Keeping your elbows in and pointed toward the ceiling, slowly lower the bar until it rests just above the level of your forehead. Press the bar back up until it reaches the starting position, contracting your triceps as you reach the top of the move.

Expert tips:

- Keep your upper arms perpendicular to the floor at all times—this maintains roughly equal tension on all three heads of the triceps.
- This move can also be performed with a straight bar.

A

B

Drag Curl

This move targets the biceps, with an emphasis on the long head of the muscle.

Equipment needed: Barbell

Start: Grasp an E-Z curl bar with a palms-up, shoulder-width grip and allow it to hang in front of your body. Assume a comfortable stance, with a slight bend in your elbows and knees.

Movement: Keeping your upper arms close to your sides and stable throughout the move, slowly bring your elbows back behind your body as far as possible, curling the bar along the line of your torso up toward your shoulders. Contract your biceps, slowly reverse the direction, and return to the starting position.

Expert tips:

- Your elbows should move back as you lift—this keeps maximum tension on the long head of the biceps.
- This move can also be performed with a standard barbell.

A   B

Pullover

This move targets the lats and the middle part of your chest.

Equipment needed: Dumbbells, bench

Start: Lie on your back on a flat bench, with your feet firmly planted on the floor. Grasp a dumbbell with both hands and raise it directly over your face.

Movement: Keeping your elbows slightly bent, slowly lower the dumbbell behind your head as far as possible without discomfort. When you feel a complete stretch in your lats, reverse the direction and return to the starting position, contracting your lats as you reach the top of the move.

Expert tips:

- Stretch only within a comfortable range of motion—overstretching can lead to shoulder injury.
- You should maintain a slight bend in your elbows throughout the movement. Do not straighten them as you lift. This will increase triceps activation at the expense of your target muscles.

A

B

VARIATION

Pullover With Stability Ball

Lie back on a stability ball so that your body is roughly parallel with the floor and perform the move as previously described.

One-Arm Row

This move targets the back muscles and is especially effective for developing the inner back musculature.

Equipment needed: Dumbbells, bench

Start: Place your left hand and left knee on a flat bench, and plant your right foot firmly on the floor. Grasp a dumbbell in your right hand with your palm facing in, and let your arm hang by your side.

Movement: Keeping your elbow close to your body and your core tight, pull the dumbbell up and back until it touches your side. Feel a contraction in your upper back and then reverse the direction, slowly returning to the start position. After finishing the desired reps on your right side, repeat the exercise with your left arm.

Expert tips:
- Keep your back slightly arched and your torso parallel with the floor throughout the movement.
- Keep your chin up at all times—this prevents rounding of the spine.
- To visualize the move, think of starting a lawn mower in a very controlled fashion.

A   B

Incline Row

This move targets the upper back muscles.

Equipment needed: Dumbbells, bench

Start: Lie on your back on an incline bench that is set at a 30-degree angle. Grasp two dumbbells with a neutral grip (palms facing each other) and allow your arms to hang straight down from your shoulders.

Movement: Keeping your elbows close to your sides, pull the dumbbells up to your hips as high as possible. Contract the muscles in your upper back and then reverse the direction, slowly returning to the starting position.

Expert tip: Do not allow your chest to come off the bench as you lift—this can injure the spine.

A   B

Incline Chest Press

This move targets the pectorals, with an emphasis on the upper part of the chest. The triceps and the front delts also receive significant activation.

Equipment needed: Dumbbells, bench

Start: Lie on your back on an adjustable bench that is set at an incline of approximately 30 to 40 degrees. Plant your feet firmly on the floor. Grasp two dumbbells and, with your palms facing away from your body, bring them to shoulder level so that they rest just above your armpits.

Movement: Simultaneously press both dumbbells directly over your chest, moving them in toward each other on the ascent. At the end of the movement, the sides of the dumbbells should gently touch together and the weights should be over the upper portion of your chest. Feel a contraction in your chest muscles and then slowly reverse the direction, returning to the starting position.

Expert tips:
- Keep your elbows flared throughout the move to maintain maximal activation of the pecs.
- As you press the weight, think of moving the dumbbells in an inverted V-pattern to increase range of motion.
- Your body should remain on the bench throughout the movement and remain stable at all times.
- To maintain continuous muscular tension, do not lock your elbows at the end of the move.

A

B

VARIATION

Incline Chest Press With Stability Ball
Lie back on a stability ball so that your torso is at a 30-degree angle to the floor and perform the move as previously described.

Flat Chest Press

This move targets the pectorals, with an emphasis on the middle part of the chest.

Equipment needed: Dumbbells, bench

Start: Lie on your back on a flat bench with your feet planted firmly on the floor. Grasp two dumbbells and, with your palms facing forward, bring them to shoulder level so they rest just above your armpits.

Movement: Simultaneously press both dumbbells directly over your chest, moving them in toward each other on the ascent. At the end of the movement, the sides of the dumbbells should gently touch together and the weights should be over the middle portion of your chest. Feel a contraction in your chest muscles and then slowly reverse the direction, returning to the starting position.

Expert tips:

- Keep your elbows flared throughout the move to maintain maximal activation of the pecs.
- As you press the weight, think of moving the dumbbells in an inverted V-pattern to increase range of motion.
- Your body should remain on the bench throughout the movement and should remain stable at all times.
- To maintain continuous muscular tension, do not lock your elbows at the end of the move.

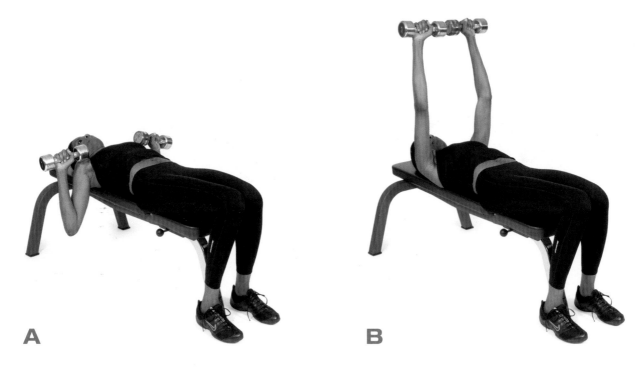

A   **B**

VARIATION

Flat Chest Press With Stability Ball
Lie back on a stability ball so that your torso is roughly parallel with the floor and perform the move as previously described.

Flat Fly

This move targets the pectorals, primarily the middle fibers. It provides better isolation for the chest muscles than the flat press since the triceps aren't involved.

Equipment needed: Dumbbells, bench

Start: Lie on your back on a flat bench, planting your feet firmly on the floor. Grasp two dumbbells and bring them out to your sides, maintaining a slight bend in your elbows throughout the move. Your palms should be facing in and toward the ceiling, and your upper arms should be roughly parallel with the floor.

Movement: Raise the weights upward in a semicircular motion, gently touching the weights together at the top of the move. At the end of the movement, the dumbbells should be over the upper portion of your chest. Contract your chest muscles and then slowly return the weights along the same path back to the starting position.

Expert tips:

- Keep your arms rounded throughout the move; do not straighten your elbows.
- As you lift the weights, think of hugging a beach ball to maintain a circular motion.
- Your body should remain on the bench throughout the movement and should remain stable at all times.
- Avoid overstretching in the starting position, which can cause injury.

A   **B**

VARIATION

Flat Fly With Stability Ball
Lie back on a stability ball so that your torso is roughly parallel with the floor and perform the move as previously described.

▶ **143**

Incline Fly

This move targets the pectorals, primarily the upper fibers of the muscle. It provides better isolation for the chest muscles than an incline press since the triceps are not involved in the exercise.

Equipment needed: Dumbbells, bench

Start: Lie on your back on an adjustable bench that is at an incline of approximately 30 to 40 degrees, planting your feet firmly on the floor. Grasp two dumbbells and bring them out to your sides, maintaining a slight bend in your elbows throughout the move. Your palms should be facing in and toward the ceiling, and your upper arms should be on the same plane as the level of the bench.

Movement: Raise the weights upward in a circular motion, gently touching the weights together at the top of the move. At the end of the movement, the dumbbells should be over the upper portion of your chest. Contract your chest muscles and then slowly return the weights along the same path back to the starting position.

Expert tips:

- Keep your arms rounded throughout the move; do not straighten your elbows.
- As you lift the weights, think of hugging a beach ball to maintain a circular motion.
- Your body should remain on the bench throughout the movement and should remain stable at all times.
- Avoid overstretching in the starting position, which can cause injury.

A   B

VARIATION

Incline Fly With Stability Ball
Lie back on a stability ball so that your upper back is resting against the ball (body inclined at about a 40-degree angle) and perform the move as previously described.

T-Bar Row

This move targets the back muscles.

Equipment needed: Barbell

Start: Place one end of a barbell in the corner of your room (you can wrap a towel around it to help prevent damage to the wall). Stand with the bar between your legs and your feet approximately shoulder-width apart, and grasp the upper portion of the bar with both hands (one hand above the other). Bend forward slightly at the hips, hold your core tight, and allow the bar to hang down in front of your body.

Movement: Keeping your elbows close to your sides, pull the bar up toward your midsection as high as possible. Pinch your shoulder blades together to contract the muscles in your upper back and then reverse the direction, slowly returning to the starting position.

Expert tips:

- It's extremely important to maintain a slight hyperextension of the lower back. Any spinal bend can result in lumbar injury.
- Keep your head up at all times—this prevents rounding of the spine.

A

B

Incline Row

This move targets the back muscles.

Equipment needed: Barbell, adjustable bench

Start: Lie on your stomach on an adjustable bench that is set at an incline of approximately 30 degrees. Grasp a barbell with a shoulder-width overhand grip (palms facing toward your body) and allow your arms to hang straight down from your shoulders.

Movement: Keeping your elbows close to your sides, pull the bar up toward your midsection as high as possible. Pinch your shoulder blades together to contract the muscles in your upper back and then reverse the direction, slowly returning to the starting position.

Expert tips:

- Do not allow your chest to come off the bench as you lift—this can injure the spine.
- Try to bring your elbows as far back as possible at the end of the movement for maximal contraction.

A   B

Reverse Bent Row

This move targets the back muscles.

Equipment needed: Barbell

Start: Grasp a barbell with a shoulder-width reverse grip (palms facing away from your body). Stand with your body angled forward, your knees bent, and your lower back slightly arched. Allow your arms to hang straight down from your shoulders.

Movement: Keeping your elbows close to your sides and your core tight, pull the bar as high up into your midsection as possible. Contract the muscles in your upper back and then reverse the direction, slowly returning to the starting position.

Expert tips:

- It's extremely important to maintain a slight hyperextension of the lower back. Any spinal bend can result in lumbar injury.
- Keep your head up at all times—this prevents rounding of the spine.

A   B

Incline Chest Press

This move targets the pectorals, with an emphasis on the upper part of the chest. The triceps and the front delts also receive significant work.

Equipment needed: Barbell, bench

Start: Lie on your back on an adjustable bench that is set at an incline of approximately 30 to 40 degrees, with your feet planted firmly on the floor. Grasp a barbell with a slightly wider than shoulder-width grip and bring it down to the upper aspect of your chest, stopping about an inch (30 cm) from touching your chest.

Movement: Press the bar directly over your upper chest, moving it in a straight line into the air. At the end of the movement, you should be holding the bar over the upper portion of your chest with your arms extended. Contract your chest muscles and then slowly return the bar along the same path back to the starting position.

Expert tips:

- Keep your elbows flared throughout the move to maintain maximal tension on the pecs.
- Your body should remain on the bench throughout the movement and should stay motionless at all times.
- To maintain continuous muscular tension, make sure you do not lock your elbows at the end of the move.
- It's wise to have a spotter for this movement to ensure safety.

A

B

Flat Chest Press

This move targets the pectorals, with an emphasis on the middle part of the chest. The triceps and the front delts also receive significant work.

Equipment needed: Barbell, bench

Start: Lie on your back on a flat bench, with your feet planted firmly on the floor. Grasp a barbell with a slightly wider than shoulder-width grip and bring it down to the middle of your chest, stopping about an inch (30 cm) before the bar touches your chest.

Movement: Press the bar directly over your chest, moving it in a straight line into the air. At the end of the movement, you should be holding the bar over the upper portion of your chest with your arms extended. Contract your chest muscles and then slowly return the bar along the same path back to the starting position.

Expert tips:

- Keep your elbows flared throughout the move.
- Your body should remain on the bench throughout the movement and should stay motionless at all times.
- To maintain continuous muscular tension, make sure you do not lock your elbows at the end of the move.
- It's wise to have a spotter for this movement to ensure safety.

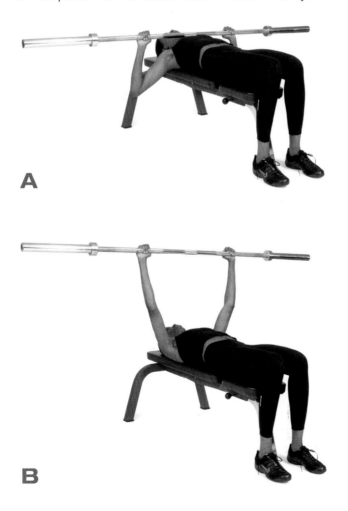

A

B

Side Bend

This move targets the obliques.

Equipment needed: Dumbbells

Start: Grasp two dumbbells and allow them to hang at your sides, with your palms facing your body. Assume a shoulder-width stance with a slight bend to your knees.

Movement: Keeping your core tight, bend your torso to the left as far as possible without discomfort. Contract your obliques and then return along the same path to the starting position. Repeat on your right side, and then alternate between sides until you reach the desired number of repetitions.

Expert tips:
- The movement should take place solely at your waist—your hips shouldn't move at all.
- Your upper body should remain upright at all times—don't sway forward or backward.

A

B

Roll-Out

This move targets the abdominal muscles.

Equipment needed: Barbell

Start: Load a pair of small plates weighing 5 pounds (2 kg) onto the ends of a barbell. Grasp the middle of the bar with an overhand, shoulder-width grip and kneel down so your shoulders are directly over the bar. Your upper back should be rounded and your butt should be held as high off the floor as possible.

Movement: Keeping your knees fixed on the floor and holding your arms taut, roll the bar forward as far as comfortably possible without allowing your body to touch the floor. Reverse the direction by forcefully contracting your abs, returning along the same path back to the starting position.

Expert tips:

- The action should take place solely at the waist—not the hips. Otherwise, your abs work statically rather than actively, diminishing results.
- The contraction happens as you pull back to the starting position—the rolling part of the movement stretches the abs.

Squat

This move targets the quads and glutes. Secondary emphasis is on the hamstrings.

Equipment needed: Dumbbells

Start: Grasp two dumbbells and allow your arms to hang down by your sides, with your palms facing your hips. Assume a shoulder-width stance with your toes pointed slightly outward.

Movement: Keeping your core tight, slowly lower your body until your thighs are approximately parallel with the ground. When you reach a seated position, reverse the direction by straightening your legs and return to the starting position, contracting your quadriceps at the top of the move.

Expert tips:

- Your knees should travel in the same plane as your toes at all times.
- Your lower back should be slightly arched and your heels should stay in contact with the floor at all times.
- Look up as you perform the move—this prevents rounding of the upper spine.
- If you have trouble holding the weights, try using lifting straps.

A

B

VARIATION

Wall Squat With Dumbbells and Stability Ball
Place a stability ball against the wall, position your body so that the ball sits in the small of your back, and perform the move as described for the standing version. This variation is particularly beneficial for targeting the quadriceps, since it allows you to place your feet farther away from the body.

One-Leg Squat

This move targets the quads and the glutes. Secondary emphasis is placed on the hamstrings. This is an excellent move to promote static balance and core stability.

Equipment needed: Dumbbells, bench

Start: Grasp two dumbbells and allow your arms to hang down by your sides, with your palms facing your hips. Place your right instep on a bench or chair.

Movement: Keeping your core tight, slowly lower your body until your left thigh is approximately parallel with the ground. Your lower back should be slightly arched and your left heel should stay in contact with the floor at all times. When you reach a seated position, reverse the direction by straightening your left leg and return to the starting position. After performing the desired number of repetitions, repeat on the opposite side.

Expert tips:
- Make sure your knee travels in line with the plane of your toes.
- Look up as you perform the move—this prevents rounding at the upper spine.
- Do not allow your front knee to travel beyond your big toe. This increases stress to the joint capsule.
- You can increase the difficulty of the exercise by raising the bench's height.

A   B

Sumo Squat

This move targets the quads and glutes. Because of the wide stance, there also is significant activation of the inner thigh muscles (adductors). The hamstrings receive secondary stimulation.

Equipment needed: Dumbbells

Start: Grasp the stem of a dumbbell with both hands and allow it to hang down in front of your body. Take a wide stance that is similar to that of sumo wrestlers in Japan. Your feet should extend approximately a foot (30 cm) or more beyond the shoulders, and your toes should point out at about a 30-degree angle.

Movement: Keeping your core tight, slowly lower your body until your thighs are approximately parallel with the ground. Your lower back should be slightly arched and your heels should stay in contact with the floor at all times. When you reach a seated position, reverse the direction by straightening your legs and return to the starting position.

Expert tips:

- Your knees should travel in the same plane as your toes.
- Your lower back should remain slightly arched and your heels should stay in contact with the floor at all times.
- Look up as you perform the move—this prevents rounding at the upper spine.
- If you have trouble holding the weights, try using lifting straps.

A   B

Split Squat Lunge

This move targets the thighs and glutes. It's a good move to develop balance.

Equipment needed: Dumbbells

Start: Grasp two dumbbells and allow them to hang down by your sides. Take a long stride forward with your left leg and raise your right heel so that your right foot is on its toes.

Movement: Keeping your shoulders back, your core tight, and your chin up, slowly lower your body by flexing your left knee and hip. Continue your descent until your right knee is almost touching the floor. Reverse the direction by forcibly extending the left hip and knee until you return to the starting position. After performing the desired number of reps, repeat the process on your right side.

Expert tips:

- Make sure your front knee travels in line with the plane of your toes.
- Focus on dropping down on your rear leg as opposed to bending the front leg. This keeps the front knee from pushing too far forward, which can place undue stress on the joint capsule.
- Look up as you perform the move—this prevents rounding at the upper spine.

A   B

Lunge

This move targets the thighs and glutes. It's a good move for developing dynamic balance.

Equipment needed: Dumbbells

Start: Grasp two dumbbells and allow them to hang down by your sides, with your palms facing your body. Assume a shoulder-width stance, with your shoulders back and your chin up.

Movement: Keeping your core tight, take a long step forward with your right leg, slowly lowering your body by bending your right knee and hip. Continue your descent until your right knee forms a 90-degree angle and your left knee is almost touching the floor. Reverse the direction by forcibly stepping back with the right leg, bringing it backward until you return to the starting position. Perform the move in the same way on your left side, and then alternate between legs until you reach the desired number of repetitions.

Expert tips:

- Make sure your front knee travels in line with the plane of your toes.
- Focus on dropping down on your rear leg. This keeps the front knee from pushing too far forward, which can place undue stress on the joint capsule.
- Look up as you perform the move—this prevents rounding at the upper spine.

A   B

Reverse Lunge

This move targets most of the lower-body muscles, with particular emphasis on the quads and the glutes. It's an excellent exercise for improving dynamic balance.

Equipment needed: Dumbbells

Start: Grasp two dumbbells and allow them to hang down by your sides, with your palms facing your body. Assume a shoulder-width stance, with your shoulders back and your chin up.

Movement: Keeping your core tight, take a long step backward with your right leg, slowly lowering your body by bending your right knee and hip. Continue your descent until your right knee is almost touching the floor and your left leg forms a 90-degree angle. Reverse the direction by forcibly extending the right hip and knee, bringing the leg forward until you return to the starting position. Perform the move the same way on your left side, and then alternate between legs until you reach the desired number of repetitions.

Expert tips:

- A longer stride emphasizes more of the glutes; a shorter stride targets the quads.
- Look up as you perform the move—this prevents rounding at the upper spine.

B   A

Side Lunge

This move targets the muscles of the lower body, with a particular emphasis on the adductors of the inner thigh. It's a good exercise for lateral balance and can be beneficial for sports such as tennis and soccer.

Equipment needed: Dumbbells

Start: Assume a wide stance that extends approximately a foot (30 cm) or more beyond shoulder width. Place your left foot in a position that is perpendicular to your right foot. Grasp two dumbbells and hold one in front of your body and one behind your body.

Movement: Keeping your right leg straight, slowly bend your left knee out to the side until your left thigh is parallel with the floor. Reverse the direction by forcibly extending your left hip and knee, straightening the leg until you reach the starting position. When the desired number of repetitions is reached, repeat the process on the opposite side.

Expert tips:

- Make sure your front knee travels in line with the plane of your toes.
- Focus on dropping down on your straight leg. This keeps the flexing knee from pushing too far forward, which can place undue stress on the joint capsule.
- Look up as you perform the move—this prevents rounding at the upper spine.

A

B

Step-Up

This move targets the thighs and the glutes. It also taxes your cardiorespiratory system—you'll be gasping hard by the end of your set!

Equipment needed: Dumbbells, bench

Start: Grasp a pair of dumbbells and allow them to hang at your sides. Stand facing the side of a flat bench with your feet shoulder-width apart. Step up on the bench with your left foot.

Movement: Immediately, follow with your right foot. Now both feet are flat on the bench. Step back down in the same order (left foot, right foot), returning to the starting position. Continue stepping up and down for the desired number of repetitions.

Expert tips:
- A higher step increases stimulation of the glutes.
- Look up as you perform the move—this prevents rounding at the upper spine.

A

B

Standing Calf Raise

This move targets the calves.

Equipment needed: Dumbbells, wooden block

Start: Stand on a step (such as a block of wood or a staircase) and allow your heels to drop below your toes. Hold onto a stationary object with one hand and hold a dumbbell in the other hand.

Movement: Rise as high as you can on your toes until your calves are fully extended. Contract your calves and then slowly reverse the direction, returning to the starting position.

Expert tips:

- Never bounce during the stretched position of the move—this can cause severe injury to the Achilles tendon.
- Keep your toes pointed straight ahead—significant outward or inward rotation places the knee in a position of poor tracking and can lead to injury. Contrary to popular belief, the shift will not work the calf muscles any differently.

A   **B**

VARIATION

One-Leg Standing Calf Raise
Keeping your left leg behind your body, hold onto a stationary object with one hand and hold a dumbbell in the other hand. Perform the move with your right leg just as you would for the two-leg version. After completing the desired number of repetitions, repeat with the opposite leg.

Seated Calf Raise

This move targets the calves, with an emphasis on the soleus muscle.

Equipment needed: Dumbbells, bench, wooden block

Start: Sit at the edge of a flat bench with the balls of your feet on a block of wood or a step. Place a dumbbell on your thighs, hold it in place, and drop your heels as far below your toes as possible.

Movement: Rise as high as you can on your toes until your calves are fully extended. Contract your calves and then slowly reverse the direction, returning to the starting position.

Expert tips:

- Never bounce during the stretched position of the move—this can cause severe injury to the Achilles tendon.
- Keep your toes pointed straight ahead—significant outward or inward rotation places the knee in a position of poor tracking and can lead to injury. Contrary to popular belief, the shift will not work the calf muscles any differently.
- For added comfort, place a folded towel on your thighs underneath the dumbbells.

A **B**

VARIATION

One-Leg Seated Calf Raise
Keeping only your right foot on the step, perform the move as described for the two-leg version. After completing the desired number of repetitions, repeat with your left leg.

Back Squat

This move targets the thighs and the glutes, with secondary emphasis on the hamstrings. It is the quintessential lower-body exercise and is one of the most functional movements you can perform, activating over 200 major muscles in the body.

Equipment needed: Barbell

Start: Rest a straight bar high on the back of your neck, grasping the bar with both hands. Assume a shoulder-width stance, with your feet turned slightly outward.

Movement: Keeping your core tight, slowly lower your body until your thighs are parallel with the ground. Your lower back should be slightly arched and your heels should stay in contact with the floor at all times. When you reach a seated position, reverse the direction by straightening your legs and return to the starting position.

Expert tips:

- Your knees should travel in the same plane as your toes at all times.
- If you have trouble keeping your heels down, place a 1-inch (2.5 cm) block of wood or a weight plate underneath them.
- Wrap a towel around the bar if it feels uncomfortable on your neck.
- It's wise to have a spotter for this movement to ensure safety.

A   B

Front Squat

This is a great movement for targeting the frontal thighs while minimizing activation of the glutes.

Equipment needed: Barbell

Start: Rest a straight bar across your upper chest, holding it in place with both hands. Assume a shoulder-width stance, with your feet turned slightly outward, your shoulders back, and your chin up.

Movement: Keeping your core tight, slowly lower your body until your thighs are parallel with the ground. Your lower back should be slightly arched and your heels should stay in contact with the floor at all times. When you reach a seated position, reverse the direction by straightening your legs and return to the starting position.

Expert tips:

- Your knees should travel in the same plane as your toes at all times.
- Your heels should stay in contact with the floor at all times. If you have trouble keeping your heels down, place a 1-inch (2.5 cm) block of wood or a weight plate underneath them.
- Wrap a towel around the bar if it feels uncomfortable on your chest.
- It's wise to have a spotter for this movement to ensure safety.

A   B

Hack Squat

This move targets the thighs and glutes.

Equipment needed: Barbell

Start: Hold a barbell behind your body at the level of your upper thighs. Grasp it with a shoulder-width grip, with your palms up and facing back. Assume a shoulder-width stance with your head and eyes up, your knees slightly bent, and your feet planted firmly on the floor.

Movement: Keeping the bar tucked against your butt and upper thighs, squat down until your upper thighs are parallel with the floor. Contract your thighs and then return slowly along the same path to the starting position.

Expert tips:

- Your knees should travel in the same plane as your toes at all times.
- Your heels should stay in contact with the floor at all times. If you have trouble keeping your heels down, place a 1-inch (2.5 cm) block of wood or a weight plate underneath them.
- If you have trouble holding the bar throughout the entire set, consider using lifting straps.

A

B

Split Squat Lunge

This move targets the thighs and the glutes. It's a good exercise to develop balance.

Equipment needed: Barbell

Start: Rest a barbell across your shoulders, grasping the bar on both sides to maintain balance. Take a long stride forward with your left leg and raise your right heel until only the toes of your right foot are touching the ground. Hold your shoulders back and your chin up.

Movement: Keeping your core tight, slowly lower your body by flexing your left knee and hip, continuing your descent until your right knee is almost touching the floor. Reverse the direction by forcibly extending the left hip and knee until you return to the starting position. After performing the desired number of reps, repeat the process on your right side.

Expert tips:

- Make sure your knee travels in line with the plane of your toes.
- Focus on dropping down on your rear leg. This keeps the front knee from pushing too far forward, which can place undue stress on the joint capsule.
- It's wise to have a spotter for this movement to ensure safety.

A   B

Lunge

This move targets the thighs and the glutes. It's a good exercise for developing dynamic balance.

Equipment needed: Barbell

Start: Rest a barbell across your shoulders, grasping the bar on both sides to maintain balance. Assume a shoulder-width stance, with your shoulders back and your chin up.

Movement: Keeping your core tight, take a long step forward with your left leg, slowly lowering your body by flexing your left knee and hip. Continue your descent until your right knee is almost touching the floor. Reverse the direction by forcibly extending the left hip and knee, bringing the leg backward until you return to the starting position. Perform the move the same way on your right side, then alternate between legs until you reach the desired number of repetitions.

Expert tips:

- Make sure your knee travels in line with the plane of your toes.
- Focus on dropping down on your rear leg. This keeps the front knee from pushing too far forward, which can place undue stress on the joint capsule.
- It's wise to have a spotter for this movement to ensure safety.

A   B

Reverse Lunge

This move targets most of the lower-body muscles, with particular emphasis on the quads and the glutes. It's an excellent exercise for improving dynamic balance.

Equipment needed: Barbell

Start: Rest a barbell across your shoulders, grasping the bar on both sides to maintain balance. Assume a shoulder-width stance, with your shoulders back and your chin up.

Movement: Keeping your core tight, take a long step backward with your right leg, slowly lowering your body by flexing your right knee and hip. Continue your descent until your right knee is almost touching the floor. Reverse the direction by forcibly extending the right hip and knee, bringing the leg forward until you return to the starting position. Perform the move the same way on your left side, then alternate between legs until you reach the desired number of repetitions.

Expert tips:

- A longer stride works the glutes; a shorter stride targets the quads.
- It's wise to have a spotter for this movement to ensure safety.

B   A

Good Morning

This move targets the glutes and hamstrings.

Equipment needed: Barbell

Start: Rest a barbell across your shoulders, grasping the bar on both sides to maintain balance. Assume a shoulder-width stance, with your head up and your knees and back straight.

Movement: Keeping your lower back taut throughout the movement, slowly bend forward at the hips until your body is roughly parallel with the floor. In a controlled fashion, reverse the direction, contracting your glutes as you raise your body up along the same path back to the starting position.

Expert tips:
- Wrap a towel around the bar if it feels uncomfortable on your neck.
- Move only at the hips, not the waist! The action is purely hip extension, and any spinal movement will place the vertebrae at risk of injury. In this movement, a tight core is of utmost importance.
- This move is not recommended for those with existing lower back injuries or pain.
- Focus on pushing your butt backward as you descend into the move—this increases the activation of the glutes and hamstrings.
- It's wise to have a spotter for this movement to ensure safety.

A

B

Stiff-Legged Deadlift

This move targets the glutes and hamstrings.

Equipment needed: Barbell

Start: Stand with your feet shoulder-width apart. Grasp a straight bar and let it hang in front of your body.

Movement: Keeping your knees straight and your core tight, slowly bend forward at the hips and lower the barbell until you feel an intense stretch in your hamstrings. Then, reverse the direction, contracting your glutes as you rise upward to the starting position.

Expert tips:

- You should only bend forward at the hips, not at the lower back. The action is purely hip extension, and any spinal movement will place the vertebrae at risk of injury.
- There is rarely a need to stand on a box as many people do. This is only necessary if you can touch your toes without flexing your spine—a feat very few people are capable of doing.
- Focus on pushing your butt backward as you descend into the move—this increases the activation of the glutes and hamstrings.

A

B

Welcome to the Machines

If you really want to go all out and build the ultimate home gym, a multifunction resistance machine is the final piece. These all-in-one units attempt to simulate the variety of machines found in health clubs, and the better ones do a pretty good job of it. But with prices starting at around $1,000, you have to decide if the benefits outweigh the hefty expenditure.

Advocates of multifunction machines argue that nothing is better at developing muscle. They claim that muscles can't tell whether they're being worked by a dumbbell or a flywheel, and then use this logic to claim that machines are safer and more convenient than free weights. Although this argument might seem logical on the surface, closer scrutiny reveals otherwise.

Consider the biomechanical differences between a free-weight exercise, such as a squat, and a machine-based movement, such as a leg press. To complete a squat, you must stabilize your body in all three planes of movement: backward and forward (sagittal plane), side to side (frontal plane), and twisting crosswise (transverse plane). Maintaining balance in these planes requires a significant contribution from the stabilizer muscles in your trunk and extremities—over 200 muscles in all. The end result is not only better synergistic muscle development, but also an improved ability to carry out daily tasks. Remember also that metabolic function is related to the amount of muscle that is activated during training. The recruitment of so many ancillary muscles maximizes metabolic activity, revving up your body's ability to burn fat both during and after exercise.

Now let's look at the performance of the leg press. Here, the action is carried out almost solely by the muscles of your lower body; the machine stabilizes your torso and arms, keeping them stationary throughout performance. Because this movement doesn't require balance, it stimulates significantly less muscle and thus burns less fat than a squat. And since the move doesn't approximate most real-life actions (when do you ever have to push an object with your feet in a straight, linear fashion?), it doesn't prepare you as well for activities of daily living.

As for the matter of safety, it's true that because machines require less skill for performance, they can provide a degree of extra safety for beginners. However, this is only true for the short term. Once your neuromuscular system grows accustomed to free-weight movement patterns—a phenomenon that occurs fairly rapidly with dedicated training—this ceases to be an issue. If you employ proper technique and stay within your means, your risk of injury with free weights will be almost nonexistent.

Bottom line: Nothing produces better results than a bench and a set of dumbbells or barbells, regardless of your fitness goals. If you're forced to choose, it's a no-brainer—go with the free weights. Thankfully, you usually don't need to choose one over the other. There's no reason you can't use both (other than cost and space, of course!). And that's a big plus because machines actually provide a terrific complement to free-weight training. When used in tandem, they elicit different patterns of muscle recruitment in a way that keeps muscles off guard, forcing them to continually adapt to new stimuli. This helps prevent the dreaded exercise plateau and stave off exercise-induced boredom.

Using machines is also an excellent way to achieve a degree of muscular isolation. Although their fixed path of motion isn't optimal from a functional standpoint, it does force the target muscles to perform the majority of the work. This allows you to develop specific areas of the body in a way that's impossible with free weights—a factor that's especially beneficial if you aim to enhance your physique aesthetics.

In most cases, you should strive to integrate both free weights and machines into your workouts. Variety is the spice of fitness, and the more variation you can employ, the better. As a rule of thumb, use dumbbell and barbell exercises as the foundation of your routine, and then selectively add in machine-based movements.

To a large extent, the precise mix between the two modalities depends on your fitness goals. For example, body-sculpting regimens generally benefit from a healthy dose of machine exercises, which foster better muscular symmetry. Core stability routines, on the other hand, should employ few, if any, machine-based movements, since their activation of stabilizer muscles is nearly nonexistent. Assess what you want to achieve from your exercise program and adjust the blend of exercises accordingly.

Quality Considerations for Multifunction Machines

Take these key considerations into account before you buy a multifunction machine:

■ *Resistance.* The first thing to consider is the manner in which a machine applies resistance during exercise. There are three main types of resistance used in home units: plate-loaded, variable, and fixed-stack resistance. Plate-loaded equipment, such as the Smith or Hammer Strength machines, are too cumbersome for most home gyms. Variable-resistance units tend to be space efficient, but they have a nonfunctional strength curve that doesn't simulate the normal pattern of muscular action (see the sidebar on variable resistance for more information). This leaves fixed-stack units, which have a manageable footprint and employ a pulley system that helps keep continuous tension on your muscles throughout the range of motion (definitely a good thing!). They're also convenient to use: Just insert a pin into the weight stack and you're ready to roll. All things being equal, most home users are best served by a fixed-stack model. One thing you shouldn't worry about is the unit's weight maximum. Machines usually come with stacks of at least 200 pounds (91 kg), which should be more than sufficient for the fitness needs of most women.

- *Construction.* The majority of multifunction gyms are built on a steel frame. To avoid flexing under load, frames should have a minimum tubular-steel gauge of 11 (gauge is a measure of the steel's thickness) and should be welded rather than bolted in areas where stress might be an issue. Cables should be of aircraft quality: coated with nylon and able to withstand at least 2,500 pounds (1,134 kg) of force. You definitely don't want a frayed cable to snap when you're in the middle of a lift! Weight stacks should be made of cast iron, with a cover to prevent injury. This feature is especially important if you have small children.

- *Exercises.* Given the large capital outlay, multifunction units should provide a full range of movements for all areas of your body. However, you won't necessarily need every possible exercise. As a rule, the more exercise options a unit has, the higher the cost will be. Decide what you need and don't pay for the things that you don't. One indispensable option is a cable pulley apparatus. Cables bridge the gap between free weights and machines, allowing you to perform movements in all planes while maintaining constant muscular tension—the best of both worlds. They're highly functional and allow performance of movements that can't be replicated with other modalities. Opt for a machine with at least one dedicated cable station. Better yet, spend a little more and get a unit with both high and low pulley stations. It's worth the extra investment. The best units also have cross cables in the seated area of the unit that allow you to perform bilateral movements, such as the shoulder press with cable (page 178) and crossover fly with cable (page 189)—a real plus if you can afford it.

- *Smoothness.* A multifunction machine should have a smooth feel during both concentric (positive) and eccentric (negative) phases of movement. The makeup of the pulley system is paramount to its smoothness. High-end pulley systems are made of nylon rather than plastic, and contain sealed bearings. Beyond this, the best thing

Variable-Resistance Machines

As the name implies, variable-resistance machines vary the resistance applied to muscles at different points throughout a lift. In home-gym units, variable resistance is usually provided by rods or bands. Here's how it works: Rods of varying stiffness are linked to cables that you pull or push through a given range of motion. The more the rods are bent during a lift, the greater the resistance to your muscles. This means you encounter less resistance at the start of a movement than the finish of the movement. The problem is that your muscles aren't designed to work this way. For instance, does lifting a package start out easy and get progressively harder? Of course not. And since the transfer of exercise to functional movement depends on how closely the move approximates the task, it's pretty clear that variable resistance isn't very functional. On the plus side, many variable units allow for movement in all three planes, facilitating better recruitment of stabilizer muscles. They also tend to be a bit less expensive and somewhat more space efficient than comparable fixed-stack units. My advice: Unless you are restricted by space or budget, go with a fixed-stack machine.

you can do is to take the machine for a test drive before purchase. Try out a variety of exercises. Is the motion fluid throughout the range of motion? Are there any sticking points? A machine made with cheap parts will encounter excessive friction, which gives it a jerky and uneven feel. If the unit doesn't handle smoothly in the store, it will probably only get worse over time.

■ *Adjustability.* A shortcoming of multifunction machines is that they are made to conform to a certain body type—generally that of an average male. Although some machines can be adjusted, this capacity varies between models, and women sometimes have trouble performing certain moves with proper technique because of their proportions. Therefore, you must make sure a unit ergonomically accommodates your height, size, and limb length. You shouldn't feel cramped or confined in any way. The seat should adjust easily so that you can execute all exercises with proper technique. Since machines lock your joints into a fixed plane of movement, any compromise in form fails to work your muscles optimally and significantly increases your prospect of injury.

■ *Stations.* Different machines come with single-station or multistation capabilities. Single-station units have one weight stack (see figure 5.1) and multistation units have two or more (see figure 5.2). You should only purchase a multistation unit if you intend for more than one person to use the machine simultaneously. If not, stick with the single-station option. You'll save money without sacrificing benefit.

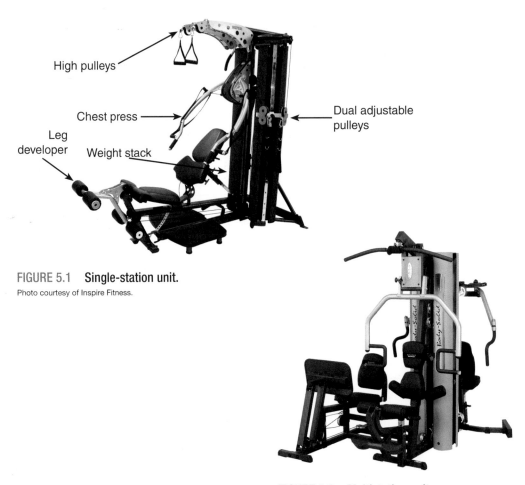

High pulleys

Chest press

Dual adjustable pulleys

Leg developer

Weight stack

FIGURE 5.1   **Single-station unit.**
Photo courtesy of Inspire Fitness.

FIGURE 5.2   **Multistation unit.**
Photo courtesy of Body-Solid, Inc.

- *Warranty.* Since there aren't a lot of moving parts, with normal use, a well-made multifunction unit should need little to no service for years to come. High-quality machines come with a standard lifetime warranty on the frame and at least a three-year warranty on parts and labor. Consider this the minimum benchmark. The manufacturer's reputation is even more important. Buy from a company that has proven itself in the field over a number of years. Parts can be hard to come by if the company goes out of business, which potentially makes the unit obsolete.

- *Size.* It should go without saying that multistation machines take up a fair amount of room—up to 200 square feet (61 sq m), depending on the model. Some are tall, requiring added vertical clearance. Attachments for exercises, such as the leg press, further increase horizontal space requirements. You must take these factors into account before you make a purchase. You don't want to bring a machine home only to find out that it doesn't fit in your workout room. Remember, you'll need to leave at least several feet of clearance on each side of the unit.

Buyer's Guide for Multifunction Machines

Although discount models abound, you'll be hard-pressed to find a good multifunction machine for less than $1,000. Depending on the breadth of exercises and the number of attachments, expect to spend at least $1,500 for a good fixed-stack unit. Often, the units cost significantly more. As with most exercise equipment, the quality of a multifunction gym will generally be equal to its cost. Don't be lured by sales or come-ons from no-name brands. Ultimately, if you don't enjoy the workout experience, the machine will become nothing more than a bulky, expensive clothes hanger.

Once you've decided on a particular unit, make sure to get a variety of different bars and handles for use in lat pull-downs, rows, and other cable-based movements. Include a long bar, a short bar (preferably with an S-curve), a v-bar, a rope, and loop handles (see figure 5.3, *a-e*). The cost of these items is insignificant when compared to the overall equipment purchase (you can often get the salesman to throw these in as part of the deal), and you'll gain a tremendous benefit from the additional exercises you can perform.

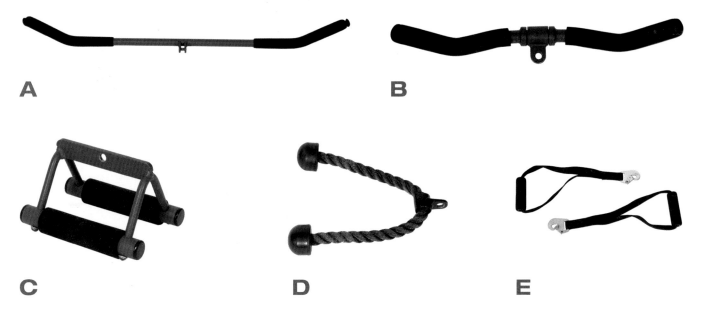

A **B**

C **D** **E**

FIGURE 5.3   Machine unit accessories: *(a)* long bar, *(b)* short bar with S-curve, *(c)* v-bar, *(d)* rope, and *(e)* loop handles.

Machine Buyer's Guide

Ideally, your multifunction unit should include the following features:

- A fixed-stack weight unit with at least one—and preferably dual high and low—cable station
- Cross cables
- Construction of 11-gauge tubular steel with nylon-coated cables of aircraft quality and cast-iron weight stacks
- A full complement of exercises for the upper and lower body
- A pulley system made of nylon that contains sealed bearings
- Complete adjustability so you can perform all exercises with proper technique
- A lifetime warranty on the frame and at least a three-year warranty on parts and labor

Functional Trainers

A fairly new entry to the home-gym market is the so-called *functional trainer* (see figure 5.4). These machines are composed of two sets of cables attached to moveable arms that can be adjusted in a multitude of positions. Without question, the units are a terrific addition to any home gym. The cable-based design is efficient and is highly adaptable to the performance of dozens of different exercises. The drawbacks: These machines don't allow the performance of certain basic gym movements, such as the leg press or leg extension, that can be beneficial if your goal is body sculpting. At this point, they're also quite expensive—usually more than several thousand dollars—which puts them out of reach for many consumers.

FIGURE 5.4 Functional trainer.
Photo courtesy of www.GoldsGymFitness.com.

Shoulder Press

This move targets the deltoids, with an emphasis on the front delts. Secondary emphasis is placed on the upper trapezius and the triceps.

Equipment needed: Multifunction machine

Start: Sit upright in the seat of a multifunction machine with your back supported by the pad. Grasp the machine handles with your palms facing away from your body and your elbows flared out to the sides. Adjust the seat height so that the handles are approximately in line with your shoulders.

Movement: Keeping your elbows flared, press the handles directly up and over your head, contracting your deltoids at the top of the move. Then, slowly return the handles back to the starting position.

Expert tips:

- Don't lock your elbows at the top of the move—doing so reduces tension on the target muscles.
- Keep your elbows flared to the sides as you lift—allowing them to move forward changes the scope of the exercise.

A

B

Shoulder Press With Cable

This move targets the deltoids, with an emphasis on the front delts. Secondary emphasis is placed on the upper trapezius and the triceps. Because of the greater stabilization and independence of the arms required, it increases total-body muscular activation more than a shoulder press with a standard machine.

Equipment needed: Multifunction machine

Start: Sit upright in the seat of a multifunction machine with your back supported by the pad. Grasp the loop handles of the cables with your palms facing away from your body and your elbows flared out to the sides. Adjust the seat height so that the handles are approximately in line with your shoulders.

Movement: Keeping your elbows flared, press the handles directly up and over your head, contracting your deltoids at the top of the move. Then, slowly return the handles back to the starting position.

Expert tips:

- Don't lock your elbows at the top of the move—doing so reduces tension to the target muscles.
- Don't arc the handles outward as you press them up—this increases stress to the connective tissues in the shoulder joint.
- Keep your elbows flared to the sides as you lift—allowing them to move forward changes the scope of the exercise.

A

B

Upright Row With Cable

This move targets the medial (middle) delts and places secondary emphasis on the biceps.

Equipment needed: Multifunction machine

Start: Grasp two loop handles (or the ends of a rope) attached to the low-pulley apparatus of a multifunction machine. Keep your feet shoulder-width apart, your torso erect, your knees slightly bent, and your core held tightly. Allow your arms to hang down from your shoulders in front of your body, but don't lock your elbows.

Movement: Slowly pull the loop handles up along the line of your body until your upper arms approach shoulder level. Keep your elbows higher than your wrists at all times. Contract your delts and then slowly lower the loop handles along the same path back to the starting position.

Expert tips:

- Initiate the action by lifting the elbows, not the wrists, to ensure optimal stimulation of the target muscles.
- Be careful not to lift your elbows beyond a position that is parallel with the ground. Doing so can lead to shoulder impingement, which may injure the rotator cuff.
- Keep your hands as close to your body as possible throughout the entire move.
- You can perform the move with a straight bar if you desire.

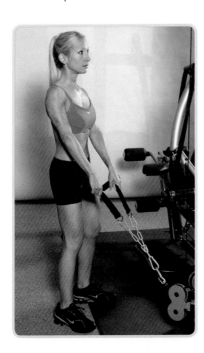
A

B

One-Arm Lateral Raise With Cable

This move targets the medial (middle) deltoid.

Equipment needed: Multifunction machine

Start: Grasp a loop handle attached to the low-pulley apparatus of a multifunction machine with your right hand. Stand so that your left side is facing the pulley, with your feet approximately shoulder-width apart, your torso erect, your knees slightly bent, and your core held tightly.

Movement: Maintain a slight bend to your elbow throughout the movement. Raise the handle across your body, up, and out to the side until it reaches the level of your shoulder. Contract your delts at the top of the movement and then slowly return the handle to the starting position. After completing the desired number of reps, repeat the process on your left side.

Expert tips:

- Think of pouring a cup of milk as you lift. Your pinky should be higher than your thumb at the top of the move—this keeps maximum tension on the medial deltoids.
- Keep your upper arms directly out to the sides at all times—allowing them to gravitate inward switches the emphasis to the front delts at the expense of the medial delts.

A

B

Kneeling Bent Lateral Raise With Cable

This move targets the posterior (rear) deltoid.

Equipment needed: Multifunction machine

Start: Grasp a loop handle attached to the low-pulley apparatus of a multifunction machine with your right hand and kneel down on your hands and knees. Stabilize your torso with your left arm. Position your right arm by your side with the elbow slightly bent.

Movement: Maintain a slight bend to your elbow and a tight core throughout the movement. Raise the handle out to your right side until the arm is parallel with the ground. Contract your delts at the top of the movement and then slowly return the handle back to the starting position. After completing the desired number of reps, repeat the process on your left side.

Expert tip: Avoid the tendency to bring your elbows in toward the body as you lift. Your elbows should remain away from the body throughout the move to keep tension on the rear delts.

A

B

Hammer Curl With Cable

This move targets the upper arms, with an emphasis on the brachialis.

Equipment needed: Multifunction machine

Start: Grasp two loop handles (or the ends of a rope) attached to the low-pulley apparatus of a multifunction machine. Press your elbows into your sides with your palms facing each other. Keep your feet shoulder-width apart, your torso erect, your knees slightly bent, and your core held tightly.

Movement: Keeping your arms stable throughout the move, curl the loop handles up toward your shoulders and contract your biceps at the top of the move. Slowly reverse the direction and return to the starting position.

Expert tips:

- Don't allow your upper arms to move forward as you lift—this brings your shoulders into the movement at the expense of your arm muscles.
- Keep your wrists straight as you lift—don't roll them to complete the move.

A

B

One-Arm Curl With Cable

This move targets the biceps.

Equipment needed: Multifunction machine

Start: Grasp a loop handle attached to the low-pulley apparatus of a multifunction machine. Press your right elbow into your right side, with your palm facing up. Keep your feet shoulder-width apart, your torso erect, your knees slightly bent, and your core held tightly.

Movement: Keeping your upper arms stable throughout the move, slowly curl the handle up toward your shoulders. Contract your biceps, slowly reverse the direction, and return to the starting position. After completing the desired number of reps, repeat the process on your left side.

Expert tips:

- If you desire, you can begin with your palm facing your side and then actively supinate your hand as you lift.
- Keep your wrist straight as you lift—don't roll your wrist!
- Don't allow your upper arm to move forward as you lift—this brings your shoulder into the movement at the expense of your arm muscles.

A

B

Overhead Triceps Extension With Cable

This move targets the triceps, particularly the long head of the muscle.

Equipment needed: Multifunction machine

Start: Grasp two loop handles (or the ends of a rope) attached to the low-pulley apparatus of a multifunction machine and turn your body away from the machine. Press your elbows close to your ears, bend your elbows, and allow your hands to hang down behind your head as far as comfortably possible, with your palms facing each other. Bring one foot in front of the other, with your torso erect and your knees slightly bent.

Movement: Keeping your elbows close to your ears, slowly straighten your arms as fully as possible. Contract your triceps and then slowly lower the weight along the same path back to the starting position.

Expert tips:

- Make sure your elbows stay pinned to your ears as you lift—if your elbows flare, you'll reduce stress to the triceps.
- Your upper arms should remain completely stationary throughout the move—any forward movement will diminish tension on the triceps.
- If you desire, you can perform this exercise one arm at a time. This may help you alleviate stress on the elbow and focus on each arm individually.

A

B

Press-Down With Cable

This move targets the triceps, particularly the medial and lateral heads.

Equipment needed: Multifunction machine

Start: Use an overhand grip to grasp two loop handles (or the ends of a rope) attached to the high-pulley apparatus of a multifunction machine. Keep your feet shoulder-width apart, your torso erect, your knees slightly bent, and your core held tightly. Press your arms against your sides with your elbows bent at a 90-degree angle and your palms facing one another.

Movement: Keeping your elbows at your sides, slowly straighten your arms as far as possible without discomfort. Contract your triceps, reverse the direction, and return to the starting position.

Expert tips:

- Don't allow your arms to move out as you lift—this brings the chest muscles into play at the expense of your triceps.
- For an added contraction, you can turn your palms out so they face away from each other at the end of the move.
- The move can be done with a variety of attachments, including a curved bar and a straight bar.

A

B

Triceps Kickback With Cable

This move targets the triceps, particularly the medial and lateral heads.

Equipment needed: Multifunction machine

Start: Grasp a loop handle attached to the low-pulley apparatus of a multifunction machine. Bend your torso forward so that it is roughly parallel with the ground. Press your right arm against your side with your right elbow bent at a 90-degree angle and your palm facing backward. Keep your feet shoulder-width apart, your torso erect, and your knees slightly bent.

Movement: Keeping your upper arm stable, raise the handle by straightening your arm until it is parallel with the floor. Then, reverse the direction and return the weight to the starting position. After finishing the desired number of repetitions, repeat the process on your left side.

Expert tips:

- Don't let your upper arm sag as you lift—this will diminish tension to the target muscles.
- Don't flick your wrist at the top of movement—this is a common performance error that only fatigues the forearm muscles before the triceps and reduces the effectiveness of the move.
- Keep your back slightly arched throughout the movement. Never round your spine— this places undue stress on the lumbar area and could lead to injury.

A

B

Incline Chest Press

This move targets the pectorals, particularly the upper portion. Secondary emphasis is placed on the shoulders and the triceps.

Equipment needed: Multifunction machine

Start: Lie on your back on the seat of a multifunction machine that is set with an approximately 30-degree incline, aligning your upper chest with the handles on the machine. Grasp the handles with a slightly wider than shoulder-width grip. Keep your palms facing away from your body and your elbows flared.

Movement: Keeping your back flat against the support pad, press the handles forward, stopping just before you fully lock your elbows. Feel a contraction in your chest muscles at the end of the movement and then slowly reverse the direction, returning to the starting position.

Expert tips:

- Most multifunction units have the capacity to move the grade of the bench to 30 or 40 degrees to optimally target the upper chest in the incline press. However, the grade varies depending on the machine. The most important thing to remember is that the action should move in line with the upper portion of your chest. A muscle always contracts maximally when the action is carried out in line with its fibers.

- Keep your elbows flared as you lift—allowing them to move forward changes the scope of the exercise.

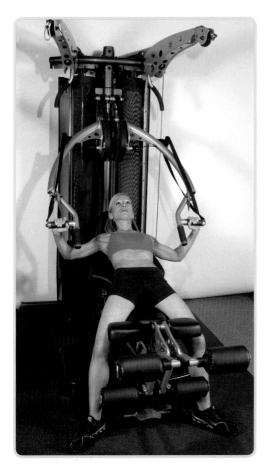

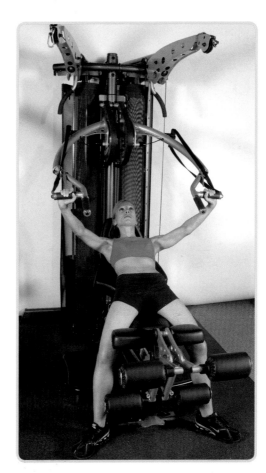

A

B

Chest Press With Cable

This move targets the pectorals, particularly the middle portion. Secondary emphasis is placed on the shoulders and the triceps.

Equipment needed: Multifunction machine

Start: Sit upright in the seat of a multifunction machine with your body facing away from the pad. Grasp the machine's loop handles with your palms facing away from your body and your elbows flared. Adjust the seat height so that the handles are aligned with the middle of your chest.

Movement: Keeping your back flat against the support pad, press the handles forward, stopping just before you fully lock your elbows. Feel a contraction in your chest muscles at the end of the movement and then slowly reverse the direction, returning to the starting position.

Expert tips:

- To shift the activation to the upper-chest musculature, press the handles slightly upward.
- The actual starting position of this move depends on your specific machine. You may need to begin by sitting upright, by lying flat, or by moving in some variation between the two positions. The most important thing to remember is that the action should move in line with the middle portion of your chest. A muscle always contracts maximally when the action is carried out in line with its fibers.
- Keep your elbows flared as you lift—allowing them to move forward changes the scope of the exercise.

A

B

Crossover Fly With Cable

This move targets the pectorals, particularly the middle portion.

Equipment needed: Multifunction machine

Start: Grasp the handles of the overhead-pulley apparatus of a multifunction machine. Stand with your feet about shoulder-width apart, your torso bent slightly forward at the waist, and your arms slightly bent and held out to the sides so they are approximately parallel with the floor.

Movement: Keeping your upper body motionless and your core tight, pull both handles down and across your body, creating a semicircular movement. Bring your hands together at a level slightly higher than your hips and squeeze your chest muscles so that you feel a contraction in the cleavage area. Then, slowly reverse the direction, allowing your hands to return along the same path back to the starting position.

Expert tip: Your elbows should remain slightly bent and fixed throughout the move—don't flex or extend them at any time. This effectively makes the exercise a pressing movement rather than a fly.

A

B

Front Lat Pull-Down

This move targets the back muscles, particularly the lats.

Equipment needed: Multifunction machine

Start: Grasp a pair of loop handles attached to the high-pulley apparatus of a multifunction machine. Keep your hands slightly greater than shoulder-width apart, your palms turned forward, your core tight, and your elbows flared out to the sides. Sit in the machine, and fully straighten your arms so you feel a complete stretch in your lats. Maintain a slight backward tilt and keep your lower back arched throughout the move.

Movement: Pull the handles down to your shoulders, bringing your elbows to your sides. Contract your lats and then slowly reverse the direction, returning to the starting position.

Expert tips:
- To increase the activation of muscles in the middle of your back (the rhomboids and the middle traps), draw your elbows back slightly as you pull down and forcefully squeeze your shoulder blades together.
- This move can be done with a long bar depending on the configuration of your machine.
- This move can be done with closer or wider grips to hit the muscles slightly differently.

A   B

VARIATIONS

◄ Neutral-Grip Lat Pull-Down
Grasp the loop handles with a neutral grip (palms facing each other) and perform the move as previously described.

Reverse-Grip Lat Pull-Down ▶
Grasp the loop handles with a reverse grip (palms facing your body) and perform the move as previously described.

Seated Row With Cable

This move targets the back muscles, particularly the inner back musculature of the rhomboids and the middle traps.

Equipment needed: Multifunction machine

Start: Grasp the loop handles attached to the low-pulley apparatus of a multifunction machine with your palms facing each other. Sit on the floor and place your feet against a stable part of the machine. Fully straighten your arms so that you feel a complete stretch in your lats. Make sure your posture is erect, with a slight arch in your lower back.

Movement: Maintaining a slight bend in your knees, pull the handles in toward your lower abdomen, keeping your elbows close to your sides and your lower back tight. As the handles touch your body, squeeze your shoulder blades together and then reverse the direction, slowly returning to the starting position.

Expert tips:

- Don't lean forward on the return. This interjects momentum into the move on the concentric action, reducing tension to the target muscles.
- Never round your spine—this places the discs in a precarious position and can lead to serious injury.
- This move can be performed with a variety of different handle attachments, such as the v-bar and the curved bar.

A **B**

Seated Row

This move targets the back muscles, particularly the inner back musculature of the rhomboids and the middle traps.

Equipment needed: Multifunction machine

Start: Sit with your body facing the pad of a multifunction machine. Press your chest against the pad and grasp the machine handles with a neutral grip (palms facing each other). Adjust the seat height so that when you grasp the handles, your arms are fully extended and you feel a stretch in your lats.

Movement: Keeping your elbows close to your sides and your lower back slightly arched, pull the handles back as far as possible without discomfort. Squeeze your shoulder blades together and then reverse the direction, slowly returning to the starting position.

Expert tip: Don't swing your body forward at the beginning of the move. I see this mistake far too often. It only serves to overstress the lower back muscles and inject unnecessary momentum into the move.

A

B

Reverse Low Row With Cable

This move targets the back muscles, particularly the inner back musculature of the rhomboids and the middle traps.

Equipment needed: Multifunction machine

Start: Grasp a straight bar attached to the low-pulley apparatus of a multifunction machine with a reverse grip (palms facing up). Step back from the machine and straighten your arms so you feel a stretch in your lats. Bend forward slightly at the hips for balance and keep a slight bend to your knees.

Movement: Keeping your core tight and your elbows close to your sides, pull the bar toward your midsection. Squeeze your shoulder blades together to contract your back muscles and then reverse the direction, slowly returning to the starting position.

Expert tip: It's absolutely essential that your upper body remains immobile during this move. Any unwanted movement can overstress the lower back muscles and potentially cause injury.

A

B

Straight-Arm
Pull-Down With Cable

This move targets the back muscles, particularly the lats.

Equipment needed: Multifunction machine

Start: Take an overhand grip on a straight bar attached to a high pulley. Slightly bend your elbows and bring the bar to eye level. Your feet should be approximately shoulder-width apart, your knees slightly bent, and your core tight.

Movement: Keeping a slight forward tilt to your upper body, pull the bar down in a semicircle until it touches your upper thighs. Contract your back muscles and then reverse the direction, slowly returning to the starting position.

Expert tip: This move can be performed with a variety of different handle attachments, such as the rope, curved bar, and loop handles.

A

B

Kneeling Crunch With Cable

This move targets the abdominals, with a focus on the upper portion.

Equipment needed: Multifunction machine

Start: Begin by facing a high-pulley apparatus and then kneel down, sitting back on your heels. Grasp two loop handles (or the ends of a rope) attached to the pulley and keep your elbows next to your ears and your torso upright.

Movement: Keeping your lower back immobile, slowly curl your shoulders down, bringing your elbows down toward your knees. Contract your abs and then slowly uncurl your body, returning to the starting position.

Expert tip: Curl only from your upper torso—your hips should remain fixed throughout the move. This maintains tension on the abs.

A

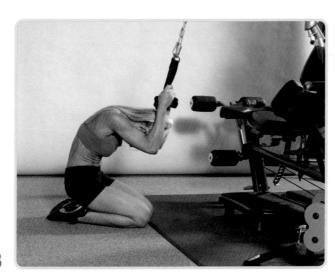

B

Kneeling and Twisting Crunch With Cable

This move targets the abdominals and the obliques.

Equipment needed: Multifunction machine

Start: Begin by facing a high-pulley apparatus, and then kneel down and sit back on your heels. Grasp two loop handles (or the ends of a rope) attached to the pulley and keep your elbows next to your ears and your torso upright.

Movement: Keeping your lower back immobile, slowly curl your shoulders down, twisting your body to the right as you bring your elbows toward your knees. Contract your abs and then slowly uncurl your body, returning to the starting position. Alternate between twisting to the right and to the left for the desired number of repetitions.

Expert tip: Curl only from your upper torso—your hips should remain fixed throughout the move. This maintains tension on the target muscles.

A

B

Side Bend With Cable

This move targets the obliques.

Equipment needed: Multifunction machine

Start: Grasp a loop handle attached to the low-pulley apparatus of a multifunction machine with your left hand. With your left side facing the machine, take a small step away from the machine so that there is tension in the cable. Keep your feet shoulder-width apart, your torso erect, and your knees slightly bent.

Movement: Keeping your core tight, bend your torso as far to the right as possible without discomfort. Contract your obliques and then return along the same path to the starting position. After finishing the desired number of reps, repeat on the opposite side.

Expert tips:
- The movement should take place solely at your waist—your hips shouldn't move at all during the move.
- Your upper body should remain in the same plane at all times—don't sway forward or backward.

A

B

Low-to-High Woodchop With Cable

This move targets the obliques.

Equipment needed: Multifunction machine

Start: Grasp two loop handles (or the ends of a rope) attached to the low-pulley apparatus of a multifunction machine. Keep your feet shoulder-width apart, your torso erect, and your knees slightly bent. Position your body so that your left side faces the machine, and extend your arms as far as comfortably possible across your body to the left.

Movement: Keeping your lower body stable, pull the band up and across your torso to the right with a motion as if you were chopping wood. Contract your obliques and then return along the same path back to the starting position. After finishing the desired number of reps, repeat on the opposite side.

Expert tips:

- To keep constant tension on the obliques, make sure the action takes place at your waist, not your hips.
- If you would like to transfer these skills to a sport that involves hip action, combine motions of the hips and the waist.

A

B

VARIATION

High-to-Low Woodchop With Cable
Grasp two loop handles (or the ends of a rope) attached to the high-pulley apparatus of a multifunction machine and perform the move as previously described.

Leg Press

This move targets the glutes and the quads, with secondary emphasis on the hamstrings.

Equipment needed: Multifunction machine

Start: Sit in the leg-press attachment of a multifunction machine. Place your feet on the footplate with a shoulder-width stance. Keeping your back pressed firmly against the padded seat, slowly bring your knees in toward your chest.

Movement: With your toes angled slightly outward and without bouncing, press the weight down in a controlled fashion and contract your quads, stopping just before you lock your knees.

Expert tip: Placing your feet high on the footplate increases stimulation of the glutes; keeping your feet low emphasizes the quads.

A

B

Leg Extension

This move targets the quadriceps.

Equipment needed: Multifunction machine

Start: Sit upright in a multifunction machine so that the undersides of your knees touch the edge of the seat. Bend your knees and place your instep underneath the roller pad located at the bottom of the machine. Grasp the machine's handles for support, tighten your core, and straighten your back.

Movement: Keeping your thighs and upper body immobile, lift your feet upward until your legs are almost parallel with the ground. Contract your quads and then reverse the direction, returning to the starting position.

Expert tips:

- Because of the extreme shear forces associated with this move, it is not recommended for those with knee problems. When in doubt, check with your physician.
- There is no benefit to turning your feet in or out. Keep them pointed straight ahead.

A

B

VARIATION

One-Leg Extension

Bend your right knee and place your right instep underneath the roller pad located at the bottom of the machine. Keep your left leg back so that it is off the roller pad. Perform the move as previously described. After performing the desired number of reps, repeat the process on your left side.

Prone Leg Curl

This move targets the hamstrings.

Equipment needed: Multifunction machine

Start: Lie facedown on a multifunction machine, with your heels hooked underneath the roller pads. Grasp a sturdy part of the machine (such as the bench pad) for stabilization.

Movement: Keeping your thighs pressed to the machine's surface and your upper body immobile, curl your feet upward, stopping just before your feet touch your butt, or as far as comfortably possible. Contract your hamstrings and then reverse the direction, returning to the starting position.

Expert tip: Keep your toes pointed away from your shins—this will reduce the leverage of the calf muscles (gastrocnemius) and increase stimulation of the hamstrings.

A

B

VARIATION

Prone One-Leg Curl
Lie facedown on a leg-curl machine, hook your right heel underneath the roller pad, and keep your left leg immobile. After finishing the desired number of repetitions, repeat the process on your left side.

Standing Adductor Raise With Cable

This move targets the inner thigh muscles.

Equipment needed: Multifunction machine

Start: Attach a cuff to the low-pulley apparatus of a multifunction machine and then secure the cuff to your left ankle. Position yourself so that your left side faces the machine and grasp something sturdy for support. Assume a stance that is slightly wider than shoulder-width, with your body erect and your core held tightly.

Movement: Keeping your upper body motionless, pull your left leg toward and across the midline of your body, as far to the right as possible. Contract the muscles of your left inner thigh and then reverse the direction, returning your leg to the starting position. After performing the desired number of reps, repeat the process on your right side.

Expert tip: Don't lean to complete the move—this introduces momentum into the lift, decreasing stimulation of the target muscles.

A

B

Standing Abductor Raise With Cable

This move targets the glutes, particularly the gluteus medius and minimus, as well as the outer thigh muscles.

Equipment needed: Multifunction machine

Start: Attach a cuff to the low-pulley apparatus of a multifunction machine and then secure the cuff to your right ankle. Position yourself so that your left side faces the weight stack and grasp something sturdy for support. Keep your body erect and your core tight. Allow your right leg to come across your body so it crosses over your left leg.

Movement: Keeping your upper body motionless, pull your right leg across your body and directly out to the side. Contract your glutes and then slowly return the weight along the same path back to the starting position. After finishing the desired number of repetitions, reverse the process and repeat on the left side.

Expert tips:

- To shift tension to the external rotator muscles (piriformis, gemellus, and obturators), rotate your little toe out as you perform the move.
- Don't lean to complete the move—this introduces momentum into the lift, decreasing stimulation of the target muscles.

A

B

Glute Back Kick With Cable

This move targets the glutes, particularly the glueteus maximus, and hamstrings.

Equipment needed: Multifunction machine

Start: Attach a cuff to the low-pulley apparatus of a multifunction machine and then secure the cuff to your right ankle. Face the machine and grasp something sturdy for support.

Movement: Keeping your upper body motionless and your right leg straight, bring your right foot back as far as comfortably possible without moving your upper torso. Contract your glutes. Slowly return to the starting position. After finishing the desired number of reps on your right side, repeat with your left leg.

Expert tip: To decrease activation of the hamstrings and thereby increase activation of the glutes, bend the working knee slightly while performing the move.

A

B

Toe Press

This move targets the calf muscles.

Equipment needed: Multifunction machine

Start: Sit upright in a leg-press machine, pressing your back firmly against the padded seat. Place the balls of your feet a comfortable distance apart on the bottom of the footplate, keeping your heels off the footplate. Straighten your legs, unlock the carriage-release bars, and drop your heels below your toes.

Movement: Keeping your knees immobile, press your toes as far up as you can. Contract your calves and then slowly reverse the direction, returning to the starting position.

Expert tips:

- Never bounce during the stretched position of the move—this can cause severe injury to the Achilles tendon.
- Keep your toes pointed straight ahead—significant outward or inward rotation places the knee in a position of poor tracking and can lead to injury. Contrary to popular belief, the shift will not work the calf muscles any differently.

A

B

Add the Cardio

There's good reason why cardio units are the most popular type of home fitness equipment. A high-quality unit can enhance your training experience by providing a combination of convenience, variety, comfort, and safety. These factors can keep you motivated to achieve your goals for years to come.

However, before you run out and snatch up a snazzy new treadmill or elliptical trainer, you should know that you can get a terrific aerobic workout for little or no money. For this reason, I didn't include cardio equipment in any of the four budgets. As mentioned, you should prioritize obtaining equipment for strength training before you consider purchasing a cardio unit. Walking, jogging, and running outdoors are great activities that burn fat and improve cardiorespiratory function, and they won't cost you a dime. The same thing goes for callisthenic exercises, such as skipping in place, squat thrusts, and jumping jacks. For less than 10 bucks, you can buy a jump rope and burn a ton of calories while exercising both your upper and lower extremities. Just make sure your ceilings have ample clearance before you start! For a couple hundred dollars, you can purchase a mountain bike that will provide transportation as well as a great workout. Still think you'd benefit from owning a cardio unit? Consider the following general factors:

- *Size.* Unless you have an unlimited amount of space in your home, you'll need to think about the dimensions of your chosen unit. Some models are designed to be more space-friendly than others. Some even fold up for easy storage. Unfortunately, there's usually a trade-off for space efficiency. For example, space-saver treadmills tend to have undersized decks and space-saver elliptical machines have limited stride lengths. These shortcomings can impede the quality of your workout. Your best bet is to find units that fit into your available space and then evaluate them in terms of performance. If the units don't meet your specifications, consider a different modality, such as a bike rather than a treadmill, or perhaps forgo any purchase for now. If you're going to spend a substantial amount of money on a piece of equipment, it's not worth settling for a sub-par workout.

- *Features.* Advances in technology have brought cardio equipment into the modern age. You can now purchase units with such wide-ranging features as wireless heart rate monitors, cup holders, TVs, MP3 outlets, and interactive video games. The variety of choices is akin to those you find when purchasing an automobile: Some units are stripped-down base models, and others come standard with an array of features. Usually, feature-rich equipment costs more. Only you can decide which features are most important to you. Make a wish list and then compare the costs and the benefits of each feature.

▪ *Stability.* There's no way you'll get a good workout with a cardio unit that shakes and shimmies. These units are both uncomfortable and unsafe. The stability of a cardio unit is generally a function of how much weight it can support. As a rule, the greater a unit's weight capacity, the sturdier it will be. Look for a unit with a weight capacity rating that is greater than 300 pounds and test it by pushing on the sides. If it sways back and forth on its base, chances are it won't hold up well under use.

▪ *Console.* A cardio unit's console displays lots of information about your workout, including an estimate of the calories you burned, the distance you traveled, and the time you spent exercising. Although it's easy to get enamored by fancy computerized gadgetry, don't let it sway your purchasing decision. Your most important considerations should be whether the machine is functional and easy to use. Make sure you can readily locate and operate the buttons. Look for LED displays that are well lit and easy to read. You shouldn't have to squint to decipher your intensity level or exercise time. In short, focus on issues that tangibly affect the quality of your workout. The rest is merely window dressing.

▪ *Programs.* Most cardio units have built-in programs that target popular goals, such as burning fat or climbing hills, by automatically varying the training resistance. On the plus side, these convenient programs can make your workouts more challenging. Unfortunately, since a machine can only make general assumptions about your individual goals and abilities, even the best programs are limited in scope. If your first priority is total convenience, having an array of programs may be worth the additional expense. Otherwise, you're better off creating a routine of your own that is consistent with your goals and abilities. You will see better results and will probably save some money in the process. See the cardio routine in chapter 12 for a detailed program to optimally burn fat.

▪ *Warranty.* Nothing can be more frustrating than purchasing a cardio unit only to endure a seemingly endless string of repairs. After all, what good comes from owning a piece of equipment that's constantly on the fritz? You can generally assess the quality of a unit's workmanship by the length of its warranty. Why? Basic economics. It simply isn't cost-effective for manufacturers to offer extended warranties on units that are made poorly. Eventually, they would go bankrupt with the cost of repairs. Look for a model with a warranty of at least one year for labor and three years for parts. Also remember that a warranty is only as good as the manufacturer standing behind it. A fly-by-night company might promise the moon, but that warranty won't be worth the paper it's printed on if they go out of business next month. You also might find it difficult or impossible to find replacement parts for a cheap unit. Buying from a reputable manufacturer gives you the peace of mind that your purchase won't soon become a fitness dinosaur.

The Big Three

Treadmills, elliptical machines, and stationary bikes are the "big three" of home cardio equipment, garnering more than three-fourths of the market's sales. The following section examines each modality in depth, outlining the pluses and minuses and detailing factors to consider.

Treadmills

Treadmills, which account for more than half of all consumer purchases, are by far the most popular piece of home fitness equipment (see figure 6.1). If you enjoy walking, jogging, or running outdoors, you may find a treadmill to be an attractive alternative. Sure, it's nice to feel close to nature, training in the fresh air and sunshine. But what about inclement weather? Ever slogged through slushy snow? Tried to work up a sweat in the cold rain? Endured oppressive heat and humidity, just to get in a workout? If you own a treadmill, the elements cease to be an issue. You can exercise in comfort regardless of what's happening outside.

Display console
Motor horsepower
Shock absorption
Folding deck

FIGURE 6.1 **Treadmill.**
Photo courtesy of Smooth Fitness.

Treadmills also help alleviate some of the ground-reaction forces associated with outdoor running. These forces may be as much as four times a person's body weight, which means that a woman who weighs 125 pounds (57 kg) exerts more than 500 pounds (227 kg) of force every time her foot hits the pavement! If you have wide hips, the stress to your knees is even greater. Please see the sidebar on Q-angle for more information. The treadmill's cushioned surface dissipates these forces, reducing the incidence of injury. Better yet, you won't have to worry about turning your ankle by stepping into a divot in the ground or wrenching your knee on a crack in the asphalt.

As a bonus, treadmill exercise is an excellent bone-builder. Its weight-bearing workout applies loads to your skeletal system in a way that sufficiently stimulates bones to increase their density. The catch: The only areas that adapt are the ones subjected to the load. In the case of a treadmill workout, you will see density improvements in the bones of your lower limbs, but little or no change in upper-body bone density. Therefore, in order to build bone from head to toe, you must combine treadmill training with upper-body strength training.

Take these considerations into account before buying a treadmill:

- *Motor.* The strength of a treadmill's motor is a function of its horsepower. For example, a motor with 1.5 horsepower has to work twice as hard as one with 3.0 horsepower to put out the same amount of power. A treadmill with insufficient

Knee Stability and the Q-Angle

Due to an increased Q-angle (the angle formed by the thigh bone between the knee and the hip), women are predisposed to knee injuries. Since most women have wider hips than men to accommodate the demands of childbirth, they also have larger Q-angles. A large Q-angle denotes lateral displacement of your femur (thigh bone), heightening patellar forces during impact activities. As a rule, the wider your hips are, the greater your potential risk of injury.

Although you can improve knee stability with a regimented strength-training program, you should take safety precautions during cardiorespiratory activities. Keep in mind that aerobic activities consist of repetitive motions. Performing the same movement for extended periods of time can overload the joints, making them vulnerable to injury. Consider the following suggestions for reducing the injury risk and optimizing aerobic adaptations:

- If you run a lot outdoors, don't get a treadmill.
- If your job entails climbing stairs all day, don't get a stair climber.
- If you ride a bike to work or around town, don't get a stationary bike.

horsepower may break down due to overheating and excessive stress. You can gauge a treadmill's horsepower by looking at peak duty and continuous duty. Continuous duty, which rates a motor's ability to sustain power over the course of a workout, is the more important of the two. Peak duty only estimates maximum power potential. If you plan to walk or jog on your treadmill, a motor with a continuous duty rating of 2.0 horsepower should be sufficient. If you intend to run, choose a model with a rating of at least 2.5.

- *Deck.* The comfort of your workout largely depends on the quality of the treadmill's deck. Decks should be well-cushioned and flexible enough to absorb impact during use. Proper cushioning eases stress on your joints and other soft-tissue structures, reducing the incidence of shin splints or chondromalacia of the knee. Look for a deck that is at least three-fourths of an inch (2 cm) thick. If you're a runner, choose one with a thickness of an inch or more (at least 2.5 cm). A reversible deck is preferable because it effectively doubles the treadmill's lifespan, saving you money in the long run.

- *Belt.* A high-quality belt is vital to smooth operation. Belts usually come in either one-ply or two-ply. Two-ply is superior, with extra stitching that helps prevent wearing and stretching during continuous use. Moreover, make sure that the belt's length is adequate for your stride and usage patterns. If you're of average height and just plan to walk leisurely, a 50-inch (127 cm) belt length should be sufficient. On the other hand, if you're an avid runner with a height of 5 feet 11 inches (180 cm), you'd be better served by a belt at least 58 inches (147 cm) long.

- *Incline.* Virtually all treadmills come with an incline function that allows you to simulate walking or running uphill. Incline, also called grade, is normally expressed as a percentage. Flat ground is represented by 0 percent; the higher the percentage, the steeper the incline. Casual exercisers will do well with the standard maximum incline of 10 percent. If you're looking for a more challenging workout, choose a treadmill that is capable of at least a 15 percent incline. Walking on a surface with a 15 percent grade burns approximately twice as many calories as walking on a level incline. Powered inclines are preferable to those that are manually operated. The convenience of pushing a button to change the grade is worth the extra expense.

- *Automatic stop.* When it comes to exercise, one thing you never want to skimp on is safety. Therefore, make sure your treadmill has an emergency stopping mechanism. This simple device connects you to the machine with a nylon cord that has a clip on one end and a key on the other. Before exercise, fasten the clip to your clothing and insert the key into a slot on the treadmill's console. If you should

Buyer's Guide for Treadmills

Ideally, your treadmill should have the following features:

- A motor with at least 2.0 horsepower
- A fiberboard deck with a platform at least three-fourths of an inch (2 cm) thick
- A belt at least 50 inches (127 cm) long
- An incline capability of at least 10 percent
- An emergency stopping mechanism

slip or fall, the key disengages from the slot, stopping the motor. I've seen this neat little invention save people from potentially serious injuries more than once. No two ways, it's a must-have.

■ *Cost.* Browse the sporting-goods section of any discount store or warehouse club, and you'll find treadmills selling for as little as a few hundred dollars. While these low prices might seem enticing, the units invariably have a poor cost-to-benefit ratio. Poor construction diminishes their performance capability, comfort, and life expectancy. Ultimately, you'll be disappointed with your purchase. High-quality treadmills start at around $1,200. Anything less simply isn't built to last. If this price exceeds your budget, consider a bike, which is considerably cheaper.

Elliptical Trainers

Elliptical trainers are quickly becoming the hottest commodity in the home-exercise market. Sales are rising at a clip of 20 percent—faster than any other modality.

Like the treadmill, elliptical trainers are designed to mimic the human gait during locomotion with one major difference: Your feet never leave the pedals (see figure 6.2). Some people compare this experience to running on a cloud.

Eliminating ground-reaction forces spares your lower limbs from the relentless pounding associated with jogging or running. And since ellipticals can be operated in both forward and backward directions, you can vary movement patterns enough to reduce repetitive-motion trauma to your joints. This all adds up to fewer joint problems in the hips, knees, and ankles, which is an especially important consideration if you suffer from lower-limb injuries or arthritis.

Take these key considerations into account before buying an elliptical trainer:

■ *Drive system.* The drive system of an elliptical machine is the mechanism by which it applies resistance during exercise. There are two basic types of drive systems: front drive and rear drive. As the names imply, front-drive units have systems in the front and rear-drive units house their systems in the back of the machine. Until recently, rear drives had a significant edge on performance, providing a smoother workout. However, front-drive technology is rapidly advancing, and some of the newer models now approach the performance of rear-drive units of comparable price. If you decide to buy a front-drive elliptical machine, opt for one with twin rollers. The rollers are subjected to a great deal of wear, and single-wheel units don't stand up well under constant use.

■ *Stride length.* Your stride length is the measurement between your feet at their greatest distance during the elliptical movement. The stride length of most units ranges from 14 to 22 inches (36-56 cm). The benefit of a greater stride length is that it works your leg muscles through a complete range of motion, which is especially important if you are tall or have long legs. To some degree, your height dictates just how long a stride length you need. See table 6.1 for specific recommendations for stride length.

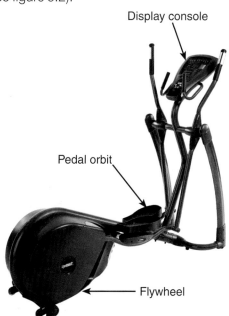

Display console

Pedal orbit

Flywheel

FIGURE 6.2 Elliptical trainer.
Photo courtesy of Smooth Fitness.

TABLE 6.1

Stride Recommendations for Elliptical Trainers

Height	Stride length
≤5 ft 2 in (157 cm)	16 in (41 cm)
5 ft 3 in to 5 ft 9 in (160-175 cm)	18 in (46 cm)
≥5 ft 10 in (178 cm)	20 in (51 cm)

> ### Buyer's Guide for Elliptical Trainers
>
> Ideally, your elliptical trainer should have the following features:
>
> - A drive system that delivers a smooth ride (front drives should have twin rollers)
> - A stride length consistent with your height (see table 6.1 on page 211)
> - Articulating foot pedals with a slip-resistant surface
> - Capability for upper-body action

- *Pedals.* Your ankle is a hinge joint that is capable of only one degree of movement. High-quality elliptical machines have articulating foot pedals that ergonomically conform to the natural movement pattern of your ankle, which keeps your foot planted throughout the range of motion. When you try out the unit, pay close attention to foot positioning. If your heel lifts at any time, the unit probably isn't compatible with your normal stride. Also, make sure the pedals have slip-resistant surfaces. This important safety feature can save you from mishap and comes at minimal cost.

- *Upper-body action.* One of the advantages of elliptical trainers is their ability to simultaneously work both lower and upper extremities. The moving handlebars allow you to pump your arms back and forth as your feet glide along the tracks. By increasing the number of working muscles, you burn more fat—a win-win situation. Unfortunately, not all units have a feature for the upper extremities. Some elliptical machines have fixed handlebars; only your legs move. Although you still can get an excellent workout without arm action, I think the feature is worth the extra cost.

- *Cost.* Don't be penny-wise but dollar-foolish. Although you can find elliptical trainers at discount prices, they invariably skimp on craftsmanship, leaving you dissatisfied with their performance and durability. Figure to spend at least $1,000 for a unit that delivers high-end performance. A cheaper model will tend to break down frequently, putting you on a first-name basis with the service technician. Stick with name brands from manufacturers who have established a good reputation in the field. I guarantee that you'll be happier in the long haul.

Stationary Bikes

Stationary bikes are often criticized as being poor fat burners, but this isn't quite the case. True, a high-intensity treadmill workout can burn about 100 more calories an hour than a comparable bike workout. However, that same bike workout still burns more than 600 calories per hour—not too shabby!

Moreover, it is shortsighted to make a purchase solely based on the absolute number of calories a unit can help you burn. Consider the issue of comfort. Studies show that people tend to find bikes more comfortable than other modalities. No big surprise here. After all, sitting is easier than standing, right? Some bikes even let you recline, further enhancing the level of comfort. This can make exercise less burdensome, potentially leading to better adherence.

Bikes are also very space efficient. They take up a mere 10 square feet (3 sq m), which is about half of the area of an elliptical trainer and only a third of the space for a treadmill. If you're cramped for space, a bike very well might be your best—or perhaps

Buyer's Guide for Stationary Bikes

Ideally, your stationary bike should have the following features:

- A fully adjustable, ergonomically-designed seat
- Adjustable handlebars if the unit is upright
- Buttons that control electromagnetic resistance
- Extra-wide, self-leveling pedals
- A belt-operated drive system

only—option. Add in the fact that bikes are inherently safe (it's virtually impossible to lose your balance or fall when seated) and are less expensive than treadmills and elliptical machines, and you'll see that bikes have a lot to offer.

Take these key considerations into account before buying a stationary bike:

- *Type.* Stationary bikes can be categorized into two basic types: upright and recumbent (see figure 6.3, *a-b*). Uprights are similar to road bikes; you sit tall on the seat with your feet placed in a position that is roughly parallel to your torso. Recumbent bikes, on the other hand, keep you in a reclined position so that your feet pedal in front of your body. Which is better? The answer depends on your needs. Recumbent bikes get the nod in terms of comfort. The contoured seat tends to be easier on your butt—you won't feel saddle-sore after a workout—and the back rest supports your spine in an ergonomically correct position, easing stress to the lumbar area. The constant forward lean associated with uprights places your lumbar region under prolonged stress, which can lead to or exacerbate back problems. In terms of burning fat, the advantage shifts to upright bikes. Since they require more core stabilization, uprights activate a greater amount of muscle mass, heightening caloric expenditure. You can further increase fat burning by pedaling in a standing position, which can't be done on a recumbent bike. Ultimately, the choice comes down to personal preference; evaluate the pluses and minuses and decide which bike better suits your needs.

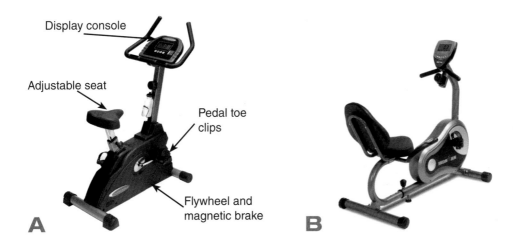

FIGURE 6.3   Stationary bikes: *(a)* upright and *(b)* recumbent.
(a) Photo courtesy of Body-Solid, Inc.
(b) Photo courtesy of Star Trac Fitness.

■ *Adjustability.* A bike should conform to your body type. Make sure the seat is fully adjustable and allows your knees to remain directly over your feet when you pedal. You should be able to extend your legs just short of locking your knees without rocking from side to side. On upright bikes, the handlebars should be roughly the same width as your shoulders and should adjust vertically so that you can maintain an upright position while riding. Remember, compromising your form can lead to injury, so don't take this issue lightly.

■ *Resistance.* The best stationary bikes create resistance in the form of electromagnetic current, utilizing electricity to increase or decrease drag around the flywheel. Since the current never makes direct contact with the flywheel, no friction is produced. This means less wear and tear on the bike's internal parts as well as smoother and quieter operation. Choose a model that lets you control resistance with the push of a button. It's a real pain in the glutes to manually adjust a knob or lever every time you need to vary workout intensity.

■ *Pedals.* The pedals on the bike should be wide enough so that the balls of your feet are positioned directly over the pedal axels. Look for models with self-leveling pedals, which help maintain proper alignment of the feet throughout the pedaling cycle. This increases comfort and control.

■ *Drive system.* A stationary bike's drive system is the mechanism that connects the pedals to the flywheel. Drive systems are usually controlled by either a belt or a chain. Go with a belt-driven unit, which gives a smoother ride and tends to require less maintenance than comparable chain drives.

■ *Cost.* Stationary bikes are by far the most affordable of the big three modalities of home cardio machines. They are a good buy if you're strapped for cash or would simply rather devote your resources to other pieces of equipment. Quality uprights go for as low as $500. Recumbent bikes tend to be priced somewhat higher, starting in the neighborhood of $700. If you opt for an upright bike, be sure to get a seat with extra gel padding. They cost less than 20 bucks and help prevent rubbing and chafing. Chances are, the salesman will throw one in with your purchase if you ask.

The Rest of the Field

There's more to cardio equipment than the big three. Stair climbers, rowers, and ski machines also make fine additions to a home gym. Here's a rundown of each machine.

Stair Climbers

Many women have been scared away from the stair climber by unsubstantiated claims that it gives users a big butt. Hogwash! In truth, stair climbing is a terrific aerobic workout that has little or no effect on the size of the muscles in your derriere. It's also the most space efficient of all the cardio modalities, requiring as little as 5 square feet (1.5 sq m) of floor space (see figure 6.4). Of the handful of manufacturers, StairMaster is by far the leader in the field. Their units are smooth, feature-rich, and built to last. They do have one downfall: At prices starting around $2,600, they are quite expensive. However, you can find a variety of miniature steppers for a fraction of the cost. These units are extremely portable (some are small enough to be stored in a closet!) and provide a decent workout.

FIGURE 6.4 Stair climber.
Photo courtesy of Nautilus, Inc.

Unfortunately, they tend to be hard on the joints and rather unstable. A new generation of *tread climbers* are attempting to combine the actions of a stair climber and a treadmill. Although the concept is intriguing, problems have been cited with reliability and biomechanics. Until all the kinks have been worked out, I'd advise you to stay away from these units.

Rowers

As you might expect from the name, rowing machines attempt to replicate the act of open-water rowing. A pulley cord is attached to a handle at one end of the unit, opposing a seat that glides back and forth along a fixed rail (see figure 6.5). When you pull on the handle, the cord extends and the seat slides backward as if you were propelling a boat down a river. Since rowers involve both the upper and lower body, they provide one of the most efficient ways to burn fat. Add in the fact that they have a reasonable footprint of about 15 square feet (5 sq m), and you may find a lot to like about these machines. The downside? It is difficult to maintain proper form over an extended training session, and the effort can place excessive strain on your lower back. Moreover, upper-body aerobic exercise has been shown to produce significantly elevated blood pressure levels when compared to lower-body aerobics, and thus it may not be suitable for those with existing cardiovascular disease. If you choose to row, you must pay strict attention to technique in order to avoid injury. The best machines have flywheel tanks that are filled with water to simulate the experience of rowing. Prices for high-quality units start at around $1,000. Other modes of

FIGURE 6.5   **Rower.**
Photo courtesy of BodyCraft.

resistance include piston-, air-, and magnetic-based technology. These units are considerably less expensive than those that use water as resistance. The better ones provide a good total-body aerobic workout. Expect to spend a minimum of around $500. Air- and magnetic-based units are preferable to those that use pistons.

Ski Machines

Ski machines come in two basic forms: those that attempt to simulate cross-country (Nordic) skiing and those that mimic downhill skiing. Avid skiers will find that the latter variety can serve as a great way to achieve sport-specific conditioning. The side-to-side motion helps to improve lower-body strength and balance, which translates into better performance on the slopes. Cross-country ski machines provide more of a total-body workout, and thus are the better fat burners. Their design is uncomplicated: Dual strips of wood slide along rollers to approximate the linear Nordic skiing motion, while either elastic cords or swiveling poles provide continuous arm action (see figure 6.6). I'm partial to models that employ independent leg motion. They allow you to train with a higher level of intensity than dependent units. The downside is that it is difficult to master coordination of movement. This is a big reason why ski machines haven't caught the fancy of the general public. With a footprint of about 20 to 30 square feet (6-9 sq m), they also take up a fair amount of space. Units of decent quality start around $500, with the better ones in the range of $1,000.

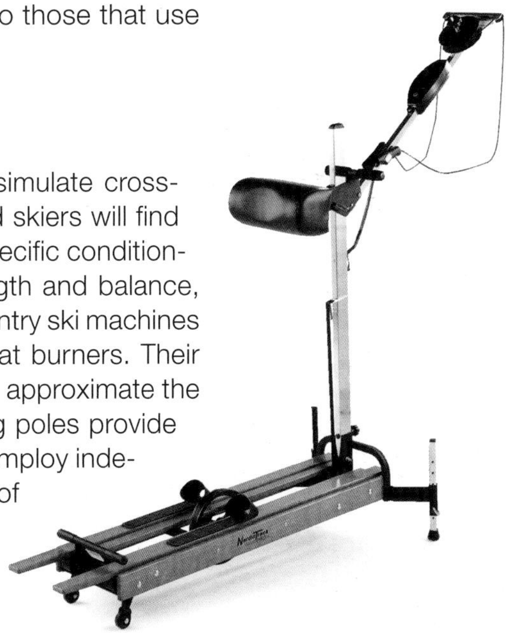

FIGURE 6.6   **Ski machine.**
Photo courtesy of The NordicTrack Company.

The Toning Myth

A common misperception is that cardio machines (such as the treadmill, elliptical trainer, and stationary bike) help to tone your body. The truth is that unless you're a complete couch potato, endurance exercise of any kind won't do much in the way of toning and sculpting. Here's why: To develop your muscles, you need to challenge them beyond their present state. By definition, aerobics is an endurance activity. Your muscles are never sufficiently challenged to overcome an overload response—an essential factor in promoting muscle development. So, although cardio produces excellent benefits for the heart and vascular system and expedites weight loss, it won't tone up your muscles to any sufficient degree. If you want lean muscle tone, you need to lift weights!

The Big Decision

So which cardio modality is best? Only you can answer that question. Try out a variety of modalities at your favorite sporting-goods store. Spend at least 10 to 15 minutes assessing whether you'd want to use each machine over the long term. Remember, adherence is paramount; you can't get fit if you don't train!

The Final Stretch

Honestly now, how often do you stretch? If you're like most, the answer probably lies somewhere between not much and not at all. Perhaps you don't think flexibility is important, that you'd rather focus your efforts on cardio and weightlifting—activities that have a tangible effect on your appearance. That's understandable. After all, you have only so much time to spend working out, right?

While this line of thinking is all too common, it can have a negative impact on your health and wellness. Maintaining optimal joint mobility brings about a multitude of benefits, including decreased musculoskeletal pain, increased tolerance to stretching, reduced risk of injury, better posture, and enhanced athletic performance. Important stuff, no doubt. That said, there is some debate about whether performing specific stretching exercises is really necessary for achieving these ideals. A case can actually be made that it's not—provided you lift weights on a regular basis. Contrary to popular belief, resistance training actually helps to make you more flexible. As long as you train through a complete range of motion, your joints are taken through their full stretch capacity on each repetition, facilitating better joint mobility. This has been borne out in research: Studies consistently show that those who lift weights are, on average, more limber than those who don't. In effect, lifting weights acts as its own form of flexibility training; stretching is already incorporated into the movements.

So does this mean you shouldn't worry about performing flexibility exercises if you lift? No pun intended, but that would be stretching the truth. Resistance training enhances flexibility only so much. Additional improvements come about only by incorporating targeted stretching movements into your routine. And the fact is that most people need supplemental stretching to keep their bodies in balance.

Activities of daily living tend to create imbalances between muscle groups: Certain muscles become tight in relation to their antagonists. The modern-day workplace is a major culprit here. Long periods of sitting at a desk tend to cause tightness and hyperactivity in the hip flexor and lower back muscles (a phenomenon that constitutes the so-called lower cross syndrome). This pulls the pelvis forward, causing excessive lordosis (swayback) and associated lower back pain. Lower cross syndrome is often accompanied by upper cross syndrome, which manifests as tight internal rotator muscles (the pecs and anterior deltoids), resulting in pinched shoulders and a hunched back. The results of these syndromes are stooped posture, reduced functional capacity, and a haggard appearance. If corrective action is not taken (that is, a combined program of strength training *and* stretching), the integrity of your joints becomes compromised and degenerative arthritis can set in. Not a pretty picture.

With these facts in mind, let's revisit the question posed earlier: Do *you* need to stretch? Ultimately, this will depend on your goals and abilities. If you're happy with your current level of flexibility and have no muscular imbalances to speak of, then perhaps performing specific flexibility exercises would be superfluous. But if you're like most people and have tightness between muscle groups or have a functional need for improved range of motion, then spending some time stretching is certainly warranted. It's also important to realize that flexibility is specific to a particular joint. You may have good upper-body flexibility and poor lower-body flexibility, or you may have an isolated part of the body such as the hamstrings or lower back that is tight. In cases such as this, you should focus your stretching efforts on the afflicted area. As you'll see, a little stretching goes a long way.

The ABCs of Stretching

The goal of any flexibility program should be to achieve an optimal balance between mobility and stability within a functional range of motion. Just as a lack of flexibility can be detrimental, so can being hypermobile. As a general rule, a joint that is too flexible will be unstable; the associated muscles can't maintain joint integrity, increasing susceptibility to injury. As with most things in life, more is not necessarily better. Often, it's worse.

Flexibility exercise can take many forms, including methods that employ dynamic, active, isometric, and passive techniques. For our purposes here, I'll focus on passive stretching. Passive stretching is ideal for home training because it is highly effective, it is simple to perform, it doesn't require a partner, and it is generally regarded as the safest form of stretching. Performance involves assuming a stretched position and holding that position using only your weight, the support of another part of your body, or an external apparatus. When properly implemented, this allows for a gradual elongation of muscle tissue, permitting you to safely stretch your body to its utmost degree.

The key to passive stretching is to carry out movements in a slow, controlled fashion. When you stretch, ease your joints into a comfort zone and then maintain the position for the duration of the set. Go only to the point where you feel tension in the muscle—not to where you experience unbearable pain. Forcing a joint beyond the boundaries of its range of motion can overload muscles and connective tissue beyond their normal elasticity, heightening the potential for strain. The structures in muscles begin to break down when stretched beyond 1.5 times their normal resting length, while ligamental breakdown begins at a stretch of only 6 percent of resting length. Overstretching also initiates a phenomenon called the stretch reflex—an internal body mechanism that protects muscles from exceeding their lengthening capacity. The stretch reflex works by sending a neural impulse to the spinal cord that in turn signals the stretched muscle to contract—the opposite effect of what you're trying to accomplish when the goal is increased flexibility.

A majority of studies indicate that holding stretches for 30 seconds maximizes results; any less reduces gains in flexibility, while stretching for longer than 30 seconds offers no additional benefits. In most instances, one set is all that's required for optimal results. That's one of the beauties of stretching: You can realize improvements in flexibility by training just minutes a day.

To enhance results, you can isometrically contract the antagonist muscle before stretching the target muscle—a technique borrowed from a system of flexibility training called proprioceptive neuromuscular facilitation (PNF). Doing so brings about a phenomenon called reciprocal inhibition, where the muscle being stretched relaxes and thus is better able to elongate. For example, before performing a biceps stretch (see page 223), you would actively tighten your triceps, hold the contraction for 10 to 15 seconds, and then proceed immediately to stretching the opposing muscle (in this case, the biceps). For the hamstring and glute stretch (see page 224), you would tighten your quads before initiating the stretch. Give this technique a try and you'll see improvements in range of motion over what you could otherwise accomplish.

When to Stretch

One notion currently accepted as gospel in many fitness circles is that you should stretch before a workout in order to prevent training-related injuries. This tenet has been followed by everyone from recreational fitness enthusiasts to professional athletes for the better part of a century. Research, however, says otherwise. Stretching before exercise does little to reduce the incidence of injuries during the ensuing workout. The preventive benefits of enhanced flexibility on injury are cumulative. They come about from performing regimented stretching movements over time, not from an acute bout before a workout.

So when should you stretch? Generally speaking, timing really doesn't matter. As the Nike slogan says, just do it!

It's generally okay to stretch before a workout. Just make sure you warm up first. When soft-tissue structures are cold, they are at their most brittle and thus subject to breakage. A warm-up increases core temperature, thereby diminishing a joint's resistance to flow (viscosity). This is accomplished via the uptake of synovial fluid, which provides the joint with lubrication. Think of it as oiling a squeaky door hinge: The door opens much more easily after it's been lubricated. So 5 to 10 minutes of light cardiorespiratory activity or calisthenics will suffice in adequately warming up the tissues. The activity should work any muscle that will be stretched. So if you're planning to stretch the lower body, opt for activities such as walking, jogging, or cycling. Rowing is a good option before upper-body stretching. Jumping jacks, skipping rope, and squat thrusts work well when you're going to stretch the entire body.

Another option is to stretch at the end of a workout. Since core temperature is already elevated, your muscles and connective tissue are primed to stretch—there's no need to warm up. Postworkout stretching also can serve as a cool-down, gradually decreasing your heart and breathing rates and returning your body to a rested state. A

Preexercise Stretching and Exercise Performance

Some exercise pros have cautioned against stretching before lifting weights. This opinion is based on studies that show preexercise stretching can lead to reductions in subsequent total force production during a workout. But a closer examination of the research reveals that things aren't what they seem on the surface. That is, the stretching protocols employed in these studies were highly excessive—spending upward of 30 minutes stretching a single joint.

Subsequent studies using more modest stretching protocols showed little if any decrements in performance. Given that optimal gains in flexibility are achieved through stretching a particular joint for no more than a minute or so, there's little need to worry that stretching before training will impair your abilities. Unless you're a competitive powerlifter gearing up for an event, stretching before exercise is as good a time as any.

cool-down is particularly important after aerobic training. It reduces the stress placed on the body and can help to prevent a sudden drop in blood pressure. Moreover, it aids in the redistribution of blood throughout the body. Otherwise, blood can pool in the muscles trained, potentially leading to cramping and stiffness.

You also can integrate flexibility training directly into your strength workouts by employing a technique that I refer to as *selective muscular stretching.* Selective muscular stretching involves stretching the muscle trained in between sets of lifting weights. The process is simple: As soon as you complete a set, immediately stretch the muscle being trained and hold it throughout the rest period. Not only is this an efficient way to enhance flexibility, but it can also help to restore blood flow to working muscles, thereby improving muscular recovery between sets.

Bottom line: Provided your muscles are warm, any time is a good time to stretch, whether it's before, during, or after a workout or on your days off from training. Moreover, you can stretch seven days a week, if desired. Since passive stretching doesn't significantly tax your neuromuscular system, it won't have any negative effects on recovery.

Stretching Equipment

Numerous gizmos are on the market claiming to help you increase flexibility, and some of them are quite pricey. While these units can offer added convenience and variety for stretching, you generally don't need to spend a lot of money on equipment to derive optimal joint flexibility.

The stretching exercises detailed in this book involve only your own body weight. They're simple to perform and highly effective. If desired, you can employ some basic equipment outlined in the $100 budget. The stability ball, for example, can be a terrific apparatus for facilitating flexibility, especially for those who find it difficult to move into and out of floor-based stretching positions. Resistance bands also can aid in stretches. By looping a band around your feet or torso, you can deepen many stretches. That said, by no means are these implements essential. Provided you follow the stretching protocol as directed, you can achieve improvements in flexibility without any additional investment.

Longer and Leaner?

Wouldn't it be great if a stretching routine could reshape your body so it became long and lean? Some fitness pros would have you believe that Pilates is just such a regimen. According to the claims, Pilates training lengthens muscles, giving you a dancer's physique that is willowy and flowing.

Unfortunately, the prospect of becoming longer and leaner through exercise is a physiological impossibility. The fact is that your genetic structure is inherent. Each muscle in your body has a predetermined shape predicated on such factors as fiber-type composition, tendon insertions, and muscle belly length. You simply cannot alter these properties unless you somehow find a mad scientist who's invented a new form of gene therapy. This is not to imply that Pilates can't have a place in a workout routine. If integrated into a comprehensive exercise program, it can enhance general fitness levels, including flexibility. But don't fall prey to marketing propaganda. Exercise, no matter what form, can only improve on your inherent structure—it can't alter genetics.

Stretching Exercises

Chest Stretch. Stand upright with your back straight, feet shoulder-width apart, and knees slightly bent. Place your arms behind your back and clasp your hands together. Keeping your body erect, extend your arms and try to lift them as high as comfortably possible until you feel a distinct stretch in your chest. Hold this position for the desired time.

Shoulder Stretch. Stand upright with your back straight, feet shoulder-width apart, and knees slightly bent. Grasp your right wrist or elbow with your left hand. Without turning your body, slowly pull your right arm across your torso as far as comfortably possible. Hold this position for the desired time and then repeat the process with your left arm.

Upper Back Stretch. Stand upright with your back straight, feet shoulder-width apart, and knees slightly bent. Clasp your hands together with palms facing forward and extend both arms out in front of your body so they form a 90-degree angle with your torso. Flare your lats forward so that you feel a distinct stretch throughout your upper back. Hold this position for the desired time. For an added stretch, rotate your arms to the right and left without turning your body.

Lower Back Stretch. Lie back on the floor. Slowly pull your knees to your chest as far as comfortably possible until you feel a distinct stretch in your lumbar region. Hold this position for the desired time. For an added stretch, you can place a folded towel under the base of the spine.

Ab Stretch. Stand upright with your back straight, feet shoulder-width apart, and knees slightly bent. Place your hands on your sides and slowly lean back as far as comfortably possible. Hold this position for the desired time. For an added effect and to enhance the stretch on the oblique muscles, lean to your left and then to your right.

Triceps Stretch. Stand upright with your back straight, feet shoulder-width apart, and knees slightly bent. Raise your right arm over your head and bend your elbow so that your right hand is behind your head. With your left hand, grasp your right wrist or elbow and pull it down as far as comfortably possible, pointing your right elbow toward the ceiling. Hold this position for the desired time and then repeat the process with your left arm.

Biceps Stretch. Stand upright with your back straight, feet shoulder-width apart, and knees slightly bent. Extend your right arm forward. Place your left palm underneath your right elbow. Slowly straighten your right arm as much as comfortably possible, pressing your elbow down into your left hand. Hold this position for the desired time and then repeat the process with your left arm.

Quadriceps Stretch. Stand upright with your back straight, feet shoulder-width apart, and knees slightly bent. If necessary, grasp a stationary object (such as a chair) with your right hand for support. Bend your left knee and bring your left foot toward your butt. Grasp your left ankle or foot with your left hand and slowly lift your foot as high as comfortably possible. Hold this position for the desired time and then repeat the process with your right leg.

Hip Flexor Stretch. Stand upright with your back straight, feet shoulder-width apart, and knees slightly bent. Take a long stride forward with your right foot, raising your left heel off the floor. Keeping your left leg completely straight and torso erect, bend your right knee until you feel a stretch in the top of your left thigh. (Do not allow your right knee to travel past the plane of your toes. If you need additional range of motion, widen your stance.) Hold this position for the desired time and then repeat the process on the opposite side.

Hamstring and Glute Stretch. Sit on the floor with your legs straight and lower back in neutral position. Keeping your head up, slowly bend forward at the hips and allow your hands to travel down along the line of your body as far as comfortably possible. When you feel a distinct stretch in your hamstrings, grab your legs and hold this position for the desired time.

Calf Stretch. Stand upright with your back straight, feet shoulder-width apart, and knees slightly bent. Step back with your left leg behind your body as far as you can while keeping your feet flat on the floor. Bend your right knee and slowly lean forward without lifting your left heel. Hold this position for the desired time and then repeat the process with your right leg.

PART III

Strategies and Ultimate Home Routines

Target Your Ultimate Body at Home

After reading parts I and II of this book, you should possess all the knowledge needed to build the ultimate home gym, one that's tailored to your needs, abilities, and budget. Congratulations, you're halfway home. Now it's time to put the equipment you purchased to good use and build your body to its ultimate potential.

The next few chapters provide detailed workouts targeting the four most common fitness goals: general conditioning, body sculpting, core stability, and weight loss. These cutting-edge routines bridge science and experience to deliver the best results in the shortest amount of time possible. Thousands of women have used variations of these routines with me over the years, enjoying terrific success. If you put in the effort, I guarantee superior results.

Workouts are provided for four budget levels, encompassing equipment purchases of $100, $500, $1,000, and $2,500 or more. Just match the workout to your budget and you're ready to roll. Everything is mapped out for you, including exercises, sets, reps, and intensity levels. If you don't like a particular exercise for some reason, simply substitute a similar movement that targets the appropriate musculature. It's that easy.

Set SMART Goals

But wait a sec. Before you just dive into one of the routines headfirst, let's take a step back and think down the road a bit. Exercise isn't a quick fix for improving your appearance and health; to enjoy lasting benefits, fitness must become a way of life. Live the fitness lifestyle and you'll change your life forever!

Sadly, the statistics on exercise adherence aren't good. About 80 percent of all people who set up a home gym stop using it within a few months. It's a familiar pattern. After a short time, the novelty of training starts to wear off. Enthusiasm wanes. You begin to skip workouts. Little by little, the number of exercise sessions you miss increases until you stop training altogether and leave your equipment to collect dust. Don't become a statistic. You can overcome the odds and become a lifelong fitness success story. All it takes is a commitment to setting goals. Goals, the reasons for wanting to exercise, are a function of your motivation.

First and foremost, understand that motivation comes from within. No one can motivate you to do something you don't want to do. You can have a beautiful home gym with the best equipment money can buy, yet it won't mean a thing if it doesn't help you achieve a meaningful goal. Think about it: Why would you want to put in all that time, sweat, and effort if there's no payoff at the end?

Setting goals clarifies what you're looking to gain from exercise, helping to sustain motivation over a period of time, and even making your workouts more enjoyable. Every time you feel too tired to work out, revisit your goals. Think about how good you'll feel afterward, and how you'll be one step closer to fitting into that slinky dress, improving your cardiorespiratory health, or reaching the green from the ninth hole at the local golf course. If your goals are meaningful, you'll be able to overcome inertia and get your butt into the gym so you can reap the rewards that are sure to follow.

Now, this isn't to say there won't be some bumps along the way. Life's travails can sometimes interfere with your exercise program. Sickness, work issues, and other crises can set back your training efforts for days or even weeks. However, if you have well-defined goals that are important to you, you will be inclined to get back into your routine quickly and stick with it over the long haul.

For goal setting to have any real value, goals must be both quantifiable and attainable. If one of these criteria is unmet, the goal is not specific, and therefore is not meaningful. You will have difficulty achieving nonspecific goals, which will result in frustration. Let's discuss these criteria in greater detail.

> ## Expert Tip
>
> You can test the validity of your goals by using the acronym, SMART, which stands for *specific, measurable, attainable, realistic,* and *timely*. Provided each of these criteria are met, you have a viable goal.

- *In order for a goal to be quantifiable, it must be specific and measurable.* For example, losing 20 pounds in three months is a quantifiable goal. You can weigh yourself today and again three months from now to see whether you have met your goal. The scale will indicate your degree of weight loss in a measurable context. Other examples of quantifiable goals include dropping a dress size in six weeks, increasing your bench press by 10 percent, and reducing total cholesterol by 50 points. Conversely, wanting to look good is not a quantifiable goal. The desire is subjective and cannot be measured by any definable standards. A goal that is doomed by ambiguity won't reinforce your motivation to train.

- *In order for a goal to be attainable, it must be realistic and timely.* The goal to lose 20 pounds in three months is attainable. Trying to lose 90 pounds in three months is not. Squatting 100 pounds might be an attainable goal, but squatting 500 pounds probably isn't. If a goal is unattainable, it can serve as a demotivator, making you feel as if all your sweat and effort is pointless. It is better to set modest goals that are readily within your reach. This practice gives you a feeling of accomplishment and spurs you on to loftier goals.

Whatever goals you decide to pursue, break them down into short time frames of no more than three months. By limiting the horizon of your goals, you will be able to accomplish them in a reasonable period of time. This promotes positive feedback and boosts self-confidence. For example, reducing your cholesterol by 50 points might appear to be a daunting task, but if you think about cutting it by 10 points a month for five months, the goal seems much more attainable. After a mere 30 days, you can celebrate the fact that you've achieved the first portion of your goal and can set your sights on the next objective.

Once you've formulated your goals, commit them to paper and post them where you'll see them. This provides a sense of accountability. You can't forget about them or sweep them under a rug. They are there in black and white, reminding you why you need to train.

Whenever possible, create incentives that help you reach your goals. For example, if you want to lose weight, buy an expensive dress that's several sizes too small. The thought of that beautiful dress sitting unused in your closet should motivate you to get in the gym. Alternatively, have your husband or boyfriend agree to take you away on a romantic vacation if you drop a certain number of dress sizes. Involving others in your fitness efforts creates a support network that will spur you on to greater heights.

Once you accomplish a goal, you should immediately set a new one. This will keep you focused and motivated. Review your goals periodically to make sure that they are consistent with your present objectives. Goals often change as your fitness level progresses. Reevaluate your position to ensure that you stick with your program.

Visualize Success

Visualization is a technique that can be used to reinforce your goals and sustain your motivation to train. Essentially, it is an organized form of daydreaming. Many athletes use this technique to actualize their potential. For example, a basketball player might visualize swishing a last-second jump shot, and a baseball player might visualize hitting a game-winning home run. The technique works beautifully in an exercise setting to increase adherence and improve training performance.

Visualization is best practiced in an environment that is quiet and free of distractions. It can be done standing, sitting, or lying down. When you are ready, close your eyes and relax your muscles. Begin to think about your goal. Is it related to your physique? If so, visualize your entire body—your arms, legs, shoulders, and so on—and create an image of how you want it to look. Picture yourself in great shape, walking on the beach in a bikini or wearing a sexy dress at an event. Maybe your goal is to improve your functional capacity. Cool. See yourself effortlessly lifting your four-year-old and toting him around the park or the zoo. Regardless of which image you choose, make it as real as possible. Imagine how good you'll feel when others compliment you on your appearance, or the sense of power you'll derive after performing tasks you've never been able to do before. If your goal is reasonable, do not limit your visualization of what you can accomplish. Let your imagination be your internal source of motivation.

Photos can enhance the practice of visualization. It is said that a picture is worth a thousand words. Well, a picture can also help to reinforce a specific mental image. This is especially relevant if you have goals related to your physique. Find a picture of yourself when you looked your best and put it on your refrigerator, dresser, or anywhere in full view. Every time you see this picture, it will remind you of your potential and help you keep the image fresh in your mind.

Once you've mastered the technique of visualization, use it during your workout to create a positive mindset. Before pumping out a set of presses or squats, picture yourself performing the lift better than ever before. Focus on the image that you want to achieve. Let nothing stand in the way of attaining your goal. This may sound hokey at first, but believe me, it works. Try it and you'll see.

You should also realize that imagery can work in reverse to create self-fulfilling prophecies of failure. If you have a negative outlook, your performance is bound to suffer. If you think that you can't perform a lift, you will almost certainly fall short in your efforts. Push these types of thoughts from your mind. If you believe you can do something, ultimately, you will do it!

Follow the Ten Commandments of Fitness

In addition to goal setting and visualization, several other principles are important to your fitness results. You've no doubt heard the biblical story of Moses traveling up the mountain to receive the Ten Commandments—immutable doctrines that all people should live by. Well, a similar but lesser-known list exists for exercise. Treat these commandments as if they were inscribed in stone by the fitness gods. They should form the basis of every exercise routine, whether you are training to become an Olympic athlete or are simply looking to tone up and get healthy. Read them over. Follow them to the letter. They'll go a long way toward helping you get the most from all that hard work in your new gym.

1   Train According to Your Goals

You shouldn't set foot in your gym without first understanding the principle of specificity. This central tenet of exercise states that in order to achieve a fitness goal, you must make your training specific to that goal. The movements you choose, the energy systems you use, and the intensity of your training should closely parallel what you're trying to accomplish.

For example, a 20-something aspiring fitness competitor should train in a manner that optimizes body composition. A postmenopausal woman looking to improve bone density should focus on strength moves that load the skeletal system. Specificity also

THE TEN COMMANDMENTS OF FITNESS

1	Train According to Your Goals	6	Rest After Intense Training
2	Fuel Your Body Before Exercise	7	Regiment a Training Schedule
3	Warm Up Before Intense Training	8	Vary Your Routine
4	Continually Challenge Your Muscles	9	Develop a Mind-to-Muscle Connection
5	Train With Proper Form	10	Know the Major Muscle Groups

applies to sports: To optimize performance, a volleyball player needs to train differently from a golfer who, in turn, should train differently from a swimmer. The closer the match between your routine and your primary goals, the better your results will be.

Make sure to keep specificity in mind when choosing your training routine. Revisit the goals you established earlier in the chapter. Prioritize them. If your prime interest at the moment is to develop better functional capacity, opt for the conditioning routine. If you're itching to look great in a bikini this summer, go with the body sculpting routine. If you're most concerned with the health and posture of your lower back, the core stability routine is your best choice.

2 Fuel Your Body Before Exercise

You wouldn't think of putting watered-down gas into a Lamborghini, would you? Of course not. A finely tuned car like that would buck and kick like a rodeo bronco if it received bad fuel. Then why do so many people choose to scarf down junk foods when the human body is infinitely more complex than an automobile?

Pretraining nutrition is essential for getting the most out of your efforts. Specifically, if you do not begin a workout with an adequate supply of energy for your muscles and brain, you simply cannot perform at your best. A complete discussion of nutrition is beyond the scope of this section, but those who are interested in more information can consult my book, *28-Day Body Shapeover*.

Carbohydrate is the primary fuel for high-intensity training. During high-intensity exercise, your body uses energy at a very fast rate, and it can't supply enough oxygen to process fat as a fuel source. It relies instead on glycogen, or stored carbohydrate, which doesn't require oxygen to be broken down for energy.

Ensure that your body's glycogen stores are fully stocked by ingesting an ample amount of carbs before exercise. In this way, you can access energy on demand, go all out in your training efforts, and extend your performance without hitting the wall.

Include protein in your preworkout meal as well. Although it doesn't contribute much in the way of energy, protein has both anabolic and anticatabolic effects on the body. Consuming protein prior to exercise provides your muscles with a steady stream of amino acids, which maximize performance and attenuate the breakdown of muscle tissue. This practice also primes the body for muscle development by significantly increasing the synthesis of muscle protein during the first hour after exercise.

Now let's talk specifics. Your preworkout meal should include a nutrient-dense carb and a protein source. Turkey on multigrain bread, lean steak and yams, egg whites and oatmeal, and chicken and brown rice are all terrific options that provide adequate fuel without bogging down your stomach.

Try to eat approximately two or three hours before training. This ensures that you digest the majority of your meal before you exercise and helps to prevent gastric upset.

If you are exercising early in the morning, consider eating a large piece of fruit a half-hour before you start your workout. Fruit, which has a high concentration of fructose, helps keep insulin levels stable because it is low on the glycemic index. Stable insulin levels prevent rebound hypoglycemia, a condition that can result in lightheadedness and fatigue. At the same time, fruits provide a valuable source of fuel during exercise, improving your capacity to train. Apples, pears, strawberries, and other low-glycemic fruits make excellent choices here.

Ideally, you should combine the fruit with a whey protein drink. Whey is a fast-acting protein, which means it is rapidly absorbed into the bloodstream. This expedites the flow of amino acids to your muscles without affecting your digestion. Measure out

Drink Up!

The most important nutrient to consume during training is water. As you work out, you lose a large amount of water by sweating and breathing. If you don't replenish these fluids, your exercise performance is bound to suffer. In fact, decrements in endurance and muscular strength can manifest after only a 2 percent reduction in hydration status. Extreme cases of dehydration can lead to heat stroke or circulatory collapse. Clearly, you should avoid exercise-induced dehydration at all costs.

Don't rely on thirst to tell you when to drink. Intense exercise inhibits the thirst sensors in your throat and gut; by the time you become thirsty, your body is already dehydrated. As you age, your thirst sensors also become increasingly less sensitive.

Therefore, during exercise, drink early and drink often. Consume 8 ounces of fluid immediately before your workout, and then take small sips of water every 15 or 20 minutes while training. Try to maintain a balance of fluids by matching the amount of water you drink with the rate at which you sweat. This will ensure a continued state of hydration.

approximately one-tenth of a gram of whey for each pound of your body weight. For example, someone who weighs 150 pounds should use 15 grams of whey. Better yet, put the fruit and whey into a blender, add some ice, and you have a delicious preworkout smoothie!

3 Warm Up Before Intense Training

The importance of warming up cannot be overstated. A good warm-up prepares your body for intense exercise by increasing your range of motion, improving the responsiveness of your muscles, and speeding up your recovery. Blowing off your warm-up will not only decrease the quality of your training, but will also increase your potential for injury. The harder you train, the more essential a warm-up becomes.

Begin each session with a general warm-up of 5 to 10 minutes of light cardio-respiratory activity. You can use virtually any mode of cardiorespiratory activity, but it's best to opt for one that's specific to the muscles being trained. Jumping jacks are usually a good choice because they involve the entire body. Ditto for elliptical trainers that include upper-body action. Work up a slight sweat, and then move on to your routine.

The primary purpose of the general warm-up is to elevate body temperature. Studies show a direct correlation between muscle temperature and exercise performance: the higher a muscle's temperature, the better its contractility, allowing it to produce more force. This ultimately leads to better performance. When you warm up, your joints also take in more synovial fluid, which lubricates the joint capsule, reduces joint viscosity, and improves range of motion.

During advanced stages of resistance training, it's beneficial to add a specific warm-up to the mix. The specific warm-up goes a step beyond the general warm-up, enhancing neuromuscular efficiency in performing a particular move. Execute exercises that are similar to those in your workout so your neuromuscular system can rehearse the movements before you do them at high intensity.

The movements used in a specific warm-up should be as close to the actual exercises as possible. For instance, if you plan to train your chest muscles, you should warm up with some bench presses or push-ups. Just a couple of light sets at the beginning of your routine are needed to achieve the desired benefits.

4 Continually Challenge Your Muscles

No two ways about it, the primary reason women fail in their quest to get fit is inadequate intensity of training. Many women simply don't train hard enough to improve their fitness level. They'll use absurdly light weights that don't come close to taxing their muscles (I've actually seen women talking on cell phones and reading magazines while performing arm curls and leg extensions!) and expect to achieve great results. No dice. Such a lackadaisical approach is destined for failure.

Intensity is dictated by the concept of progressive overload. In simplified terms, this means that in order to bring about change in your body, you need to continually stress your muscles beyond their present capacity. By nature, the body doesn't like change. Its desire to settle into a comfort zone is called homeostasis. If your training is not intense enough to tax your resources, the stimulus won't be great enough to force your body from its comfort zone.

Regardless of the target workout you choose to follow, you must apply progressive overload. Don't think of weights as heavy or light. Choose a weight that makes it difficult, if not impossible, to finish the last few repetitions in a given range. If the weight doesn't challenge your muscles, it's too light. The concept of progressive overload is the only way to compel your muscles to produce an adaptive response. This will bring about positive change in your physique.

5 Train With Proper Form

This should be a no-brainer, right? Wrong! It never ceases to amaze to me how many lifters, including some with years of experience, train with poor form. They throw weights around in haphazard fashion, producing movements that fail to train their muscles as they desire. Inevitably, they end up with muscular imbalances and sore joints. At some point, they usually experience a training-related injury.

Bulking Up

If you're afraid that intense training will bulk you up like an Amazon woman, relax. It's not going to happen. More than 99 percent of women lack the capacity to develop significant muscle mass. The main reason: a lack of testosterone. Testosterone is a hormone that's secreted by the testes in males and, to a lesser extent, by the ovaries in females. It has two main functions. First, testosterone is *androgenic,* or masculinizing. It promotes male-oriented characteristics such as thick facial and body hair, baldness, and deepening of the voice. Second, testosterone is *anabolic,* or building. Through a complex process, it interacts with muscle tissue at the cellular level to increase protein synthesis, the primary stimulus for muscular growth. Hence, there is a direct relationship between testosterone and muscle mass: The more testosterone you secrete, the greater your propensity to build muscle.

On average, women produce only 5 percent of the amount of testosterone that their male counterparts produce. This is nature's way of preserving femininity. As a result, it's difficult for female frames to bulk up significantly. Without an anabolic stimulus from testosterone, muscle tissue has limited impetus to *hypertrophy* (grow larger), and its growth remains modest, even with advanced training methods.

That said, *bulky* is a subjective term. What is pleasing muscle tone to one person may be too much for another. Only you can determine how much muscle tone you desire. The good news is that it's a lot easier to decrease muscle mass than to gain it. If a particular muscle group is getting too big for your liking, simply decrease the intensity of your training. In short order, detraining will take effect and your muscle will shrink to its previous size.

Perfect form involves performing an exercise so that only the target muscles are used to complete the maneuver. The weight is lifted in the most efficient manner possible, allowing muscles to contract in a direct line with their fibers. There are no extraneous body movements and no hesitations—just one continuous motion as each rep flows smoothly into the next.

Unfortunately, people naturally try to take the path of least resistance, lifting weights in the easiest possible fashion rather than in a way conducive to muscular development. Be proactive when working on form and take the following factors into account:

▪ *Rep speed.* When you're lifting a weight, remember the ABCs—Always Be in Control. Control is influenced by gravitational force which, in turn, is dictated by the concentric and eccentric phases of a repetition. Concentric reps (sometimes called positives) involve lifting a weight against the force of gravity. For example, when performing an arm curl (see page 30), you flex your arm from a fully straightened position. During the concentric phase, you shorten the target muscle until a contraction is achieved at the top of the movement. Significant exertion is required to complete the lift, so a slightly faster pace is acceptable. Take approximately 1 to 2 seconds to complete this phase.

Alternatively, eccentric reps (sometimes called negatives) move with the force of gravity. In the example of the arm curl, you straighten your arm from a fully flexed position. During the eccentric phase, the muscle lengthens and stretches at the end of the movement. Here, you should focus on resisting the pull of gravity so that momentum does not play a significant role in your performance. On average, the negative phase should last twice as long as the positive phase. Take approximately 2 to 4 seconds to complete this phase.

▪ *Breathing.* You should inhale and exhale in sync with each repetition. For best results, regiment your breathing in the following manner. Take a deep breath before starting your set. As you initiate the concentric portion of the rep, start to exhale, expelling your breath evenly. By the time you have contracted your target muscle, you should have released all the air from your lungs. Next, inhale as you return the weight to the starting position, preparing yourself for the next repetition. Continue breathing in this fashion until you have completed your set. Above all, never hold your breath throughout a lift (a phenomenon known as the Valsalva maneuver). Doing so can cut off the blood supply to your brain, resulting in headaches, dizziness, or fainting. In extreme cases, you can even rupture a blood vessel or tear a retina. Ouch! The bottom line: Even breathing incorrectly is better than not breathing at all.

▪ *Range of motion.* Unless you're training with an injury or working through a sticking point, you should always perform exercises over a complete range of motion. The repeated use of limited-range movements can cause an adaptation in which muscles get accustomed to their shortened position. They then accommodate by assuming this position as their resting length. Unless corrective measures are taken, joint mobility is compromised. Exercises performed through a complete range of motion counteract this effect and enhance flexibility. In effect, they serve as a dynamic form of stretching. Just as importantly, they elicit more forceful muscular contractions. There is a direct correlation between the amount of applied force and muscular development: The greater the force applied, the better your development will be. You will only achieve optimal results by routinely working your muscles over their full ranges. For example, in the one-arm row (see page 139), you should fully stretch your working arm toward the floor, pull the weight up as high as possible along the line of your body, and then return again to the fully stretched position.

You'll need to make a dedicated effort to learn proper technique for each movement you perform. To facilitate the process, I've furnished detailed descriptions of every exercise in this book. Commit them to memory. Make them part of your subconscious. The fact is that even minor adjustments in your form can make a big difference in your results.

6 Rest After Intense Training

In keeping with the biblical analogy, let's go back to the tale about how God created the world. As the story goes, He spent six days perfecting heaven and earth, then used the seventh day to rest. Well, God was definitely onto something. He realized that after expending all that sweat and effort on the universe, He needed some downtime to recuperate.

Okay, maybe that's not exactly how it went, but I took a few liberties here to make a point: The need for recuperation is just as important for us mortals. Our bodies need rest, especially after a grueling workout. Exercise doesn't build your muscles, it breaks them down. The stress of intense training causes small tears in the structural components of your muscles. Your body synthesizes protein to repair the damaged muscle tissue while you're resting, setting the stage for muscle development. Shortchange recuperation, and your body never has the opportunity to adequately recover from the extreme demands of training.

All too often, people ignore this fact. They spend hours upon hours in the gym, subscribing to the misguided theory that if a little bit is good, a lot must be better. Bad idea. Marathon workouts are unnecessary. They inevitably lead to a state of overtraining in which your immune system is suppressed and your progress is impaired. See the sidebar on page 236 for more information on overtraining.

Some people try to get around this predicament by employing a split routine. They train one muscle group one day, a different muscle group the next, and so on, never giving their bodies a day off. Unfortunately, this practice fails to account for the synergistic interactions between muscle groups. For instance, the biceps are integrally involved in the performance of back maneuvers, the shoulders and triceps are engaged in many exercises for the chest, and the glutes and hamstrings are used during multijoint leg movements. Other muscles function as stabilizers. In particular, the abdominals and the erector spinae (the muscles of the lower back) help stabilize the body in a number of upper- and lower-body exercises by contracting statically. Even on a secondary level, when a muscle is repeatedly subjected to intense physical stress without adequate rest, the rate at which muscle damage occurs outpaces the reparation process. The end result is impaired muscular development.

The routines outlined in this book are designed to provide just the right balance of exercise and recovery times. They should be performed three days a week on nonconsecutive days, such as Monday, Wednesday, and Friday. This timing coincides with the normal course of protein synthesis, as well as the amount of time your body needs to fully repair damaged muscle tissue, which lasts approximately 48 hours. Remember, it's the quality of training that optimizes results, not the quantity. With respect to exercise, less can be more!

Overtraining

Overtraining syndrome (OTS) is an exercise-induced malady that increases your body's production of cortisol, a stress hormone that inhibits protein synthesis and accelerates proteolysis (protein breakdown). This syndrome not only brings muscular development to a screeching halt, but it also hinders the body's ability to utilize fat for fuel—a double whammy that wreaks havoc on your body.

Glutamine stores are also rapidly depleted by OTS. Glutamine is the primary source of energy for immune cells. Without an adequate supply of glutamine to use as fuel, the immune system loses its ability to produce antibodies. Ultimately, the body's capacity to fight viruses and infections is impaired, leading to infirmity.

Unfortunately, no test can definitively determine whether you're suffering from OTS. Common symptoms include irritability, depression, chronic fatigue, reduced appetite, increased resting heart rate, and decreased exercise performance. However, someone who is overtrained may not necessarily manifest all of these symptoms. Consequently, you may become overtrained without even realizing it.

The best advice to avoid OTS is to be in tune with your body. Remain objective. Don't allow yourself to be blinded by emotion. If you're feeling weak or run-down, take a day or two off. It's better to err on the side of caution. One thing is certain: Ignoring the telltale signs that your body needs a break from training is a recipe for fitness disaster.

7 Regiment a Training Schedule

No matter how awesome your training routine is, you won't get anything out of it unless you get your butt into the gym. This is basic common sense, right? It should be. However, nearly three-fourths of the people who enter into an exercise program stop working out within the first few months!

One of the best ways to adhere to your fitness practice is to make exercise a habit. Think of it like brushing your teeth—a necessity, not an option. You should have preset training days. Write them into your schedule, just as you would an important business meeting or a family function. Unless you have a major crisis, stick to your schedule rigidly.

Don't buy into the claim made by certain fitness professionals that you need to exercise first thing in the morning. This is nonsense. Some people don't function well in the morning. If this describes you, chances are you'll sleepwalk through an early training session. The net result is a low-quality, inefficient workout that leads to poor adherence.

Ultimately, it doesn't matter when you train as long as you do it. Let your biorhythms determine when you should work out. If you are a morning person, go ahead and train early. But if you don't really get going until you've been awake for several hours, by all means, train later in the day. Do what you need to stay regimented.

8 Vary Your Routine

Ever heard that variety is the spice of life? Well, variety also is the spice of fitness. The human body is an extremely resourceful organism that intuitively adapts to repetitive stress. What's one of the most potent stressors? You've got it: exercise! If you perform the same exercise routine over and over, your body eventually becomes impervious to its effects. You reach a training plateau where your results stagnate. The longer you stay with the same routine, the less effective it becomes.

The key to sustaining progress is to constantly change workout variables. This keeps your body off guard, never giving it the opportunity to get accustomed to a particular muscular stress. When your muscles are continually forced to adjust, your results progress at a steady rate.

The routines in this book embrace the concept of variety with a technique called nonlinear periodization that manipulates exercises, reps, sets, and rest intervals from one session to the next. In effect, you'll perform a different routine each time you train.

What's more, suggestions are provided on how to alter the routines into the future to keep workouts fresh and interesting. You'll make steady progress and you'll look forward to hitting the gym each time you train.

> ## Expert Tip
>
> One of the best ways to remain focused on your exercise program is to keep a workout diary. When used on a regular basis, this practice allows you to monitor your progress and make necessary adjustments to your routine based on hard data rather than guesswork. For strength-training workouts, you should take note of exercises, sets, reps, and weight. For cardio workouts, include the exercise modality, your speed or level, the distance traveled, and your time. Also, write down how you felt during the workout, as well as anything that might have affected your results, such as illness, nutritional status, or stress level. Review the diary at the end of each month to evaluate whether your routine needs a tune-up.

9 Develop a Mind-to-Muscle Connection

There's more to weight training than simply lifting a weight from point A to point B. In fact, two women with identical routines will achieve vastly different results depending on their mental approach to training, or their *mind-to-muscle connection.*

Simply stated, a mind-to-muscle connection is the melding of mind and muscle so that they become one. Visualize the muscle you are training and feel that muscle contract throughout each repetition. Rather than thinking about where you feel a muscle working, you must picture where you are supposed to feel the stimulus.

A mind-to-muscle connection is beneficial on two levels. First, it ensures that your target muscles perform the majority of work during an exercise. Without this connection, your supporting muscles and connective tissue tend to dominate the lift, which diminishes results. Second, when you've mentally locked into a movement, your form tends to automatically fall into place. This both improves exercise performance and reduces the possibility of injury.

Developing a mind-to-muscle connection requires total concentration. From the moment you begin a set, fix your thoughts on the muscle that you are training. You must be oblivious to your surroundings, purging all outside distractions from your mind. Forget about your nail appointment, your dinner reservations, or any other diversions that might arise. The only thing that matters at this point is performing each repetition with total precision. As you train, make a concerted effort to visualize your target muscles doing the work. During the concentric phase of the movement, consciously feel the squeeze in your target muscles. During the negative phase, feel your target muscle lengthening as you return to the starting position. Make this practice a ritual throughout each set. In short order, it will become habit.

10 Know the Major Muscle Groups

Like it or not, you need to know the composition of your muscles in order to get the most from your training efforts. This knowledge helps you visualize each muscle during training, fostering a better mind-to-muscle connection. It also makes you aware of the path that weight must travel to target specific muscles, improving your ability to train with proper form. Finally, it allows you to hone in on muscular imbalances, assessing which muscles need improvement and which don't.

I'm not saying that you need to be an anatomist. There are more than 600 skeletal muscles in the human body, and many have no significant relevance to regimented exercise. Trying to learn them all would be burdensome and unnecessary. Instead, aim for a basic understanding of the major muscle groups and their functions in human movement. Here is a rundown of the ones you need to know.

Chest

The primary chest muscle is the pectoralis major, and its name is generally shortened to *pectorals* or *pecs*. It's a large, sunburst-shaped muscle with two heads, a clavicular head on the upper portion of the chest and a sternocostal head on the middle and lower portions (see figure 8.1). Both heads work to bring the arms across the midline of the body in exercises like the chest press and the fly. The sternal portion is more active in exercises performed on flat surfaces and the clavicular aspect dominates during incline movements.

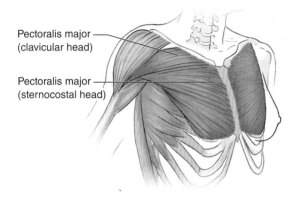

Pectoralis major (clavicular head)

Pectoralis major (sternocostal head)

FIGURE 8.1   Chest muscles.

Back

The upper back is the most complex of all the muscle groups, containing many individual muscles. The largest among these muscles is the latissimus dorsi (often called the *lats*), shown in figure 8.2. This pair of broad, flat muscles is most often associated with upper back muscularity. Its fibers have several different angles of pull, depending on the origins of the fibers, but its main functions are to pull the arms down toward the sides of the body (as in exercises like lat pull-downs) and to pull the arms down and back (as in exercises like rows and pullovers).

The teres major is often called the lats' little helper. It's a small muscle situated on the upper part of your back. Basically, anything the lats do, the teres major does as well.

The trapezius (*traps,* for short) is a long, triangular muscle that runs down the entire back of your torso. It originates at the base of the skull and attaches in numerous places along the spine and shoulder blades. Because of these different attachments, the trapezius essentially operates as three different muscles that can be classified into upper, middle, and lower regions. The upper portion is responsible for shoulder elevation (shrugging your shoulders), the middle portion is involved in the retraction of the shoulder blades (as in various rowing movements), and the lower portion is involved in depressing the shoulder blades.

The rhomboids reside in the middle of the upper back and include the rhomboid major and the rhomboid minor. These muscles lie underneath the trapezius and contribute greatly to giving your back that coveted muscular detail. Their main function is to retract the shoulder blades.

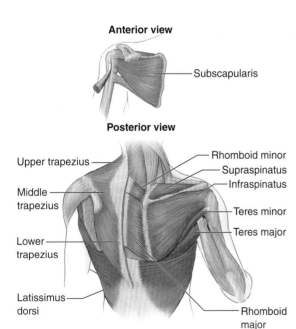

Anterior view

Subscapularis

Posterior view

Upper trapezius

Middle trapezius

Lower trapezius

Latissimus dorsi

Rhomboid minor

Supraspinatus

Infraspinatus

Teres minor

Teres major

Rhomboid major

FIGURE 8.2   Back muscles.

Shoulders

The primary shoulder muscles are the deltoids (*delts,* for short), triangular muscles that have three distinct heads (see figure 8.3). Each head has a separate function: the *anterior,* or frontal, deltoid flexes the shoulder joint (raises the arm in front of the body); the *medial,* or middle, deltoid abducts the shoulder joint (raises the arm out to the side, away from the body's midline); and the *posterior,* or rear, deltoid extends the shoulder joint horizontally (brings the arm across and toward the back of the body).

FIGURE 8.3 **Shoulder muscles.**

The muscles of the rotator cuff, which include the supraspinatus, infraspinatus, teres minor, and subscapularis, assist the delts and play an essential role in stabilizing the shoulder joint (see figure 8.2). They act together to keep the bone of the upper arm in the shoulder socket. As the name implies, they also rotate the shoulder internally and externally and raise it out to the side.

Arms

The arms can be classified into muscles on the *anterior* (front) and *posterior* (back) portions. The most glamorous muscle on the anterior part of the arm is the biceps brachii, also known as the *bis* (see figure 8.4*a*). The two main functions of the biceps are to flex (curl) the elbow and to supinate the hand (turn the palm up toward the ceiling).

The brachialis is lesser known than the biceps but is certainly no less important. Its main function is to flex the elbow.

The primary muscle on the posterior part of the arm is the triceps brachii (often called the *tris*). The tris has three distinct heads—a long head, a medial head, and a lateral head—joined to form a common tendon that attaches to the ulna, a bone in the forearm (see figure 8.4*b*). All three heads of the triceps function to straighten the elbow from a bent position (as in triceps press-downs and kickbacks). Because the long head crosses the shoulder joint, it is involved in some shoulder movements. You can target it by exercises in which you elevate your upper arm over your head (as in overhead triceps extensions).

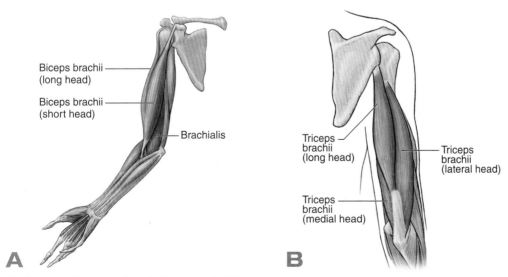

FIGURE 8.4 **Arm muscles: *(a)* biceps and *(b)* triceps.**

Abdominals

The abdominal complex is made up of four distinct muscles. The rectus abdominis, commonly known as the *six-pack muscle,* is one long sheath that runs from just underneath the breastbone (sternum) all the way down to the pelvis (see figure 8.5). Many people wrongly believe that the upper and lower portions of the rectus abdominis are two separate muscles that can be trained independently. This is not the case. Because of its configuration, the entire complex contracts as a single unit. Consequently, you cannot work one part without affecting the rest of the muscle. However, if you have a strong mind-to-muscle connection, you can accentuate one aspect more than another by altering the point of spinal movement.

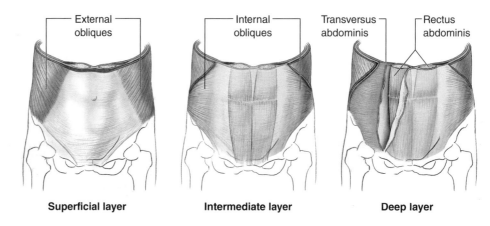

Superficial layer **Intermediate layer** **Deep layer**

FIGURE 8.5 Abdominal muscles.

The obliques consist of two separate muscles: the external obliques and the internal obliques. These waist muscles run diagonally along the sides of your body. The external obliques are the more visible of the two muscles, extending from the upper part of your ribs all the way down to your hips. The internal obliques, which lie underneath the external obliques, are somewhat hidden from view. For the most part, the muscles work together as a unit, helping you bend or twist your torso sideways.

The transversus abdominis lies deep within your abdomen. Although it is not outwardly visible, it plays a central role in containing your internal organs and also assists pulmonary function. Because of its position, you can't really apply direct stress to this muscle. Its most important role in exercise is to keep your core stable, and it receives considerable ancillary stress during training.

Front of Thigh

The frontal thighs are primarily comprised of the quadriceps (the *quads*) and the adductors. The quadriceps consists of four separate muscles: the rectus femoris, the vastus lateralis, the vastus medialis, and the vastus intermedius (see figure 8.6). These muscles are responsible for knee extension (straightening the knee from a bent position). The rectus femoris is unique in that it crosses the hip joint, so it also functions as a hip flexor. Therefore, it can be individually targeted when the hip remains extended during a knee extension (as in a sissy squat).

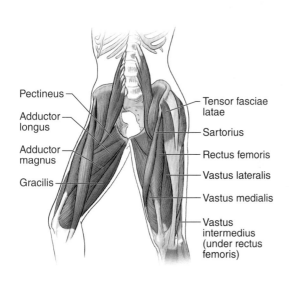

FIGURE 8.6 Muscles of the front of the thigh.

The adductors are the primary muscles of the inner thigh. They function to bring your thighs together from a spread position (as in various adduction movements). Because many women tend to store fat in this region, they often make a beeline to the adductor machine in hopes of reducing the flab. Although targeted exercises will help to tone up the adductor muscles, they won't directly strip away the fat. For more information, see the sidebar on spot reduction on page 288 in chapter 11.

Back of Thigh and Gluteal Muscles

The primary muscles on the posterior aspect of your lower body are the hamstrings and the gluteal muscles, or *glutes* (see figure 8.7). The glutes consist of three separate muscles: the gluteus maximus, the gluteus medius, and the gluteus minimus. The gluteus maximus is the largest of the gluteal muscles, covering the majority of the buttocks. Its primary function is to extend the hip joint, allowing you to straighten your hips (as in the stiff-leg deadlift) and to bring your leg backward (as in the glute back kick). The gluteus medius and gluteus minimus reside underneath and to the sides of the gluteus maximus. Their primary function is to bring the legs out and to the sides (as in the motion of the outer thigh machine that's so popular with women at the gym).

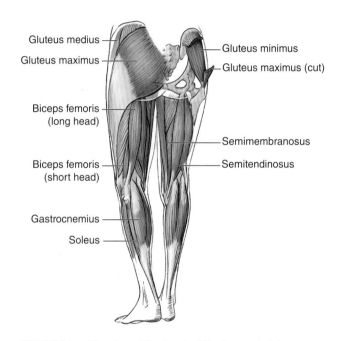

FIGURE 8.7 **Muscles of the back of the leg and glutes.**

The hamstrings complex consists of three separate muscles: the biceps femoris, the semitendinosus, and the semimembranosus. All three muscles essentially operate in concert with one another, flexing the knee (so your heel approaches your butt) and assisting the glutes in hip extension.

Calves

The calves are comprised of two main muscles. The gastrocnemius (*gastroc,* for short) is a diamond-shaped muscle with two distinct heads (see figure 8.7). The medial head, which provides most of the diamond shape, originates on the rear portion of the leg, just above the outer part of the knee. The lateral head originates on the opposite side of the knee. Both heads intermesh midway down the leg and fuse with the Achilles tendon at the ankle. The primary function of the gastroc is to raise the heel from the ground (an action called plantarflexion).

The soleus, which is somewhat hidden by the gastroc, has a much longer muscle belly that contributes greatly to the overall development of the calf. Because it does not cross the knee joint, you can train the soleus with a great degree of isolation by performing calf exercises with bent knees.

Ultimate Body Conditioning

The ultimate home routine for body conditioning is designed to enhance your physical well-being. It's ideal if you're starting to work out, coming back after a break, or looking for a change of pace from your present routine. You'll not only achieve increased energy, better reflexes, improved balance, and an enhanced overall sense of health and wellness, but you will also see a marked improvement in your performance of activities of daily living. Pretty impressive, huh?

▶ **Use this routine if . . . you are a beginner to strength training or are primarily interested in improving your general health, fitness, balance, and functional ability.**

How will these positive changes come about? To answer this question, let's compare strength training to constructing a house. First, you lay a strong foundation that acts as a base of support. Next, you erect a framework that provides structure. Finally, only after you've developed a solid groundwork on which to build, you focus on aesthetic details.

Think of body conditioning as training that lays the foundation. The focus of this routine is on the interaction of your body as a whole, developing not only your muscles, but also the supporting structural connective tissue. Connective tissues, such as tendons, ligaments, and the protective sheaths of fascia that surround muscle, maintain joint health and play an integral role in the function of your muscles. Weak connective tissue impairs your muscles' ability to transmit force, leading to a reduction in strength. It also predisposes your joints to debilitating strains and tears—injuries that can sometimes take months to heal. This is why so many athletes who abuse anabolic steroids, which strengthen muscle but not connective tissue, suffer an inordinate number of debilitating injuries. As the saying goes, "A chain is only as strong as its weakest link."

The holistic nature of the routine also helps foster better synchronization between your muscles and nerves. Precise interaction between the two is essential for optimal muscular function. In fact, during the first several weeks of training, most of the strength you gain will not be the result of increased muscle development, but rather because your neuromuscular pathways have been enhanced. Simply stated, your central nervous system will become more efficient in its activation patterns, which improves your ability to exert strength on demand.

The end result is a body made for function. Tasks that were once a chore will soon become effortless. Moving furniture, hauling packages, lifting your child—no problem. In short, you'll enjoy a better quality of life.

The routine can also serve as an excellent precursor for more advanced *split* routines, such as those used for body sculpting and sports performance. One of the biggest mistakes I see women make when they begin a fitness regimen is to focus the majority of their efforts on isolated "shaping" movements. They gravitate toward exercises for the small muscles of the inner and outer thighs, the obliques, and the arms, ignoring the larger muscle groups of the torso and lower body. While isolation movements certainly have their place in a routine, their value is limited until you develop a solid base of muscle. To understand this principle, let's revisit the analogy of building a house. A builder cannot begin to construct walls or a roof before a foundation is in place. There would be nothing to build on, right? Similarly, you can't shape what you don't yet have. As the architect of your own physique, you must build a base of muscle before you attempt to hone the shape and symmetry of your body.

Program Protocol

The home routine for body conditioning is a total-body regimen that you perform three days a week. You will train all nine of the major muscle groups every time you work out. The routines are divided according to the four basic budgets explained in chapter 2. Simply choose the budget that corresponds to the equipment that you own and follow this protocol.

Exercises

Perform one exercise for each muscle group. Since you train your entire body every time you work out, additional exercises are unnecessary and potentially counter-productive. Working out beyond the outlined routine would only impair your body's ability to recover, ultimately leading to overtraining. Remember the sixth commandment of fitness: With respect to exercise, less can be more.

This routine liberally incorporates multijoint exercises, especially for the larger muscle groups of the shoulders, back, chest, and thighs. Here's the lowdown: Some muscles function as prime movers, others as synergists, and still others as stabilizers. There are even muscles that solely exist to maintain balance by interpreting and correcting shifts in body position. Exercises that engage multiple joints mimic the tasks of daily life that require your muscles to operate in a linked chain. Therefore, functional transfer is greater than if you were to use isolation exercises, which inherently limit the involvement of supporting muscles and don't train the body to work as efficiently as a unit.

Multijoint exercises also stimulate large amounts of muscle. This has dual benefits. First, it provides an efficient means of training your body—an important consideration given the total-body composition of the routine. What's more, it heightens your metabolic rate to the max. Greater muscle involvement equates to more calories burned both during and after a workout. The upshot is an improvement in lean body composition and a better sense of overall health and fitness.

However, not all of the muscle groups lend themselves to multijoint movements. By their nature, the biceps, triceps, and calves are best targeted with single-joint moves. Thus, this routine uses isolation exercises to target these muscles, as well as for variety in larger muscle groups. Consult the exercise finder on page vi to see which exercises are multijoint and which are single joint.

You will perform exercises on both stable and unstable surfaces. The combination of the two elicits varied proprioceptive responses that condition your body to efficiently operate in an array of different environments. There is a greater focus on stable-surface training, since most real-world activities are carried out on stable ground (see the first commandment of fitness, which deals with specificity of training).

Sets

Perform three sets of each exercise. Carry out the sets in the traditional *block* fashion (as opposed to circuit-style). This means you'll perform one set of an exercise, rest, perform your second set, rest, and then do your third set. After finishing your third set, move on to the next exercise and perform subsequent sets in a similar manner.

Perhaps you're wondering why you need to perform three sets of each exercise. After all, certain fitness professionals continue to promote the theory that one set is sufficient to fully stimulate your muscles and that additional sets are superfluous. Sorry, but science says otherwise. Although single-set protocols certainly make good use of time and can produce modest results, studies have repeatedly shown the superiority of multiple-set routines in promoting muscular strength and development as you advance in your training efforts. The evidence is overwhelming: To optimize results and avoid hitting a plateau, you must train with multiple sets.

Multiple-set routines have another significant advantage over single-set routines. When you repeatedly perform an exercise, you ingrain neuromuscular patterns into your subconscious, establishing the all-important link between mind and muscle. This practice is particularly important during the early phases of training before your body becomes accustomed to producing coordinated movements between joints. Only after continual practice do exercises become second nature, allowing you to concentrate on perfecting skill and strength.

That said, we all know that life can sometimes get in the way of exercising. Occasionally, you might find yourself pressed for time, unable to get through a full routine. In these situations, you can cut back on the total number of sets to ensure you work out your entire body. Some exercise is certainly better than none. But these occurrences should be the exception rather than the rule. Considering that the routine takes less than an hour to complete, time shouldn't be a major issue. Always strive to perform the full number of sets and compromise only when absolutely necessary.

Repetitions

Repetitions span from 4 to 20 reps for each set. A wide range of repetitions is necessary to fully stimulate the full spectrum of slow- and fast-twitch muscle fibers that produce muscular endurance, strength, and power. Developing these fibers helps prepare your body for any physical challenge you might encounter, whether the activity lasts a minute or an hour.

This routine systematically groups repetitions, targeting endurance, strength, and power on different days. Day 1 has a high range that targets 15 to 20 reps per set, day 2 has a moderate scheme that targets 8 to 12 reps, and day 3 has a low range that targets 4 to 6 reps. Think of these ranges as a general guideline rather than a hard rule. As long as you adhere to the spirit of the protocol, you can go outside the prescribed range every now and then. Slight variations won't hurt, and can actually have a positive effect by challenging your body in unexpected ways.

There is one caveat to the rep protocol: If you are a beginner, stick with higher reps until you have reached a comfort level. This is especially important in free-weight exercises, which require a greater level of skill to execute. Get used to the feel of a movement. Entrench it into your subconscious. Once muscle memory is established, you can begin to utilize alternative repetition ranges, progressing first to moderate-rep sets and then to low-rep sets.

Rest

Rest for 30 to 90 seconds between sets. As a rule, an inverse relationship exists between repetitions and rest. You need less rest for higher reps and more rest for lower reps.

Since high-rep sets develop muscular endurance, it's beneficial to keep rest periods short. This practice taxes the fatigue-resistant slow-twitch muscle fibers responsible for carrying out aerobic tasks. Rest for around 30 seconds between sets, just long enough to catch your breath. Only rest longer if you are feeling dizzy or overworked. Over time, your body will adjust to the fast-paced tempo and you will move from one set to the next without incident.

Conversely, lower-rep sets require more rest in order to fully replenish your body's energy stores. Since lower-rep sets develop strength and power, all your body's resources are needed to exert maximal effort into each lift. If you start the next set before you have recovered from the previous one, you won't be able to lift as much weight. In general, 60 to 90 seconds is sufficient, but you might need upwards of 2 minutes depending on a variety of physical factors. Bottom line: Don't progress to the next set until you're sure you are ready to give it your all.

Intensity

If you are a beginner to training or if you haven't worked out for more than several months, think of the first few weeks of training as an acclimation period. Your objective should be to allow your body to adapt to the routine and adjust to the stresses of weight training. It's similar to how you would approach swimming in a cold pool. You wouldn't cannonball off the diving board without testing the water first, would you? Similarly, don't be overzealous during the early stages of training. Although you are undoubtedly eager to see results, overtaxing your body before it is ready can impose a tremendous strain on your muscles, connective tissue, and nervous system. The end result is impaired results or, worse, a training injury. Accordingly, choose a starting weight that is somewhat challenging but doesn't require supreme effort to finish the set.

Once your body has acclimated to the routine, you should employ the fourth commandment of fitness, that of progressive overload. Make sure that the amount of weight you use in a set is sufficiently challenging. At the very least, you should be struggling to complete the last few reps of each set, regardless of repetition range. On the last set of each exercise, try to push your body to momentary muscular failure—the point at which you cannot complete another repetition. This will ensure steady progress and help stave off plateau.

Going Forward

To prevent your workout from growing stale and hitting a plateau, you should strive to change exercise variables on an ongoing basis. Here are some suggestions for sustaining progress in the body conditioning routine. After completing the four-week cycle, consider implementing some or all of these concepts going forward:

- *Work one side at a time.* A good way to improve functional balance is by employing unilateral leg progressions. Simply stated, perform lower-body exercises one leg at a time rather than with both legs simultaneously. After you finish the target range of repetitions for one leg, proceed directly to training the other leg. This is an excellent way to force your body to adjust to unstable environments. Squats and leg presses lend themselves well to unilateral movements. Focus on form first, and then add more weight as time goes on.

- *Try some supersets.* If you're really ambitious, consider performing some of the exercises in the routine as supersets. This involves performing two movements back to back without resting in between sets. You'll not only heighten muscular stimulation, but you'll also make your workout more efficient—a win-win situation. Although you can use supersets in any rep range, they generally work best for developing muscle endurance. See chapter 10 for more information on supersets and how to best integrate them into a routine.

- *Aerobicize.* Try performing callisthenic exercises between sets to spruce up your body conditioning. For instance, you could do some jumping jacks between sets of shoulder presses or jog in place between lunges. In this way you make productive use of your rest intervals, revving up fat burning and improving cardio-respiratory health without increasing your workout time. It's a beautifully efficient training strategy. Realize, though, that this technique can get intense and is sometimes overwhelming. Make sure you don't overdo it and compromise the quality of your lifting, which should always be the primary focus of your routine. Take it slow at the beginning by employing light callisthenic movements, and then increase intensity over time if you see fit.

Body Conditioning Routine, $100 Budget

WEEK 1 Day 1

Exercise	Page	Sets	Reps	Rest interval
Upright row with resistance band	24	3	15-20	30 sec
Seated row with resistance band	42	3	15-20	30 sec
Standing chest press with resistance band	48	3	15-20	30 sec
Arm curl with resistance band	30	3	15-20	30 sec
Triceps kickback with resistance band	35	3	15-20	30 sec
Sumo squat	77	3	15-20	30 sec
Standing leg curl	86	3	15-20	30 sec
One-leg bent-knee toe press with resistance band	103	3	15-20	30 sec
Twisting crunch	54	3	15-20	30 sec

WEEK 1 Day 2

Exercise	Page	Sets	Reps	Rest interval
Shoulder press with resistance band	25	3	8-12	60 sec
Lat pull-down with resistance band	44	3	8-12	60 sec
Push-up	36	3	8-12	60 sec
One-arm hammer curl with resistance band	31	3	8-12	60 sec
Press-down with resistance band	33	3	8-12	60 sec
Reverse lunge	81	3	8-12	60 sec
Floor kick	84	3	8-12	60 sec
Standing calf raise	91	3	8-12	60 sec
Crunch with stability ball	66	3	8-12	60 sec

WEEK 1 Day 3

Exercise	Page	Sets	Reps	Rest interval
Pike press	22	3	4-6	90 sec
Pull-up	39	3	4-6	90 sec
Reverse push-up with stability ball	40	3	4-6	90 sec
Hammer curl with resistance band	31	3	4-6	90 sec
Overhead triceps extension with resistance band	34	3	4-6	90 sec
Split squat lunge with resistance band	96	3	4-6	90 sec
Bridge with stability ball	72	3	4-6	90 sec
Toe press with resistance band	104	3	4-6	90 sec
Reverse crunch	58	3	4-6	90 sec

Body Conditioning Routine, $100 Budget

WEEK 2 Day 1

Exercise	Page	Sets	Reps	Rest interval
Lateral raise with resistance band	27	3	15-20	30 sec
Row with resistance band and stability ball	43	3	15-20	30 sec
Standing fly with resistance band	50	3	15-20	30 sec
One-arm curl with resistance band	30	3	15-20	30 sec
Triceps dip	23	3	15-20	30 sec
Lunge	80	3	15-20	30 sec
Prone hip extension	85	3	15-20	30 sec
One-leg toe press with resistance band	104	3	15-20	30 sec
Side crunch with stability ball	67	3	15-20	30 sec

WEEK 2 Day 2

Exercise	Page	Sets	Reps	Rest interval
Standing reverse fly with resistance band	29	3	8-12	60 sec
Prone lat pull with stability ball	41	3	8-12	60 sec
Standing incline chest press with resistance band	49	3	8-12	60 sec
Concentration curl with resistance band	32	3	8-12	60 sec
One-arm overhead triceps extension with resistance band	34	3	8-12	60 sec
Leg press with resistance band	97	3	8-12	60 sec
Prone one-leg curl with resistance band	99	3	8-12	60 sec
One-leg standing calf raise	91	3	8-12	60 sec
Bicycle crunch	53	3	8-12	60 sec

WEEK 2 Day 3

Exercise	Page	Sets	Reps	Rest interval
Arnold press with resistance band	26	3	4-6	90 sec
Chin-up	38	3	4-6	90 sec
Incline push-up	37	3	4-6	90 sec
One-arm hammer curl with resistance band	31	3	4-6	90 sec
Triceps kickback with resistance band	35	3	4-6	90 sec
Squat with resistance band	95	3	4-6	90 sec
Standing abductor raise with resistance band	100	3	4-6	90 sec
Bent-knee toe press with resistance band	103	3	4-6	90 sec
Toe touch	52	3	4-6	90 sec

Body Conditioning Routine, $100 Budget

WEEK 3 Day 1

Exercise	Page	Sets	Reps	Rest interval
Bent lateral raise with resistance band	28	3	15-20	30 sec
Straight-arm pull-down with resistance band	46	3	15-20	30 sec
Standing low fly with resistance band	51	3	15-20	30 sec
Hammer curl with resistance band	31	3	15-20	30 sec
Press-down with resistance band	33	3	15-20	30 sec
Step-up	83	3	15-20	30 sec
Lying abductor raise	90	3	15-20	30 sec
One-leg seated calf raise	92	3	15-20	30 sec
Crunch	57	3	15-20	30 sec

WEEK 3 Day 2

Exercise	Page	Sets	Reps	Rest interval
Upright row with resistance band	24	3	8-12	60 sec
Lying pullover with resistance band	47	3	8-12	60 sec
Push-up	36	3	8-12	60 sec
One-arm curl with resistance band	30	3	8-12	60 sec
Overhead triceps extension with resistance band	34	3	8-12	60 sec
Split squat lunge	79	3	8-12	60 sec
Prone leg curl	87	3	8-12	60 sec
Toe press with resistance band	104	3	8-12	60 sec
Russian twist with stability ball	71	3	8-12	60 sec

WEEK 3 Day 3

Exercise	Page	Sets	Reps	Rest interval
Shoulder press with resistance band	25	3	4-6	90 sec
Neutral-grip lat pull-down with resistance band	44	3	4-6	90 sec
Reverse push-up with stability ball	40	3	4-6	90 sec
Arm curl with resistance band	30	3	4-6	90 sec
Triceps dip	23	3	4-6	90 sec
One-leg squat	76	3	4-6	90 sec
Leg curl with stability ball	93	3	4-6	90 sec
Standing calf raise with resistance band	102	3	4-6	90 sec
Kneeling crunch with resistance band	74	3	4-6	90 sec

Body Conditioning Routine, $100 Budget

WEEK 4 Day 1

Exercise	Page	Sets	Reps	Rest interval
Lateral raise with resistance band	27	3	15-20	30 sec
Reverse-grip lat pull-down with resistance band	44	3	15-20	30 sec
Standing incline chest press with resistance band	49	3	15-20	30 sec
One-arm hammer curl with resistance band	31	3	15-20	30 sec
One-arm overhead triceps extension with resistance band	34	3	15-20	30 sec
Squat	75	3	15-20	30 sec
Superwoman	55	3	15-20	30 sec
One-leg standing calf raise	91	3	15-20	30 sec
Horizontal woodchop with resistance band	73	3	15-20	30 sec

WEEK 4 Day 2

Exercise	Page	Sets	Reps	Rest interval
Arnold press with resistance band	26	3	8-12	60 sec
One-arm low row with resistance band	45	3	8-12	60 sec
Incline push-up	37	3	8-12	60 sec
Concentration curl with resistance band	32	3	8-12	60 sec
Triceps dip	23	3	8-12	60 sec
Sumo squat	77	3	8-12	60 sec
One-leg bridge	63	3	8-12	60 sec
One-leg bent-knee toe press with resistance band	103	3	8-12	60 sec
Side jackknife	59	3	8-12	60 sec

WEEK 4 Day 3

Exercise	Page	Sets	Reps	Rest interval
Pike press	22	3	4-6	90 sec
Row with resistance band and stability ball	43	3	4-6	90 sec
Standing chest press with resistance band	48	3	4-6	90 sec
One-arm curl with resistance band	30	3	4-6	90 sec
Press-down with resistance band	33	3	4-6	90 sec
Split squat lunge with resistance band	96	3	4-6	90 sec
Prone one-leg curl with resistance band	99	3	4-6	90 sec
Standing calf raise with resistance band	102	3	4-6	90 sec
Rotating crunch with stability ball	70	3	4-6	90 sec

Body Conditioning Routine, $500 Budget

Exercise	Page	Sets	Reps	Rest interval
Shoulder press with dumbbells	113	3	15-20	30 sec
Seated row with resistance band	42	3	15-20	30 sec
Push-up	36	3	15-20	30 sec
Arm curl with dumbbells and stability ball	120	3	15-20	30 sec
Triceps kickback with resistance band	35	3	15-20	30 sec
Squat with dumbbells	152	3	15-20	30 sec
Leg curl with stability ball	93	3	15-20	30 sec
Toe press with resistance band	104	3	15-20	30 sec
Reverse crunch	58	3	15-20	30 sec

Exercise	Page	Sets	Reps	Rest interval
Upright row with resistance band	24	3	8-12	60 sec
One-arm row with dumbbells	139	3	8-12	60 sec
Flat chest press with dumbbells and stability ball	142	3	8-12	60 sec
Arm curl with resistance band	30	3	8-12	60 sec
Triceps dip	23	3	8-12	60 sec
Split squat lunge with resistance band	96	3	8-12	60 sec
Standing abductor raise with resistance band	100	3	8-12	60 sec
One-leg seated calf raise with dumbbells	161	3	8-12	60 sec
Rotating crunch with stability ball	70	3	8-12	60 sec

Exercise	Page	Sets	Reps	Rest interval
Arnold press with dumbbells	114	3	4-6	90 sec
Lat pull-down with resistance band	44	3	4-6	90 sec
Incline chest press with dumbbells	141	3	4-6	90 sec
Incline curl with dumbbells	121	3	4-6	90 sec
Overhead triceps extension with dumbbells	126	3	4-6	90 sec
Reverse lunge with dumbbells	157	3	4-6	90 sec
Prone one-leg curl with resistance band	99	3	4-6	90 sec
Standing calf raise with dumbbells	160	3	4-6	90 sec
Russian twist with stability ball	71	3	4-6	90 sec

Body Conditioning Routine, $500 Budget

WEEK 2 Day 1

Exercise	Page	Sets	Reps	Rest interval
Arnold press with dumbbells and stability ball	114	3	15-20	30 sec
Prone lat pull with stability ball	41	3	15-20	30 sec
Incline fly with dumbbells and stability ball	144	3	15-20	30 sec
Preacher curl with dumbbells	122	3	15-20	30 sec
Overhead triceps extension with resistance band	34	3	15-20	30 sec
Split squat lunge with dumbbells	155	3	15-20	30 sec
Superwoman	55	3	15-20	30 sec
Seated calf raise with dumbbells	161	3	15-20	30 sec
Bicycle crunch	53	3	15-20	30 sec

WEEK 2 Day 2

Exercise	Page	Sets	Reps	Rest interval
Upright row with dumbbells	115	3	8-12	60 sec
Pullover with dumbbells	138	3	8-12	60 sec
Standing chest press with resistance band	48	3	8-12	60 sec
Hammer curl with dumbbells	125	3	8-12	60 sec
Overhead triceps extension with dumbbells and stability ball	126	3	8-12	60 sec
Sumo squat with dumbbells	154	3	8-12	60 sec
Hyperextension with stability ball	68	3	8-12	60 sec
Standing calf raise with resistance band	102	3	8-12	60 sec
Toe touch	52	3	8-12	60 sec

WEEK 2 Day 3

Exercise	Page	Sets	Reps	Rest interval
Pike press	22	3	4-6	90 sec
Chin-up	38	3	4-6	90 sec
Incline push-up	37	3	4-6	90 sec
Concentration curl with dumbbells	123	3	4-6	90 sec
Press-down with resistance band	33	3	4-6	90 sec
One-leg squat with dumbbells	153	3	4-6	90 sec
Prone hip extension	85	3	4-6	90 sec
One-leg toe press with resistance band	104	3	4-6	90 sec
Side bend with dumbbells	150	3	4-6	90 sec

Body Conditioning Routine, $500 Budget

WEEK 3 Day 1

Exercise	Page	Sets	Reps	Rest interval
Standing shoulder press with dumbbells	113	3	15-20	30 sec
Reverse-grip lat pull-down with resistance band	44	3	15-20	30 sec
Incline chest press with dumbbells and stability ball	141	3	15-20	30 sec
Standing arm curl with dumbbells	120	3	15-20	30 sec
Lying triceps extension with dumbbells	127	3	15-20	30 sec
Leg press with resistance band	97	3	15-20	30 sec
Bridge with stability ball	72	3	15-20	30 sec
Bent-knee toe press with resistance band	103	3	15-20	30 sec
Twisting crunch	54	3	15-20	30 sec

WEEK 3 Day 2

Exercise	Page	Sets	Reps	Rest interval
Lateral raise with dumbbells and stability ball	117	3	8-12	60 sec
Incline row with dumbbells	140	3	8-12	60 sec
Standing incline chest press with resistance band	49	3	8-12	60 sec
Prone incline curl with dumbbells	124	3	8-12	60 sec
Triceps kickback with dumbbells	128	3	8-12	60 sec
Side lunge with dumbbells	158	3	8-12	60 sec
Lying abductor raise	90	3	8-12	60 sec
One-leg standing calf raise with dumbbells	160	3	8-12	60 sec
Crunch with stability ball	66	3	8-12	60 sec

WEEK 3 Day 3

Exercise	Page	Sets	Reps	Rest interval
Shoulder press with resistance band	25	3	4-6	90 sec
Pull-up	39	3	4-6	90 sec
Reverse push-up with stability ball	40	3	4-6	90 sec
Hammer curl with resistance band	31	3	4-6	90 sec
Standing overhead triceps extension with dumbbells	126	3	4-6	90 sec
Reverse lunge with dumbbells	157	3	4-6	90 sec
Leg curl with stability ball	93	3	4-6	90 sec
Standing calf raise with dumbbells	160	3	4-6	90 sec
Kneeling crunch with resistance band	74	3	4-6	90 sec

Body Conditioning Routine, $500 Budget

WEEK 4 Day 1

Exercise	Page	Sets	Reps	Rest interval
Standing Arnold press with dumbbells	114	3	15-20	30 sec
Row with resistance band and stability ball	43	3	15-20	30 sec
Flat chest press with dumbbells	142	3	15-20	30 sec
Hammer curl with dumbbells and stability ball	125	3	15-20	30 sec
Triceps dip	23	3	15-20	30 sec
Step-up with dumbbells	159	3	15-20	30 sec
Floor kick	84	3	15-20	30 sec
One-leg bent-knee toe press with resistance band	103	3	15-20	30 sec
Horizontal woodchop with resistance band	73	3	15-20	30 sec

WEEK 4 Day 2

Exercise	Page	Sets	Reps	Rest interval
Shoulder press with dumbbells and stability ball	113	3	8-12	60 sec
Neutral-grip lat pull-down with resistance band	44	3	8-12	60 sec
Flat fly with dumbbells and stability ball	143	3	8-12	60 sec
One-arm curl with resistance band	30	3	8-12	60 sec
Triceps kickback with resistance band	35	3	8-12	60 sec
Squat with resistance band	95	3	8-12	60 sec
Standing leg curl	86	3	8-12	60 sec
Toe press with resistance band	104	3	8-12	60 sec
Side crunch with stability ball	67	3	8-12	60 sec

WEEK 4 Day 3

Exercise	Page	Sets	Reps	Rest interval
Arnold press with resistance band	26	3	4-6	90 sec
One-arm low row with resistance band	45	3	4-6	90 sec
Incline fly with dumbbells	144	3	4-6	90 sec
Incline curl with dumbbells	121	3	4-6	90 sec
One-arm overhead triceps extension with dumbbells	126	3	4-6	90 sec
Lunge with dumbbells	156	3	4-6	90 sec
One-leg bridge	63	3	4-6	90 sec
One-leg standing calf raise with dumbbells	160	3	4-6	90 sec
Hanging knee raise	64	3	4-6	90 sec

Body Conditioning Routine, $1000 Budget

Exercise	Page	Sets	Reps	Rest interval
Upright row with barbell	130	3	15-20	30 sec
T-bar row with barbell	145	3	15-20	30 sec
Incline fly with dumbbells and stability ball	144	3	15-20	30 sec
Hammer curl with dumbbells	125	3	15-20	30 sec
Press-down with resistance band	33	3	15-20	30 sec
Split squat lunge with barbell	165	3	15-20	30 sec
Lying abductor raise	90	3	15-20	30 sec
Standing calf raise with dumbbells	160	3	15-20	30 sec
Horizontal woodchop with resistance band	73	3	15-20	30 sec

Exercise	Page	Sets	Reps	Rest interval
Shoulder press with dumbbells and stability ball	113	3	8-12	60 sec
Incline row with dumbbells	140	3	8-12	60 sec
Reverse push-up with stability ball	40	3	8-12	60 sec
Arm curl with dumbbells and stability ball	120	3	8-12	60 sec
Triceps kickback with dumbbells	128	3	8-12	60 sec
Sumo squat with dumbbells	154	3	8-12	60 sec
Prone one-leg curl with resistance band	99	3	8-12	60 sec
One-leg seated calf raise with dumbbells	161	3	8-12	60 sec
Hanging knee raise	64	3	8-12	60 sec

Exercise	Page	Sets	Reps	Rest interval
Military press with barbell	129	3	4-6	90 sec
Lat pull-down with resistance band	44	3	4-6	90 sec
Flat chest press with dumbbells	142	3	4-6	90 sec
Drag curl with barbell	137	3	4-6	90 sec
Lying triceps extension with dumbbells	127	3	4-6	90 sec
Back squat with barbell	162	3	4-6	90 sec
Stiff-legged deadlift with barbell	169	3	4-6	90 sec
Toe press with resistance band	104	3	4-6	90 sec
Reverse crunch	58	3	4-6	90 sec

Body Conditioning Routine, $1000 Budget

Exercise	Page	Sets	Reps	Rest interval
Lateral raise with resistance band	27	3	15-20	30 sec
One-arm low row with resistance band	45	3	15-20	30 sec
Flat fly with dumbbells and stability ball	143	3	15-20	30 sec
One-arm curl with resistance band	30	3	15-20	30 sec
Triceps dip	23	3	15-20	30 sec
Lunge with dumbbells	156	3	15-20	30 sec
Prone leg curl	87	3	15-20	30 sec
Seated calf raise with dumbbells	161	3	15-20	30 sec
Toe touch	52	3	15-20	30 sec

Exercise	Page	Sets	Reps	Rest interval
Shoulder press with dumbbells	113	3	8-12	60 sec
Incline row with barbell	146	3	8-12	60 sec
Flat chest press with dumbbells and stability ball	142	3	8-12	60 sec
Arm curl with barbell	134	3	8-12	60 sec
Triceps kickback with resistance band	35	3	8-12	60 sec
Reverse lunge with barbell	167	3	8-12	60 sec
Floor kick	84	3	8-12	60 sec
One-leg toe press with resistance band	104	3	8-12	60 sec
Side crunch with stability ball	67	3	8-12	60 sec

Exercise	Page	Sets	Reps	Rest interval
Standing shoulder press with dumbbells	113	3	4-6	90 sec
One-arm row with dumbbells	139	3	4-6	90 sec
Incline chest press with dumbbells	141	3	4-6	90 sec
Preacher curl with barbell and stability ball	133	3	4-6	90 sec
Overhead triceps extension with resistance band	34	3	4-6	90 sec
Split squat lunge with dumbbells	155	3	4-6	90 sec
Standing abductor raise with resistance band	100	3	4-6	90 sec
One-leg standing calf raise with dumbbells	160	3	4-6	90 sec
Bicycle crunch	53	3	4-6	90 sec

Body Conditioning Routine, $1000 Budget

WEEK 3 Day 1

Exercise	Page	Sets	Reps	Rest interval
Upright row with resistance band	24	3	15-20	30 sec
Neutral-grip lat pull-down with resistance band	44	3	15-20	30 sec
Incline chest press with dumbbells and stability ball	141	3	15-20	30 sec
Incline curl with dumbbells	121	3	15-20	30 sec
Close-grip bench press with barbell	131	3	15-20	30 sec
Lunge with barbell	166	3	15-20	30 sec
Superwoman	55	3	15-20	30 sec
Bent-knee toe press with resistance band	103	3	15-20	30 sec
Crunch with stability ball	66	3	15-20	30 sec

WEEK 3 Day 2

Exercise	Page	Sets	Reps	Rest interval
Shoulder press with resistance band	25	3	8-12	60 sec
Pullover with dumbbells	138	3	8-12	60 sec
Incline chest press with barbell	148	3	8-12	60 sec
Hammer curl with resistance band	31	3	8-12	60 sec
Nose breaker with barbell	136	3	8-12	60 sec
Step-up with dumbbells	159	3	8-12	60 sec
Bridge with stability ball	72	3	8-12	60 sec
Standing calf raise with resistance band	102	3	8-12	60 sec
Side bend with dumbbells	150	3	8-12	60 sec

WEEK 3 Day 3

Exercise	Page	Sets	Reps	Rest interval
Standing Arnold press with dumbbells	114	3	4-6	90 sec
Reverse bent row with barbell	147	3	4-6	90 sec
Incline fly with dumbbells	144	3	4-6	90 sec
Concentration curl with dumbbells	123	3	4-6	90 sec
Press-down with resistance band	33	3	4-6	90 sec
Reverse lunge with dumbbells	157	3	4-6	90 sec
Good morning with barbell	168	3	4-6	90 sec
Standing calf raise with dumbbells	160	3	4-6	90 sec
Kneeling crunch with resistance band	74	3	4-6	90 sec

Body Conditioning Routine, $1000 Budget

WEEK 4 Day 1

Exercise	Page	Sets	Reps	Rest interval
Upright row with dumbbells	115	3	15-20	30 sec
Row with resistance band and stability ball	43	3	15-20	30 sec
Standing chest press with resistance band	48	3	15-20	30 sec
21s with barbell	135	3	21	30 sec
Triceps kickback with dumbbells	128	3	15-20	30 sec
Front squat with barbell	163	3	15-20	30 sec
Prone hip extension	85	3	15-20	30 sec
One-leg bent-knee toe press with resistance band	103	3	15-20	30 sec
Russian twist with stability ball	71	3	15-20	30 sec

WEEK 4 Day 2

Exercise	Page	Sets	Reps	Rest interval
Arnold press with dumbbells	114	3	8-12	60 sec
Reverse-grip lat pull-down with resistance band	44	3	8-12	60 sec
Push-up	36	3	8-12	60 sec
Arm curl with resistance band	30	3	8-12	60 sec
Triceps dip	23	3	8-12	60 sec
Hack squat with barbell	164	3	8-12	60 sec
One-leg bridge	63	3	8-12	60 sec
Seated calf raise with dumbbells	161	3	8-12	60 sec
Roll-out with barbell	151	3	8-12	60 sec

WEEK 4 Day 3

Exercise	Page	Sets	Reps	Rest interval
Upright row with barbell	130	3	4-6	90 sec
Chin-up	38	3	4-6	90 sec
Flat chest press with barbell	149	3	4-6	90 sec
Prone incline curl with dumbbells	124	3	4-6	90 sec
Overhead triceps extension with dumbbells	126	3	4-6	90 sec
Squat with dumbbells	152	3	4-6	90 sec
Leg curl with stability ball	93	3	4-6	90 sec
Toe press with resistance band	104	3	4-6	90 sec
Rotating crunch with stability ball	70	3	4-6	90 sec

Body Conditioning Routine, $2500 Budget

WEEK 1 Day 1

Exercise	Page	Sets	Reps	Rest interval
Shoulder press with cable	178	3	15-20	30 sec
Front lat pull-down with machine	190	3	15-20	30 sec
Flat chest press with dumbbells and stability ball	142	3	15-20	30 sec
Preacher curl with dumbbells	122	3	15-20	30 sec
Overhead triceps extension with cable	184	3	15-20	30 sec
Step-up with dumbbells	159	3	15-20	30 sec
Lying abductor raise	90	3	15-20	30 sec
Standing calf raise with resistance band	102	3	15-20	30 sec
Twisting crunch	54	3	15-20	30 sec

WEEK 1 Day 2

Exercise	Page	Sets	Reps	Rest interval
Arnold press with dumbbells	114	3	8-12	60 sec
Prone lat pull with stability ball	41	3	8-12	60 sec
Incline chest press with dumbbells	141	3	8-12	60 sec
One-arm curl with cable	183	3	8-12	60 sec
Nose breaker with barbell	136	3	8-12	60 sec
One-leg squat with dumbbells	153	3	8-12	60 sec
Prone one-leg curl with resistance band	99	3	8-12	60 sec
Standing calf raise with dumbbells	160	3	8-12	60 sec
Roll-out with barbell	151	3	8-12	60 sec

WEEK 1 Day 3

Exercise	Page	Sets	Reps	Rest interval
Military press with barbell	129	3	4-6	90 sec
Seated row with machine	192	3	4-6	90 sec
Flat chest press with dumbbells	142	3	4-6	90 sec
Drag curl with barbell	137	3	4-6	90 sec
Overhead triceps extension with resistance band	34	3	4-6	90 sec
Leg press with machine	199	3	4-6	90 sec
Glute back kick with cable	204	3	4-6	90 sec
Toe press with machine	205	3	4-6	90 sec
Side crunch with stability ball	67	3	4-6	90 sec

Body Conditioning Routine, $2500 Budget

Exercise	Page	Sets	Reps	Rest interval
One-arm lateral raise with cable	180	3	15-20	30 sec
Row with resistance band and stability ball	43	3	15-20	30 sec
Incline chest press with dumbbells and stability ball	141	3	15-20	30 sec
Arm curl with barbell	134	3	15-20	30 sec
Triceps kickback with dumbbells	128	3	15-20	30 sec
Squat with resistance band	95	3	15-20	30 sec
Good morning with barbell	168	3	15-20	30 sec
Seated calf raise with dumbbells	161	3	15-20	30 sec
Low-to-high woodchop with cable	198	3	15-20	30 sec

Exercise	Page	Sets	Reps	Rest interval
Upright row with dumbbells	115	3	8-12	60 sec
Reverse-grip lat pull-down with machine	190	3	8-12	60 sec
Crossover fly with cable	189	3	8-12	60 sec
Arm curl with dumbbells	120	3	8-12	60 sec
Press-down with cable	185	3	8-12	60 sec
Squat with dumbbells	152	3	8-12	60 sec
Leg curl with stability ball	93	3	8-12	60 sec
One-leg standing calf raise with dumbbells	160	3	8-12	60 sec
Rotating crunch with stability ball	70	3	8-12	60 sec

Exercise	Page	Sets	Reps	Rest interval
Shoulder press with machine	177	3	4-6	90 sec
One-arm row with dumbbells	139	3	4-6	90 sec
Incline chest press with barbell	148	3	4-6	90 sec
Hammer curl with cable	182	3	4-6	90 sec
Triceps kickback with resistance band	35	3	4-6	90 sec
Back squat with barbell	162	3	4-6	90 sec
Standing abductor raise with cable	203	3	4-6	90 sec
Toe press with resistance band	104	3	4-6	90 sec
Kneeling crunch with cable	195	3	4-6	90 sec

Body Conditioning Routine, $2500 Budget

WEEK 3 Day 1

Exercise	Page	Sets	Reps	Rest interval
Shoulder press with resistance band	25	3	15-20	30 sec
Neutral-grip lat pull-down with machine	190	3	15-20	30 sec
Incline fly with dumbbells	144	3	15-20	30 sec
Preacher curl with barbell and stability ball	133	3	15-20	30 sec
Triceps dip	23	3	15-20	30 sec
Leg extension with machine	200	3	15-20	30 sec
Reverse hyperextension with stability ball	65	3	15-20	30 sec
One-leg seated calf raise with dumbbells	161	3	15-20	30 sec
Bicycle crunch	53	3	15-20	30 sec

WEEK 3 Day 2

Exercise	Page	Sets	Reps	Rest interval
Upright row with barbell	130	3	8-12	60 sec
Reverse low row with cable	193	3	8-12	60 sec
Standing incline chest press with resistance band	49	3	8-12	60 sec
Hammer curl with resistance band	31	3	8-12	60 sec
Overhead triceps extension with dumbbells	126	3	8-12	60 sec
Split squat lunge with dumbbells	155	3	8-12	60 sec
Stiff-legged deadlift with barbell	169	3	8-12	60 sec
One-leg toe press with resistance band	104	3	8-12	60 sec
Side bend with cable	197	3	8-12	60 sec

WEEK 3 Day 3

Exercise	Page	Sets	Reps	Rest interval
Shoulder press with dumbbells	113	3	4-6	90 sec
T-bar row with barbell	145	3	4-6	90 sec
Incline chest press with machine	187	3	4-6	90 sec
Incline curl with dumbbells	121	3	4-6	90 sec
Press-down with resistance band	33	3	4-6	90 sec
Reverse lunge with dumbbells	157	3	4-6	90 sec
Prone one-leg curl with machine	201	3	4-6	90 sec
Standing calf raise with dumbbells	160	3	4-6	90 sec
Kneeling crunch with resistance band	74	3	4-6	90 sec

Body Conditioning Routine, $2500 Budget

WEEK 4 Day 1

Exercise	Page	Sets	Reps	Rest interval
Kneeling bent lateral raise with cable	181	3	15-20	30 sec
Seated row with resistance band	42	3	15-20	30 sec
Flat fly with dumbbells and stability ball	143	3	15-20	30 sec
Concentration curl with dumbbells	123	3	15-20	30 sec
Triceps kickback with cable	186	3	15-20	30 sec
Front squat with barbell	163	3	15-20	30 sec
Hyperextension with stability ball	68	3	15-20	30 sec
Bent-knee toe press with resistance band	103	3	15-20	30 sec
Toe touch	52	3	15-20	30 sec

WEEK 4 Day 2

Exercise	Page	Sets	Reps	Rest interval
Upright row with cable	179	3	8-12	60 sec
Incline row with dumbbells	140	3	8-12	60 sec
Chest press with cable	188	3	8-12	60 sec
Arm curl with resistance band	30	3	8-12	60 sec
Lying triceps extension with dumbbells	127	3	8-12	60 sec
Sumo squat with dumbbells	154	3	8-12	60 sec
Prone one-leg curl with resistance band	99	3	8-12	60 sec
One-leg standing calf raise with dumbbells	160	3	8-12	60 sec
Crunch with stability ball	66	3	8-12	60 sec

WEEK 4 Day 3

Exercise	Page	Sets	Reps	Rest interval
Pike press	22	3	4-6	90 sec
Seated row with cable	191	3	4-6	90 sec
Flat chest press with barbell	149	3	4-6	90 sec
Hammer curl with dumbbells	125	3	4-6	90 sec
Overhead triceps extension with resistance band	34	3	4-6	90 sec
Lunge with dumbbells	156	3	4-6	90 sec
Prone leg curl with machine	201	3	4-6	90 sec
Toe press with machine	205	3	4-6	90 sec
Kneeling and twisting crunch with cable	196	3	4-6	90 sec

10

Ultimate Body Sculpting

The ultimate home routine for body sculpting is a high-energy workout designed to help you slim down and tone up in minimal time. You should start to notice changes within a few weeks. You'll feel tighter and firmer. Your clothes will begin to fit better. Then, over the next several months, your entire shape will change, with stubborn fat giving way to lean, hard muscle. And before you know it, your body will have transformed before your very eyes!

> ▶ **Use this routine if . . .**
> **you want to shape your physique to its ultimate potential.**

I mentioned earlier that exercise is both an art and a science. Nowhere is this axiom more apt than in body sculpting. You are the artist—the sculptor—and once you understand the basic principles of exercise, you have the power to shape your physique almost any way you desire.

Of course, genetics plays a role in the process. If you are 5-foot-2 (157 cm) and large boned, you're not going to look like a runway model. Nor can you say, "I want Madonna's arms, Jennifer Lopez's butt, and Janet Jackson's abs." You would need to pick your parents in order to turn that dream into reality. But this doesn't mean you can't sport a terrific body. Within your own genetic framework, the possibilities for body sculpting are virtually unlimited. You can hide or downplay various structural flaws, accentuating your positive characteristics to create a head-turning physique. Want the illusion of a slimmer waist? No problem. Just add some muscle to your side deltoids and—voila!—you've got it. Want a slimming effect on your thighs? Develop the sweep in your calf muscles and—presto!—you'll have leaner-looking legs.

Before entering into the routine, you must understand that this is an advanced workout. If you're new to training or haven't trained regularly for more than a few months, I recommend that you start with the conditioning routine in chapter 9 to prepare your body for more strenuous activity. When you feel you're ready, you may progress to body sculpting with the confidence that the routine won't overtax your neuromuscular system.

Program Protocol

The ultimate home routine for body sculpting is a split routine that you perform three days a week. It employs multiple sets for various muscle groups on different days of the week. These routines are divided according to the four basic budgets explained in chapter 2. Simply choose the budget that corresponds to the equipment you own and follow this protocol.

Exercises

Perform two to four exercises for each muscle group. From a body sculpting perspective, you need multiple exercises to achieve a complete and balanced development of your physique. You can't, however, simply string together a hodgepodge of different movements. To bring about positive change, you must take care to assess how your movements interact with each other.

Here's the skinny: Muscles are made up of thousands and thousands of tiny, threadlike fibers. These fibers have different attachment sites and run in different directions across the muscle. Only by training a muscle from a variety of different planes and angles can you work all of its fibers to their fullest potential.

Let's take a look at a hypothetical chest-training routine that embraces this concept. Start off with an incline chest press and you'll primarily work the upper portion of your pectorals (i.e., the clavicular head). Combine this movement with a flat chest press and you'll bring the lower and middle fibers of the pectorals (the sternal head) into play. Finish up with a pec fly and even more fibers are recruited. All told, three distinct moves are involved, each with a specific purpose in sculpting your chest muscles.

On the other hand, performing both an incline barbell press and an incline dumbbell press in the same workout would be needlessly redundant. These movements essentially target the same areas of the chest. Performing both in the same session would only expend valuable energy reserves that you can and should put to better use.

The exercises in this regimen are structured to mesh synergistically. Notice how the training angles and planes of movement are varied in each session to target different areas of each muscle group. The end result is a streamlined routine with minimal overlap between movements, diminishing the potential for overtraining.

To ensure that your target muscles carry out the majority of the work, the routine focuses on exercises performed on stable surfaces. Understand that muscular development is directly related to the amount of tension placed on muscles. When you train on an unstable surface, such as a stability ball, a significant portion of the force output is diverted away from the target muscles and is taken up by the stabilizers. Reduce force output and you reduce tension; reduce tension and you impair your ability to tone up. Bottom line: For body sculpting purposes, stable-surface training is the preferred mode with one exception—abdominal training. Core activation is significantly increased when you perform abdominal exercises on unstable surfaces. Therefore, the stability ball should play a prominent role in targeting the abs.

You'll also notice a lot of single-joint exercises in the routine. These movements allow you to selectively target a muscle (or even a specific part of a muscle) at the exclusion of secondary muscles, aiding your efforts to develop muscular symmetry. Consult the exercise finder on pages vi to xi to see which exercises use a single joint and which use multiple joints.

Sets

Perform 6 to 12 sets for each muscle group. Smaller muscle groups, such as the biceps and calves, need fewer sets to fully stimulate the muscle fibers, but larger muscle groups, such as the thighs and back, require a greater volume of sets. See table 10.1 for the suggested volume for each muscle group.

Unless otherwise noted, carry out sets in traditional block fashion (in which you perform a set of a specific exercise, rest, perform the next set for the same exercise, rest, and continue in this fashion before moving on to the next exercise). This routine also includes specialized techniques called double-drop sets, supersets, and giant sets. Here is an overview of these techniques:

TABLE 10.1

Suggested Exercise Volume for Muscle Groups

Muscle group	Number of sets
Back	10-12
Chest	10-12
Quads	10-12
Shoulders	8-10
Abdominals	8-10
Hamstrings	8-10
Biceps	6-8
Triceps	6-8
Calves	6-8

■ *Double-drop sets.* These sets help stimulate the target muscle beyond the limits of traditional block sets. The concept is simple: After performing the desired number of reps, drop the weight by approximately 20 to 30 percent and perform as many additional reps as you can. When you are unable to complete any more reps at the reduced weight, drop the weight by another 20 to 30 percent and rep out whatever you can. For example, say you normally perform a lateral raise with an 8-pound weight. When you do the double-drop set, you'll begin with 8-pound dumbbells for the prescribed number of repetitions, immediately drop down to 5-pound dumbbells for as many reps as you can, and then drop down to 3-pound dumbbells to muscular failure. Once you finish a set of double drops, you'll know why they're often called burn sets!

■ *Supersets.* In these sets, you'll perform two exercises consecutively without resting in between. This high-energy technique injects greater intensity into your routine while heightening fat burning. Since your muscles begin to recuperate several seconds after you complete a set, move quickly from one exercise to the next during supersetted movements. The following list outlines the three basic categories of supersets:

— *Compound supersets.* In compound supersets, you perform back-to-back exercises for the same muscle group. The biggest advantage of this type of superset is that it allows you to prefatigue a muscle so that the smaller supporting muscles don't give out before the prime mover. For example, you might perform an incline chest fly, immediately followed by an incline chest press. The single-joint fly prefatigues the pectoral muscles, ensuring that the inherently weaker triceps will endure the ensuing multijoint pressing movement. The downside of performing compound supersets is that fatigue from lactic-acid buildup limits the amount of weight you can use for the second exercise of the superset. It's a worthy trade-off if you're not seeking maximal strength.

— *Agonist and antagonist supersets.* The terms *agonist* and *antagonist* describe opposing muscle groups in which one muscle contracts while the other relaxes. Examples include biceps and triceps, chest and back, and quadriceps and hamstrings. Supersets involving groups of agonist and antagonist muscles take advantage of a phenomenon called *reciprocal inhibition,* in which the antagonist's contraction leads to a more forceful contraction of the agonist in the next set. For example, if you perform a biceps curl followed by a triceps kickback, reciprocal inhibition causes the triceps to contract with greater force if trained immediately after the biceps exercise. Reversing the order would lead to a stronger contraction of the biceps. The upshot: better muscle development.

— *Unrelated muscle supersets.* In unrelated muscle supersets, you do exactly what the name implies. You perform consecutive sets of exercises for muscle groups that have no significant relationship to one another. This type of superset usually combines an upper-body movement with a lower-body movement. For example, you might perform a seated row for your back, followed immediately by a squat for your thighs; or do an arm curl, followed by a standing calf raise. Although these supersets are good for increasing the efficiency of your workout, they don't directly enhance the training experience.

■ *Giant sets.* These sets take supersets one step further. Instead of two consecutive exercises, a giant set involves performing three or more different exercises in succession. You'll move directly from one exercise to the next without resting between them. This practice not only heightens both exercise intensity and muscle development, but it also significantly heightens metabolic activity, thereby maximizing fat burning both during and after the workout.

Repetitions

Perform 8 to 20 reps for each set. The routine employs two distinct ranges of repetitions: a moderate-rep, hypertrophy-oriented scheme (8 to 10 reps per set) and a high-rep, muscle-endurance–oriented scheme (15 to 20 reps per set).

Moderate reps target the fast-twitch, type-II fibers—the ones that have the greatest potential for muscular development. These fibers have also been shown to maximize the release of anabolic hormones vital to the growth process.

During high-rep schemes, on the other hand, a greater amount of work is carried out by fatigue-resistant, slow-twitch, type-I fibers. These fibers have a limited ability for growth, but they contribute to giving your body a dense, hard appearance when properly developed.

To ensure optimal stimulation of all fibers, you'll alternate between the two ranges of repetitions on a weekly basis: Do high reps one week and moderate reps the next. This practice brings about a balance of shape and tone that looks great whether in clothes or on the beach.

Rest

Rest for 30 to 60 seconds between sets. High-rep workouts employ 30-second rest intervals. The objective here is to maintain a brisk pace to your workout and to keep things moving. If you aren't still winded before beginning your next set, you're resting too long.

On moderate-rep sets, rest periods will be a more modest 60 seconds. This gives your muscles and central nervous system a little more time to recuperate, so you can come back strong for successive sets. Avoid resting much longer than this, though. Studies have shown that, when used in conjunction with moderate reps, rest intervals of 60 seconds maximally spike anabolic hormone levels and enhance metabolic stress—factors believed to be triggers for muscle development.

Intensity

In order to sculpt your body to its ultimate potential, you need to train hard—harder than you would for virtually any other fitness goal. This means that you should perform the majority of sets until you reach momentary muscular failure—the point at which you are physically unable to perform another rep.

Don't allow your mind to give up before your body does. You must push past the pain threshold. This is a difficult proposition when your muscles are burning from lactic-acid buildup. But this is exactly what is required to optimize results. If you perform the desired number of repetitions and still have the strength to pump out another, you have not sufficiently taxed your muscle and results will be compromised. Stay mentally strong. When your muscles start to protest, ignore them! Think about the payoff. Once the workout is over, you'll be glad you did.

Going Forward

In order to prevent your workout from growing stale and hitting a plateau, you should strive to change exercise variables on an ongoing basis. Here are some suggestions for sustaining progress in the body sculpting routine. After completing the four-week cycle, consider implementing some or all of these concepts going forward.

- *Change the split.* The way in which you split up your routine has a direct effect on muscle development. Performing the same split over and over inevitably leads to boredom and stagnation. This routine groups agonist muscles with their antagonists, but numerous other combinations would fare just as well. Consider the following options:

  — *Front, side, and rear.* Train your abs and quads on day 1; your shoulders, biceps, and triceps on day 2; and your back, hamstrings, and calves on day 3.

  — *Push and pull.* Train your chest, shoulders, and triceps on day 1; your back, biceps, and abs on day 2; and your quads, hamstrings, and calves on day 3.

  — *Upper, lower, and upper.* Train your shoulders, quads, and triceps on day 1; your back, calves, and abs on day 2; and your chest, hamstrings, and biceps on day 3.

Don't be afraid to experiment with other splits. As I've repeatedly noted throughout this book, variety is the spice of fitness.

- *Reprioritize the order.* As a general rule, it's best to train large muscle groups first in your routine. The reason: Training smaller muscles first reduces their capacity to serve as supporting muscle movers in exercises for the larger muscle groups. Ultimately, your supporting muscles fatigue before your prime movers do, and you fall short of maximally stimulating the target muscle. However, this rule goes by the wayside during the advanced stages of body sculpting. Instead, prioritize your routine to train lagging muscles first. In this way, you'll have more energy to train these muscles and hence derive better results from your efforts. Evaluate your physique and assess which muscles need more development. Then, if warranted, go ahead and train your biceps before your back or your calves before your thighs to bring these muscles into alignment with the rest of your body.

- *Get some rest.* Continually training until you reach momentary muscular failure places a great deal of stress on your body. It can tax your neuromuscular system, wear down your joints, and suppress your immune function. Before you know it, you're wallowing in an overtrained state (see page 236 for more information on overtraining). To counteract this effect, you should take a week off every three months or so. Avoid all strenuous activity during this week, limiting your exercise to low-intensity pursuits that don't challenge your reserves, such as jogging or swimming. If you're feeling run-down, you might even employ a transition phase by switching to a less-intense routine like the conditioning routine for a few weeks. Your goal is to come back strong so that you can continue to make progress and avoid that dreaded plateau.

Body Sculpting Routine, $100 Budget

WEEK 1 Day 1 (Chest, Back, and Abs)

Exercise	Page	Sets	Reps	Rest interval
Reverse-grip lat pull-down with resistance band	44	4	8-10	60 sec
Seated row with resistance band	42	4*	8-10	60 sec
Lying pullover with resistance band	47	3	8-10	60 sec
Incline push-up	37	4	8-10	60 sec
Standing incline chest press with resistance band	49	3	8-10	60 sec
Standing low fly with resistance band	51	3	8-10	60 sec
Crunch with stability ball	66	3	8-10	60 sec
Side jackknife	59	3	8-10	60 sec
Horizontal woodchop with resistance band	73	2	8-10	60 sec

*Perform the final set as a double-drop set.

WEEK 1 Day 2 (Quads, Glutes, Hamstrings, and Calves)

Exercise	Page	Sets	Reps	Rest interval
Reverse lunge	81	4	8-10	60 sec
Leg extension with resistance band	98	4	8-10	60 sec
Sissy squat	78	4	8-10	60 sec
Bridge with stability ball	72	3	8-10	60 sec
Prone one-leg curl with resistance band	99	3	8-10	60 sec
Standing abductor raise with resistance band	100	2	8-10	60 sec
Standing calf raise with resistance band	102	4	8-10	60 sec
One-leg bent-knee toe press with resistance band	103	4	8-10	60 sec

WEEK 1 Day 3 (Shoulders, Biceps, and Triceps)

Exercise	Page	Sets	Reps	Rest interval
Pike press	22	4	8-10	60 sec
Upright row with resistance band	24	3*	8-10	60 sec
Bent lateral raise with resistance band	28	3	8-10	60 sec
One-arm curl with resistance band	30	4	8-10	60 sec
Hammer curl with resistance band	31	3	8-10	60 sec
Overhead triceps extension with resistance band	34	3	8-10	60 sec
One-arm press-down with resistance band	33	3	8-10	60 sec
Triceps kickback with resistance band	35	2	8-10	60 sec

*Perform the final set as a double-drop set.

Body Sculpting Routine, $100 Budget

WEEK 2   Day 1 (Chest, Back, and Abs)

Exercise	Page	Sets	Reps	Rest interval

Superset:
  Prone lat pull with stability ball
  Neutral-grip lat pull-down with resistance band
	
	41
	44
		4	15-20	30 sec

Row with resistance band and stability ball	43	4	15-20	30 sec
Reverse push-up with stability ball	40	3	15-20	30 sec

Superset:
  Standing chest press with resistance band
  Standing fly with resistance band
	
	48
	50
		4	15-20	30 sec

Giant set:
  Toe touch
  Reverse crunch
  Side crunch with stability ball
	
	52
	58
	67
		3	15-20	30 sec

WEEK 2   Day 2 (Quads, Glutes, Hamstrings, and Calves)

Exercise	Page	Sets	Reps	Rest interval

Superset:
  Leg press with resistance band
  Squat
	
	97
	75
		4	15-20	30 sec

Lying adductor raise	88	3	15-20	30 sec

Giant set:
  Superwoman
  Prone leg curl
  Lying abductor raise
	
	55
	87
	90
		3	15-20	30 sec

One-leg toe press with resistance band	104	4	15-20	30 sec
One-leg seated calf raise	92	3	15-20	30 sec

WEEK 2   Day 3 (Shoulders, Biceps, and Triceps)

Exercise	Page	Sets	Reps	Rest interval

Superset:
  Shoulder press with resistance band
  Lateral raise with resistance band
	
	25
	27
		3	15-20	30 sec

Standing reverse fly with resistance band	29	3	15-20	30 sec
Arm curl with resistance band	30	4	15-20	30 sec
One-arm hammer curl with resistance band	31	4	15-20	30 sec

Superset:
  Press-down with resistance band
  Triceps dip
	
	33
	23
		3	15-20	30 sec

One-arm overhead triceps extension with resistance band	34	2	15-20	30 sec

Body Sculpting Routine, $100 Budget

WEEK 3   Day 1 (Chest, Back, and Abs)

Exercise	Page	Sets	Reps	Rest interval
Chin-up	38	4	8-10	60 sec
One-arm low row with resistance band	45	4	8-10	60 sec
Straight-arm pull-down with resistance band	46	4	8-10	60 sec
Incline push-up	37	4	8-10	60 sec
Standing chest press with resistance band	48	3	8-10	60 sec
Standing fly with resistance band	50	3	8-10	60 sec
Kneeling crunch with resistance band	74	3	8-10	60 sec
Rotating crunch with stability ball	70	3	8-10	60 sec
Russian twist with stability ball	71	2	8-10	60 sec

WEEK 3   Day 2 (Quads, Glutes, Hamstrings, and Calves)

Exercise	Page	Sets	Reps	Rest interval
Split squat lunge with resistance band	96	4*	8-10	60 sec
Leg extension with stability ball	94	4	8-10	60 sec
Side lunge	82	3	8-10	60 sec
One-leg bridge	63	3	8-10	60 sec
Leg curl with stability ball	93	3	8-10	60 sec
Hyperextension with stability ball	68	3	8-10	60 sec
Toe press with resistance band	104	4	8-10	60 sec
Bent-knee toe press with resistance band	103	3	8-10	60 sec

*Perform the final set as a double-drop set.

WEEK 3   Day 3 (Shoulders, Biceps, and Triceps)

Exercise	Page	Sets	Reps	Rest interval
Arnold press with resistance band	26	4	8-10	60 sec
One-arm lateral raise with resistance band	27	3*	8-10	60 sec
Bent lateral raise with resistance band	28	3	8-10	60 sec
One-arm curl with resistance band	30	4	8-10	60 sec
Concentration curl with resistance band	32	4	8-10	60 sec
One-arm overhead triceps extension with resistance band	34	4	8-10	60 sec
Triceps kickback with resistance band	35	4	8-10	60 sec

*Perform the final set as a double-drop set.

Body Sculpting Routine, $100 Budget

WEEK 4   Day 1 (Chest, Back, and Abs)

Exercise	Page	Sets	Reps	Rest interval
Superset: 　Lat pull-down with resistance band 　Push-up	 44 36	4	15-20	30 sec
Superset: 　Seated row with resistance band 　Standing incline chest press with resistance band	 42 49	3	15-20	30 sec
Superset: 　Lying pullover with resistance band 　Standing low fly with resistance band	 47 51	3	15-20	30 sec
Superset: 　Bicycle crunch 　Helicopter with stability ball	 53 69	3	15-20	30 sec
Reverse pendulum	60	2	15-20	30 sec

WEEK 4   Day 2 (Quads, Glutes, Hamstrings, and Calves)

Exercise	Page	Sets	Reps	Rest interval
Superset: 　Sumo squat 　Split squat lunge	 77 79	4	15-20	30 sec
One-leg extension with resistance band	98	4	15-20	30 sec
Superset: 　Prone hip extension 　Floor kick	 85 84	3	15-20	30 sec
Standing leg curl	86	3	15-20	30 sec
Superset: 　Standing calf raise 　Seated calf raise	 91 92	4	15-20	30 sec

WEEK 4   Day 3 (Shoulders, Biceps, and Triceps)

Exercise	Page	Sets	Reps	Rest interval
Superset: 　Upright row with resistance band 　Lateral raise with resistance band	 24 27	3	15-20	30 sec
Standing reverse fly with resistance band	29	3	15-20	30 sec
Arm curl with resistance band	30	4	15-20	30 sec
One-arm hammer curl with resistance band	31	4	15-20	30 sec
Superset: 　Triceps dip 　Overhead triceps extension with resistance band	 23 34	3	15-20	30 sec
One-arm press-down with resistance band	33	2	15-20	30 sec

Body Sculpting Routine, $500 Budget

WEEK 1 Day 1 (Chest, Back, and Abs)

Exercise	Page	Sets	Reps	Rest interval
Reverse-grip lat pull-down with resistance band	44	4	8-10	60 sec
One-arm row with dumbbells	139	4	8-10	60 sec
Prone lat pull with stability ball	41	3	8-10	60 sec
Flat chest press with dumbbells	142	4*	8-10	60 sec
Incline chest press with dumbbells and stability ball	141	3	8-10	60 sec
Standing fly with resistance band	50	4	8-10	60 sec
Rotating crunch with stability ball	70	3	8-10	60 sec
Side bend with dumbbells	150	3	8-10	60 sec
Hanging knee raise	64	2	8-10	60 sec

*Perform the final set as a double-drop set.

WEEK 1 Day 2 (Quads, Glutes, Hamstrings, and Calves)

Exercise	Page	Sets	Reps	Rest interval
Lunge with dumbbells	156	4*	8-10	60 sec
One-leg squat with dumbbells	153	4	8-10	60 sec
Sissy squat	78	3	8-10	60 sec
Hyperextension with stability ball	68	4	8-10	60 sec
Leg curl with stability ball	93	3	8-10	60 sec
Standing abductor raise with resistance band	100	3	8-10	60 sec
Standing calf raise with dumbbells	160	4*	8-10	60 sec
One-leg bent-knee toe press with resistance band	103	3	8-10	60 sec

*Perform the final set as a double-drop set.

WEEK 1 Day 3 (Shoulders, Biceps, and Triceps)

Exercise	Page	Sets	Reps	Rest interval
Shoulder press with dumbbells	113	4	8-10	60 sec
Lateral raise with resistance band	27	3*	8-10	60 sec
Prone reverse fly with dumbbells	119	3	8-10	60 sec
One-arm curl with resistance band	30	3	8-10	60 sec
Hammer curl with dumbbells	125	2*	8-10	60 sec
Concentration curl with dumbbells	123	2	8-10	60 sec
Press-down with resistance band	33	3	8-10	60 sec
One-arm overhead triceps extension with dumbbells	126	3	8-10	60 sec
Triceps kickback with dumbbells	128	2	8-10	60 sec

*Perform the final set as a double-drop set.

Body Sculpting Routine, $500 Budget

WEEK 2   Day 1 (Chest, Back, and Abs)

Exercise	Page	Sets	Reps	Rest interval

Superset:
    Lat pull-down with resistance band
    Incline chest press with dumbbells
	
	44
	141
		4	15-20	30 sec

Superset:
    Incline row with dumbbells
    Push-up
	
	140
	36
		4	15-20	30 sec

Superset:
    Straight-arm pull-down with resistance band
    Flat fly with dumbbells and stability ball
	
	46
	143
		3	15-20	30 sec

Giant set:
    Crunch with stability ball
    Side crunch with stability ball
    Helicopter with stability ball
	
	66
	67
	69
		3	15-20	30 sec

WEEK 2   Day 2 (Quads, Glutes, Hamstrings, and Calves)

Exercise	Page	Sets	Reps	Rest interval

Superset:
    Reverse lunge with dumbbells
    Sumo squat with dumbbells
	
	157
	154
		4	15-20	30 sec

Standing adductor raise with resistance band	101	3	15-20	30 sec

Superset:
    Prone hip extension
    Prone leg curl
	
	85
	87
		3	15-20	30 sec

Lying abductor raise	90	2	15-20	30 sec

Superset:
    Toe press with resistance band
    Bent-knee toe press with resistance band
	
	104
	103
		4	15-20	30 sec

WEEK 2   Day 3 (Shoulders, Biceps, and Triceps)

Exercise	Page	Sets	Reps	Rest interval
Shoulder press with resistance band	25	4	15-20	30 sec

Superset:
    Lateral raise with dumbbells
    Bent lateral raise with dumbbells
	
	117
	118
		3	15-20	30 sec

Superset:
    Arm curl with dumbbells
    Hammer curl with resistance band
	
	120
	31
		2	15-20	30 sec

Preacher curl with dumbbells	122	3	15-20	30 sec

Superset:
    Triceps dip
    Overhead triceps extension with resistance band
	
	23
	34
		4	15-20	30 sec

Body Sculpting Routine, $500 Budget

WEEK 3   Day 1 (Chest, Back, and Abs)

Exercise	Page	Sets	Reps	Rest interval
Chin-up	38	4	8-10	60 sec
One-arm low row with resistance band	45	4	8-10	60 sec
Lying pullover with resistance band	47	3	8-10	60 sec
Incline push-up	37	4	8-10	60 sec
Standing chest press with resistance band	48	4	8-10	60 sec
Incline fly with dumbbells	144	3*	8-10	60 sec
Toe touch	52	3	8-10	60 sec
Twisting crunch	54	3	8-10	60 sec
Horizontal woodchop with resistance band	73	2	8-10	60 sec

*Perform the final set as a double-drop set.

WEEK 3   Day 2 (Quads, Glutes, Hamstrings, and Calves)

Exercise	Page	Sets	Reps	Rest interval
Split squat lunge with dumbbells	155	4*	8-10	60 sec
Side lunge with dumbbells	158	4	8-10	60 sec
Leg extension with stability ball	94	3	8-10	60 sec
One-leg bridge	63	4	8-10	60 sec
Prone one-leg curl with resistance band	99	4	8-10	60 sec
Standing calf raise with resistance band	102	4	8-10	60 sec
Seated calf raise with dumbbells	161	3	8-10	60 sec

*Perform the final set as a double-drop set.

WEEK 3   Day 3 (Shoulders, Biceps, and Triceps)

Exercise	Page	Sets	Reps	Rest interval
Arnold press with dumbbells	114	4*	8-10	60 sec
Upright row with resistance band	24	3	8-10	60 sec
Standing reverse fly with resistance band	29	3	8-10	60 sec
Arm curl with dumbbells and stability ball	120	3	8-10	60 sec
One-arm hammer curl with resistance band	31	3	8-10	60 sec
Concentration curl with dumbbells and stability ball	123	2	8-10	60 sec
One-arm overhead triceps extension with dumbbells	126	3*	8-10	60 sec
Lying triceps extension with dumbbells	127	3	8-10	60 sec
Triceps kickback with resistance band	35	2	8-10	60 sec

*Perform the final set as a double-drop set.

Body Sculpting Routine, $500 Budget

WEEK 4 Day 1 (Chest, Back, and Abs)

Exercise	Page	Sets	Reps	Rest interval
Neutral-grip lat pull-down with resistance band	44	4	15-20	30 sec
Superset: 　Seated row with resistance band 　Pullover with dumbbells	 42 138	3	15-20	30 sec
Superset: 　Flat fly with dumbbells 　Flat chest press with dumbbells	 143 142	4	15-20	30 sec
Standing low fly with resistance band	51	3	15-20	30 sec
Superset: 　Bicycle crunch 　Reverse crunch	 53 58	3	15-20	30 sec
Russian twist with stability ball	71	2	15-20	30 sec

WEEK 4 Day 2 (Quads, Glutes, Hamstrings, and Calves)

Exercise	Page	Sets	Reps	Rest interval
Superset: 　Step-up with dumbbells 　Leg press with resistance band	 159 97	4	15-20	30 sec
Leg extension with resistance band	98	4	15-20	30 sec
Superset: 　Bridge with stability ball 　Floor kick	 72 84	3	15-20	30 sec
Standing leg curl	86	3	15-20	30 sec
One-leg standing calf raise with dumbbells	160	4	15-20	30 sec
One-leg seated calf raise with dumbbells	161	4	15-20	30 sec

WEEK 4 Day 3 (Shoulders, Biceps, and Triceps)

Exercise	Page	Sets	Reps	Rest interval
Superset: 　Shoulder press with dumbbells and stability ball 　Lateral raise with dumbbells and stability ball	 113 117	4	15-20	30 sec
Bent lateral raise with resistance band	28	3	15-20	30 sec
Superset: 　Incline curl with dumbbells 　Overhead triceps extension with dumbbells	 121 126	3	15-20	30 sec
Superset: 　Arm curl with resistance band 　Lying triceps extension with dumbbells	 30 127	3	15-20	30 sec
Superset: 　Prone incline curl with dumbbells 　Triceps dip	 124 23	2	15-20	30 sec

Body Sculpting Routine, $1000 Budget

WEEK 1 Day 1 (Chest, Back, and Abs)

Exercise	Page	Sets	Reps	Rest interval
Pull-up	39	4	8-10	60 sec
T-bar row with barbell	145	4	8-10	60 sec
Pullover with dumbbells	138	3	8-10	60 sec
Flat chest press with barbell	149	4*	8-10	60 sec
Incline chest press with dumbbells	141	3	8-10	60 sec
Standing fly with resistance band	50	3	8-10	60 sec
Crunch with stability ball	66	3	8-10	60 sec
Side jackknife	59	3	8-10	60 sec
Roll-out with barbell	151	2	8-10	60 sec

*Perform the final set as a double-drop set.

WEEK 1 Day 2 (Quads, Glutes, Hamstrings, and Calves)

Exercise	Page	Sets	Reps	Rest interval
Back squat with barbell	162	4*	8-10	60 sec
Reverse lunge with barbell	167	4	8-10	60 sec
Leg press with resistance band	97	3	8-10	60 sec
Stiff-legged deadlift with barbell	169	4	8-10	60 sec
Prone one-leg curl with resistance band	99	3	8-10	60 sec
Lying abductor raise	90	2	8-10	60 sec
Toe press with resistance band	104	4	8-10	60 sec
One-leg seated calf raise with dumbbells	161	3	8-10	60 sec

*Perform the final set as a double-drop set.

WEEK 1 Day 3 (Shoulders, Biceps, and Triceps)

Exercise	Page	Sets	Reps	Rest interval
Arnold press with dumbbells	114	4*	8-10	60 sec
Lateral raise with resistance band	27	3	8-10	60 sec
Standing reverse fly with resistance band	29	3	8-10	60 sec
Arm curl with barbell	134	3*	8-10	60 sec
Incline curl with dumbbells	121	2	8-10	60 sec
Hammer curl with resistance band	31	2	8-10	60 sec
Overhead triceps extension with dumbbells	126	4	8-10	60 sec
Triceps kickback with resistance band	35	4	8-10	60 sec

*Perform the final set as a double-drop set.

Body Sculpting Routine, $1000 Budget

WEEK 2 Day 1 (Chest, Back, and Abs)

Exercise	Page	Sets	Reps	Rest interval

Superset:
  Lat pull-down with resistance band
  Reverse bent row with barbell
	
	44
	147
		4	15-20	30 sec

Straight-arm pull-down with resistance band	46	3	15-20	30 sec
Standing chest press with resistance band	48	4	15-20	30 sec

Superset:
  Flat fly with dumbbells
  Flat chest press with dumbbells
	
	143
	142
		3	15-20	30 sec

Giant set:
  Crunch
  Reverse crunch
  Russian twist with stability ball
	
	57
	58
	71
		3	15-20	30 sec

WEEK 2 Day 2 (Quads, Glutes, Hamstrings, and Calves)

Exercise	Page	Sets	Reps	Rest interval

Superset:
  Squat with dumbbells
  Side lunge with dumbbells
	
	152
	158
		4	15-20	30 sec

Leg extension with resistance band	98	3	15-20	30 sec

Superset:
  Reverse hyperextension with stability ball
  Leg curl with stability ball
	
	65
	93
		3	15-20	30 sec

Standing abductor raise with resistance band	100	3	15-20	30 sec

Superset:
  Standing calf raise with dumbbells
  Seated calf raise with dumbbells
	
	160
	161
		4	15-20	30 sec

WEEK 2 Day 3 (Shoulders, Biceps, and Triceps)

Exercise	Page	Sets	Reps	Rest interval
Upright row with barbell	130	3	15-20	30 sec

Giant set:
  Front raise with dumbbells
  Lateral raise with dumbbells
  Bent lateral raise with dumbbells
	
	116
	117
	118
		2	15-20	30 sec

Superset:
  Arm curl with dumbbells
  Nose breaker with barbell
	
	120
	136
		3	15-20	30 sec

Superset:
  Prone incline curl with dumbbells
  Overhead triceps extension with resistance band
	
	124
	34
		3	15-20	30 sec

Superset:
  Drag curl with barbell
  Lying triceps extension with dumbbells
	
	137
	127
		2	15-20	30 sec

Body Sculpting Routine, $1000 Budget

WEEK 3 Day 1 (Chest, Back, and Abs)

Exercise	Page	Sets	Reps	Rest interval
Reverse-grip lat pull-down with resistance band	44	4	8-10	60 sec
One-arm row with dumbbells	139	4	8-10	60 sec
Prone lat pull with stability ball	41	4	8-10	60 sec
Incline chest press with barbell	148	4*	8-10	60 sec
Push-up	36	3	8-10	60 sec
Incline fly with dumbbells	144	4	8-10	60 sec
Twisting crunch	54	3	8-10	60 sec
Rotating crunch with stability ball	70	3	8-10	60 sec
Kneeling crunch with resistance band	74	2	8-10	60 sec

*Perform the final set as a double-drop set.

WEEK 3 Day 2 (Quads, Glutes, Hamstrings, and Calves)

Exercise	Page	Sets	Reps	Rest interval
Front squat with barbell	163	4*	8-10	60 sec
Lunge with dumbbells	156	4	8-10	60 sec
Standing adductor raise with resistance band	101	4	8-10	60 sec
Good morning with barbell	168	4	8-10	60 sec
Prone leg curl	87	3	8-10	60 sec
Floor kick	84	2	8-10	60 sec
Standing calf raise with dumbbells	160	4	8-10	60 sec
One-leg bent-knee toe press with resistance band	103	3	8-10	60 sec

*Perform the final set as a double-drop set.

WEEK 3 Day 3 (Shoulders, Biceps, and Triceps)

Exercise	Page	Sets	Reps	Rest interval
Military press with barbell	129	4*	8-10	60 sec
Upright row with resistance band	24	3	8-10	60 sec
Prone reverse fly with dumbbells	119	3	8-10	60 sec
One-arm curl with resistance band	30	3	8-10	60 sec
Concentration curl with dumbbells	123	4	8-10	60 sec
Close-grip bench press with barbell	131	3	8-10	60 sec
Triceps dip	23	3	8-10	60 sec
Triceps kickback with dumbbells	128	2	8-10	60 sec

*Perform the final set as a double-drop set.

Body Sculpting Routine, $1000 Budget

WEEK 4 Day 1 (Chest, Back, and Abs)

Exercise	Page	Sets	Reps	Rest interval
Neutral-grip lat pull-down with resistance band	44	4	15-20	30 sec
Incline row with barbell	146	3	15-20	30 sec
Lying pullover with resistance band	47	3	15-20	30 sec

Superset:
  Flat fly with dumbbells and stability ball
  Flat chest press with dumbbells and stability ball
	
	143
	142
		4	15-20	30 sec

Standing low fly with resistance band	51	3	15-20	30 sec

Superset:
  Bicycle crunch
  Helicopter with stability ball
	
	53
	69
		3	15-20	30 sec

Side crunch with stability ball	67	2	15-20	30 sec

WEEK 4 Day 2 (Quads, Glutes, Hamstrings, and Calves)

Exercise	Page	Sets	Reps	Rest interval

Giant set:
  Sumo squat with dumbbells
  Step-up with dumbbells
  Sissy squat
	
	154
	159
	78
		4	15-20	30 sec

Giant set:
  Prone hip extension
  Bridge with stability ball
  Leg curl with stability ball
	
	85
	72
	93
		3	15-20	30 sec

Superset:
  Standing calf raise with resistance band
  Bent-knee toe press with resistance band
	
	102
	103
		4	15-20	30 sec

WEEK 4 Day 3 (Shoulders, Biceps, and Triceps)

Exercise	Page	Sets	Reps	Rest interval

Superset:
  Shoulder press with dumbbells
  Upright row with dumbbells
	
	113
	115
		3	15-20	30 sec

Bent lateral raise with resistance band	28	4	15-20	30 sec

Superset:
  Arm curl with resistance band
  Preacher curl with barbell and stability ball
	
	30
	133
		3	15-20	30 sec

Preacher curl with dumbbells	122	2	15-20	30 sec

Superset:
  Press-down with resistance band
  Overhead triceps extension with dumbbells and stability ball
	
	33
	126
		4	15-20	30 sec

Body Sculpting Routine, $2500 Budget

WEEK 1 Day 1 (Chest, Back, and Abs)

Exercise	Page	Sets	Reps	Rest interval
Front lat pull-down with machine	190	4*	8-10	60 sec
Seated row with cable	191	4	8-10	60 sec
Prone lat pull with stability ball	41	3	8-10	60 sec
Incline chest press with barbell	148	4	8-10	60 sec
Flat chest press with dumbbells	142	4*	8-10	60 sec
Standing low fly with resistance band	51	3	8-10	60 sec
Kneeling crunch with cable	195	3	8-10	60 sec
Rotating crunch with stability ball	70	3	8-10	60 sec
Side bend with dumbbells	150	2	8-10	60 sec

*Perform the final set as a double-drop set.

WEEK 1 Day 2 (Quads, Glutes, Hamstrings, and Calves)

Exercise	Page	Sets	Reps	Rest interval
Lunge with dumbbells	156	4	8-10	60 sec
One-leg extension with machine	200	3*	8-10	60 sec
Standing adductor raise with cable	202	3	8-10	60 sec
Good morning with barbell	168	3	8-10	60 sec
Prone one-leg curl with resistance band	99	3	8-10	60 sec
Standing abductor raise with resistance band	100	2	8-10	60 sec
Toe press with machine	205	4*	8-10	60 sec
One-leg seated calf raise with dumbbells	161	3	8-10	60 sec

*Perform the final set as a double-drop set.

WEEK 1 Day 3 (Shoulders, Biceps, and Triceps)

Exercise	Page	Sets	Reps	Rest interval
Shoulder press with machine	177	4*	8-10	60 sec
Upright row with dumbbells	115	3	8-10	60 sec
Standing reverse fly with resistance band	29	3	8-10	60 sec
Hammer curl with dumbbells	125	3*	8-10	60 sec
One-arm curl with cable	183	3	8-10	60 sec
Preacher curl with barbell and stability ball	133	2	8-10	60 sec
Press-down with resistance band	33	3	8-10	60 sec
One-arm overhead triceps extension with dumbbells	126	3	8-10	60 sec
Triceps kickback with dumbbells	128	2	8-10	60 sec

*Perform the final set as a double-drop set.

Body Sculpting Routine, $2500 Budget

WEEK 2   Day 1 (Chest, Back, and Abs)

Exercise	Page	Sets	Reps	Rest interval
Superset: Reverse-grip lat pull-down with resistance band Incline fly with dumbbells	 44 144	4	15-20	30 sec
Superset: Seated row with machine Incline chest press with dumbbells	 192 141	4	15-20	30 sec
Superset: Pullover with dumbbells Standing fly with resistance band	 138 50	3	15-20	30 sec
Superset: Roll-out with barbell Bicycle crunch	 151 53	3	15-20	30 sec
Low-to-high woodchop with cable	198	3	15-20	30 sec

WEEK 2   Day 2 (Quads, Glutes, Hamstrings, and Calves)

Exercise	Page	Sets	Reps	Rest interval
Superset: Leg press with machine Sissy squat	 199 78	4	15-20	30 sec
Step-up	83	3	15-20	30 sec
Superset: Prone leg curl with machine Hyperextension with stability ball	 201 68	4	15-20	30 sec
Lying abductor raise	90	2	15-20	30 sec
Superset: Standing calf raise with dumbbells Seated calf raise with dumbbells	 160 161	4	15-20	30 sec

WEEK 2   Day 3 (Shoulders, Biceps, and Triceps)

Exercise	Page	Sets	Reps	Rest interval
Superset: Upright row with cable Lateral raise with dumbbells	 179 117	3	15-20	30 sec
Kneeling bent lateral raise with cable	181	3	15-20	30 sec
Superset: Arm curl with barbell Prone incline curl with dumbbells	 134 124	2	15-20	30 sec
21s with barbell	135	3	21	30 sec
Superset: Overhead triceps extension with cable Lying triceps extension with dumbbells	 184 127	3	15-20	30 sec
Triceps kickback with resistance band	35	2	15-20	30 sec

Body Sculpting Routine, $2500 Budget

WEEK 3 Day 1 (Chest, Back, and Abs)

Exercise	Page	Sets	Reps	Rest interval
Lat pull-down with resistance band	44	4	8-10	60 sec
One-arm row with dumbbells	139	4	8-10	60 sec
Straight-arm pull-down with cable	194	3*	8-10	60 sec
Chest press with cable	188	4	8-10	60 sec
Reverse push-up with stability ball	40	3	8-10	60 sec
Flat fly with dumbbells	143	3*	8-10	60 sec
Crunch with stability ball	66	3	8-10	60 sec
Reverse crunch	58	3	8-10	60 sec
Side bend with cable	197	2	8-10	60 sec

*Perform the final set as a double-drop set.

WEEK 3 Day 2 (Quads, Glutes, Hamstrings, and Calves)

Exercise	Page	Sets	Reps	Rest interval
Split squat lunge with barbell	165	4*	8-10	60 sec
Side lunge with dumbbells	158	4	8-10	60 sec
One-leg squat with dumbbells	153	3	8-10	60 sec
Prone hip extension	85	3	8-10	60 sec
Leg curl with stability ball	93	3	8-10	60 sec
Standing abductor raise with cable	203	2	8-10	60 sec
One-leg standing calf raise with dumbbells	160	4	8-10	60 sec
Seated calf raise with dumbbells	161	3	8-10	60 sec

*Perform the final set as a double-drop set.

WEEK 3 Day 3 (Shoulders, Biceps, and Triceps)

Exercise	Page	Sets	Reps	Rest interval
Arnold press with dumbbells	114	4	8-10	60 sec
One-arm lateral raise with cable	180	3*	8-10	60 sec
Prone reverse fly with dumbbells	119	3	8-10	60 sec
Drag curl with barbell	137	3*	8-10	60 sec
Arm curl with dumbbells	120	2	8-10	60 sec
Concentration curl with dumbbells	123	2	8-10	60 sec
Overhead triceps extension with resistance band	34	3	8-10	60 sec
Triceps kickback with cable	186	3	8-10	60 sec
Nose breaker with barbell	136	2	8-10	60 sec

*Perform the final set as a double-drop set.

Body Sculpting Routine, $2500 Budget

WEEK 4 Day 1 (Chest, Back, and Abs)

Exercise	Page	Sets	Reps	Rest interval

Superset:
  Neutral-grip lat pull-down with machine
  Reverse low row with cable
	
	190
	193
		4	15-20	30 sec

Straight-arm pull-down with resistance band	46	3	15-20	30 sec

Giant set:
  Push-up
  Incline chest press with machine
  Crossover fly with cable
	
	36
	187
	189
		3	15-20	30 sec

Giant set:
  Kneeling and twisting crunch with cable
  Toe touch
  Reverse pendulum
	
	196
	52
	60
		3	15-20	30 sec

WEEK 4 Day 2 (Quads, Glutes, Hamstrings, and Calves)

Exercise	Page	Sets	Reps	Rest interval

Giant set:
  Back squat with barbell
  Reverse lunge with dumbbells
  Leg extension with machine
	
	162
	157
	200
		3	15-20	30 sec

Stiff-legged deadlift with barbell	169	3	15-20	30 sec
Prone one-leg curl with machine	201	3	15-20	30 sec
Glute back kick with cable	204	2	15-20	30 sec

Superset:
  Toe press with resistance band
  Bent-knee toe press with resistance band
	
	104
	103
		4	15-20	30 sec

WEEK 4 Day 3 (Shoulders, Biceps, and Triceps)

Exercise	Page	Sets	Reps	Rest interval

Superset:
  Shoulder press with cable
  Upright row with barbell
	
	178
	130
		2	15-20	30 sec

Lateral raise with resistance band	27	3	15-20	30 sec
Bent lateral raise with dumbbells	118	3	15-20	30 sec
Preacher curl with dumbbells	122	2	15-20	30 sec

Superset:
  Hammer curl with cable
  Incline curl with dumbbells
	
	182
	121
		3	15-20	30 sec

Superset:
  Press-down with cable
  Overhead triceps extension with dumbbells
	
	185
	126
		3	15-20	30 sec

Nose breaker with barbell	136	2	15-20	30 sec

11

Ultimate Core Stability

People tend to associate core stability workouts with abdominal training, often performing so-called core routines with the misguided hope of a flatter midsection. Regarding the latter, let's be perfectly clear: You can't slim down a specific area of your body with targeted exercises, no matter how often or how intensely you perform the movements. You could do crunches and side bends until the cows come home, but they won't do a thing to directly whittle away your spare tire. In reality, trying to spot-reduce with abdominal movements is just an exercise in futility. See the sidebar on spot reduction on page 288 for a detailed explanation.

▶ Use this routine if . . . you want to achieve a strong core or reduce lower back pain.

While the abs certainly play a role in core stability, they are by no means the only, or even most important, muscles that make up the core. The core is actually comprised of a group of muscles that span the length of the torso, including the transversus abdominis, the internal and external obliques, the rectus abdominis, the erector spinae, the multifidus, the quadratus lumborum, and the muscles of the pelvic floor. These muscles act together to stabilize your spine and pelvis, providing a sturdy base from which all movement begins. Only when your core is solid and stable can muscular power be transferred so that physical activity takes place.

One of the biggest benefits of core stability training is that it fosters better lower back health. Lower back pain is a condition that has reached epidemic proportions. The numbers are staggering. According to the American Academy of Orthopaedic Surgeons, 80 percent of Americans experience back pain at some point during their lives. That amounts to over 200 million people, with associated medical costs exceeding $100 billion per year!

However, most people don't realize that back problems are more a function of poor core endurance strength than inadequate absolute strength. Fact: The majority don't hurt their backs lifting a heavy object. Instead, it's the cumulative effects of poor posture that gradually take a toll on the lumbar muscles, ultimately causing them to give out.

A large percentage of back ailments can be traced to the modern workplace. Today's desk jobs have workers hunching over computers for hours on end. Over time, these habits place excessive strain on the vertebral column. Ultimately, the core muscles weaken, the hip flexors get tight, and the lumbar region loses its normal curvature—a surefire recipe for chronic back pain. Take-home message: Although six-pack abs might make you look great at the beach, they won't help much in protecting your spine.

The actual manifestation of lumbar pain is usually innocuous. You might turn the wrong way or sleep in a new position and then—bam!—a searing pain shoots through your lower back. The next thing you know, you're keeling over in agony, unable to move.

The ultimate home routine for core stability is designed to strengthen your core in a way that counteracts the effects of daily forces, preventing injuries to your lumbar region. You'll target your core muscles as a single entity, including the multifidi, the erector spinae, the quadratus lumborum, the rectus abdominis, and the deep muscles of the abdominal wall (obliques and transversus abdominis). Just as important, you'll strengthen the annuli of your spinal discs—the fibrous sheaths of connective tissue that comprise the outer portion of your vertebrae. Strong annuli keep the gel-like nuclei pulposi inside the spinal discs, preventing the dreaded effects of herniation.

The routine is particularly beneficial for women just before and after pregnancy. Approximately 70 percent of women experience back pain during pregnancy—a direct effect of carrying an extra 20 pounds (9 kg) or more in their midsections. That's like lugging around a small suitcase 24/7! Ideally, you should start strengthening your core before you conceive. Only by having a strong core at the outset will your lumbar musculature be able to withstand the constant strain placed on it, potentially sparing you months of discomfort. Labor will be easier and, following delivery, your abs will pop back into shape better than ever.

If the effects of childbearing have already taken a toll, don't fret. You can still achieve a strong core. Just be dedicated and, most of all, patient. It takes time to undo the ravages of nature, but I guarantee that if you make the commitment, you will see good results.

The Myth of Spot Reduction

Despite the inflated claims of certain hucksters, you can't spot-reduce body fat; it's a physiological impossibility. To appreciate why spot reduction doesn't work, you must understand how fat is synthesized. When you consume calories in abundance, your body converts the excess nutrients into fat-based compounds called *triglycerides,* which are then stored in fat cells called *adipocytes.* Adipocytes are pliable storehouses that either shrink or expand to accommodate fatty deposits. They are present in virtually every part of the body. There is a direct correlation between the size of adipocytes and obesity: The larger your adipocytes are, the fatter you will appear.

When you exercise, your body breaks triglycerides back down into fatty acids, which your blood transports to your muscles to use for energy. Because fatty acids must travel through the circulatory system—a time-consuming event—it is just as efficient for your body to burn fat from one area as it is from another. In other words, from an energy standpoint, the proximity of fat cells to the working muscles is completely irrelevant. The body cannot choose to use fat from a particular area. Instead, it draws from adipocytes in all regions of the body, including the face, the trunk, and the extremities.

Program Protocol

The ultimate home routine for core stability is a total-body routine that you perform three days a week. It focuses on exercises that both directly and indirectly engage the stabilizer muscles. These routines are divided according to the four basic budgets explained in chapter 2. Simply choose the budget that corresponds to the equipment you own and follow this protocol.

Exercises

Perform one exercise for the major muscles of the torso (the chest, back, and shoulders) and upper legs (the thighs, glutes, and hamstrings). You will train the core itself with multiple exercises in different planes of movement. Because of the large volume of exercises dedicated to direct core training, this routine does not specifically target the biceps, triceps, and calves. Don't worry, though, they won't be neglected. These muscles receive lots of ancillary activity during performance of the exercises for the chest, shoulders, and back—enough to sufficiently stimulate development.

You'll also note the absence of hip flexor movements in the routine. The hip flexors are powerful muscles that, when overdeveloped, can pull the spine forward, leading to a swaybacked posture in those with a weak core. What's the most common hip flexor move? The sit up! That's right—the old standard taught in virtually every gym class is one of the worst offenders for causing lower back pain and thus a poor choice for core stability. In addition to increasing hip flexor involvement, the exercise places excessive shear force on the spine, which can lead directly to spinal injury. The crunch, with its numerous variations, is a much better choice. It limits the involvement of the hip flexors and generates virtually no lumbar shear force while placing maximal tension on the abdominal muscles.

This routine focuses on exercises that can be performed on unstable surfaces. Because of the balance required to carry out these moves, your core activity will be significantly higher than it would be with comparable stable-surface training. Your abs and back will work as an integrated unit, contracting together isometrically to maintain equilibrium. The routine uses multijoint exercises whenever possible because they place the greatest demand on core stability. A cautionary note: If you suffer from lower back pain, you should begin by performing the exercises on stable surfaces. Progress to unstable surfaces only after you have built up sufficient spinal stability.

The routine also liberally uses standing exercises. When you stand, your core is highly active in maintaining posture. The benefit of these moves is that they are more functional than unstable-surface exercises, since there is greater transfer to most activities of daily living.

Sets

Perform three sets of each exercise. Instead of doing traditional block sets, you will perform the routine in a circuit format, moving fluidly from one exercise to the next, to the next, and so on. Once you've completed the entire circuit of movements, repeat the sequence two more times.

Circuit training is ideal for optimizing local muscular endurance. You will simultaneously push your muscles to work aerobically and challenge their strength. With its predominance of unstable-surface training, this routine places particular emphasis on core stamina. During nonstop activity, the abdominal and lower back muscles must work overtime to maintain balance and stability. And since the movements change from one moment to the next, your core must adapt to different stressors, furthering its development.

Repetitions

Perform 15 to 20 reps for each set. A high-rep format is essential for optimizing muscular endurance. It keeps the core muscles under constant tension for prolonged periods, enhancing their ability to resist fatigue. When performing movements that require continuous isometric contractions, such as the plank, the side bridge, and the bird dog, aim to work up to holding the position for a minute or longer. The longer you can maintain core strength in static positions, the better their endurance-oriented adaptation.

The order of the routine alternates between pushing and pulling exercises to optimize recovery of the prime movers. In the upper body, the chest and shoulder muscles are used in pushing movements and the back muscles are involved in pulling movements. A similar relationship exists in the lower body: The muscles in the front of the thighs (quadriceps) are used in pushing movements, while pulling is carried out by the muscles in the rear portion of the thighs (hamstrings). Alternating these two moves allows extra rest for the antagonist muscle, regenerating its ability to come back strong in the following set. This is particularly important in circuit training, in which moves change rapidly from one set to the next.

Rest

Rest as little as possible between sets—just long enough to catch your breath. Muscular endurance requires moving as quickly as possible between exercises. Aim to rest for 10 seconds, preferably less.

Set up your equipment in a manner that facilitates the transition from one exercise to the next. The idea is to maintain constant muscular tension in your core by forcing it to stabilize against weighted loads. If you don't feel aerobically challenged by the end of the circuit, you're taking too long between movements.

Intensity

As in any resistance-based routine, you must adhere to the overload principle and challenge your core muscles beyond their present capacity. For more information, see the fourth commandment of fitness in chapter 8. You should have difficulty completing the last few reps of each set. When performing moves that require an isometric hold, such as the plank and the side bridge, you should be struggling to maintain a proper position at the end of the set. Any less won't bring about the desired adaptation.

That said, core stability doesn't necessitate training to momentary muscular failure. The goal isn't to maximize stimulation of the arms, legs, and torso. Rather, your objective is to tax your core muscles in a way that increases their resistance to fatigue. This requires sustaining near-maximal tension for prolonged periods so that your core must work almost nonstop throughout the workout. When you begin to find the movements easier to perform, increase the resistance or the number of repetitions to remain challenged by the stimulus.

Going Forward

To prevent your workout from growing stale and hitting a plateau, you should strive to change exercise variables on an ongoing basis. Here are some suggestions for sustaining progress in the core stability routine. After completing the four-week cycle, consider implementing some or all of these concepts going forward.

- *Go for strength.* While it's true that most lower back injuries are endurance-related, this doesn't mean that absolute core strength is of no consequence. You might need to lift an extra-heavy object or move a bulky piece of furniture someday. To accomplish such tasks, your core muscles must be up to the challenge. This means some of your training should ultimately shift toward strength development. Substituting strength sets for endurance sets one session a week should do the trick. Perform 6 to 10 reps of each set with heavier weights. In time, you'll develop a core that can withstand the demands of any situation.

- *Reverse the order.* In most cases, it's not advisable to train the core muscles first in a workout. Doing so reduces core stability during non-core lifts, thereby diminishing stimulation of the target muscles. However, this isn't an issue in a core-based routine. Your primary goal is to fatigue the core musculature; the other muscle groups are of secondary concern. Take advantage of this fact. Work in reverse order, and perform the moves in the opposite sequence. This will change muscle recruitment patterns, spurring your core on to better development.

- *Destabilize the stable.* Perform standing moves on unstable surfaces to challenge your core muscles beyond their present capacity. Here is where a Bosu trainer or balance discs come in handy. Use them every other workout or so to provide a different muscular stimulus. At first, you'll have to use very light weights. Perhaps you won't be able to sustain any weight at all. That's okay. Work on using your core to balance your body until you can perform each move with precision. Once you have mastered a movement, gradually increase the amount of weight to keep your core in a constant state of adaptation.

Core Stability Routine, $100 Budget

WEEK 1   Day 1

Exercise	Page	Sets	Reps	Rest interval
Upright row with resistance band	24	3	15-20	10 sec
Row with resistance band and stability ball	43	3	15-20	10 sec
Push-up	36	3	15-20	10 sec
One-leg squat	76	3	15-20	10 sec
Bridge with stability ball	72	3	15-20	10 sec
Bicycle crunch	53	3	15-20	10 sec
Side crunch with stability ball	67	3	15-20	10 sec
Plank	61	3	Static hold	10 sec
Bird dog	56	3	Static hold	10 sec

WEEK 1   Day 2

Exercise	Page	Sets	Reps	Rest interval
Shoulder press with resistance band	25	3	15-20	10 sec
Prone lat pull with stability ball	41	3	15-20	10 sec
Standing chest press with resistance band	48	3	15-20	10 sec
Squat with resistance band	95	3	15-20	10 sec
Superwoman	55	3	15-20	10 sec
Toe touch	52	3	15-20	10 sec
Russian twist with stability ball	71	3	15-20	10 sec
Side bridge	62	3	Static hold	10 sec
Plank	61	3	Static hold	10 sec

WEEK 1   Day 3

Exercise	Page	Sets	Reps	Rest interval
Arnold press with resistance band	26	3	15-20	10 sec
Lat pull-down with resistance band	44	3	15-20	10 sec
Standing incline chest press with resistance band	49	3	15-20	10 sec
Reverse lunge	81	3	15-20	10 sec
Bridge	63	3	15-20	10 sec
Reverse hyperextension with stability ball	65	3	15-20	10 sec
Crunch with stability ball	66	3	15-20	10 sec
Bird dog	56	3	Static hold	10 sec
Side bridge	62	3	Static hold	10 sec

Core Stability Routine, $100 Budget

Exercise	Page	Sets	Reps	Rest interval
Shoulder press with resistance band	25	3	15-20	10 sec
One-arm low row with resistance band	45	3	15-20	10 sec
Reverse push-up with stability ball	40	3	15-20	10 sec
Sumo squat	77	3	15-20	10 sec
Crunch	57	3	15-20	10 sec
Horizontal woodchop with resistance band	73	3	15-20	10 sec
Side jackknife	59	3	15-20	10 sec
Plank	61	3	Static hold	10 sec
Bird dog	56	3	Static hold	10 sec

Exercise	Page	Sets	Reps	Rest interval
Standing reverse fly with resistance band	29	3	15-20	10 sec
Neutral-grip lat pull-down with resistance band	44	3	15-20	10 sec
Push-up	36	3	15-20	10 sec
Split squat lunge with resistance band	96	3	15-20	10 sec
Kneeling crunch with resistance band	74	3	15-20	10 sec
Reverse crunch	58	3	15-20	10 sec
Helicopter with stability ball	69	3	15-20	10 sec
Side bridge	62	3	Static hold	10 sec
Plank	61	3	Static hold	10 sec

Exercise	Page	Sets	Reps	Rest interval
Upright row with resistance band	24	3	15-20	10 sec
Seated row with resistance band	42	3	15-20	10 sec
Standing low fly with resistance band	51	3	15-20	10 sec
Step-up	83	3	15-20	10 sec
Rotating crunch with stability ball	70	3	15-20	10 sec
Toe touch	52	3	15-20	10 sec
Bridge with stability ball	72	3	15-20	10 sec
Bird dog	56	3	Static hold	10 sec
Side bridge	62	3	Static hold	10 sec

Core Stability Routine, $100 Budget

WEEK 3 Day 1

Exercise	Page	Sets	Reps	Rest interval
Arnold press with resistance band	26	3	15-20	10 sec
Reverse-grip lat pull-down with resistance band	44	3	15-20	10 sec
Standing chest press with resistance band	48	3	15-20	10 sec
Squat	75	3	15-20	10 sec
Bicycle crunch	53	3	15-20	10 sec
Superwoman	55	3	15-20	10 sec
Reverse pendulum	60	3	15-20	10 sec
Plank	61	3	Static hold	10 sec
Bird dog	56	3	Static hold	10 sec

WEEK 3 Day 2

Exercise	Page	Sets	Reps	Rest interval
Upright row with resistance band	24	3	15-20	10 sec
One-arm low row with resistance band	45	3	15-20	10 sec
Standing incline chest press with resistance band	49	3	15-20	10 sec
Lunge	80	3	15-20	10 sec
Twisting crunch	54	3	15-20	10 sec
Side crunch with stability ball	67	3	15-20	10 sec
Bridge	63	3	15-20	10 sec
Side bridge	62	3	Static hold	10 sec
Plank	61	3	Static hold	10 sec

WEEK 3 Day 3

Exercise	Page	Sets	Reps	Rest interval
Shoulder press with resistance band	25	3	15-20	10 sec
Prone lat pull with stability ball	41	3	15-20	10 sec
Reverse push-up with stability ball	40	3	15-20	10 sec
One-leg squat	76	3	15-20	10 sec
Crunch with stability ball	66	3	15-20	10 sec
Reverse hyperextension with stability ball	65	3	15-20	10 sec
Horizontal woodchop with resistance band	73	3	15-20	10 sec
Bird dog	56	3	Static hold	10 sec
Side bridge	62	3	Static hold	10 sec

Core Stability Routine, $100 Budget

WEEK 4 Day 1

Exercise	Page	Sets	Reps	Rest interval
Upright row with resistance band	24	3	15-20	10 sec
Row with resistance band and stability ball	43	3	15-20	10 sec
Standing fly with resistance band	50	3	15-20	10 sec
Side lunge	82	3	15-20	10 sec
Kneeling crunch with resistance band	74	3	15-20	10 sec
Side jackknife	59	3	15-20	10 sec
Russian twist with stability ball	71	3	15-20	10 sec
Plank	61	3	Static hold	10 sec
Bird dog	56	3	Static hold	10 sec

WEEK 4 Day 2

Exercise	Page	Sets	Reps	Rest interval
Shoulder press with resistance band	25	3	15-20	10 sec
Lat pull-down with resistance band	44	3	15-20	10 sec
Standing low fly with resistance band	51	3	15-20	10 sec
Sumo squat	77	3	15-20	10 sec
Reverse crunch	58	3	15-20	10 sec
Helicopter with stability ball	69	3	15-20	10 sec
Reverse pendulum	60	3	15-20	10 sec
Side bridge	62	3	Static hold	10 sec
Plank	61	3	Static hold	10 sec

WEEK 4 Day 3

Exercise	Page	Sets	Reps	Rest interval
Lateral raise with resistance band	27	3	15-20	10 sec
Neutral-grip lat pull-down with resistance band	44	3	15-20	10 sec
Push-up	36	3	15-20	10 sec
Reverse lunge	81	3	15-20	10 sec
Crunch	57	3	15-20	10 sec
Rotating crunch with stability ball	70	3	15-20	10 sec
Hyperextension with stability ball	68	3	15-20	10 sec
Bird dog	56	3	Static hold	10 sec
Side bridge	62	3	Static hold	10 sec

Core Stability Routine, $500 Budget

WEEK 1   Day 1

Exercise	Page	Sets	Reps	Rest interval
Arnold press with dumbbells and stability ball	114	3	15-20	10 sec
Row with resistance band and stability ball	43	3	15-20	10 sec
Incline chest press with dumbbells and stability ball	141	3	15-20	10 sec
Squat with dumbbells	152	3	15-20	10 sec
Crunch with stability ball	66	3	15-20	10 sec
Russian twist with stability ball	71	3	15-20	10 sec
Bridge with stability ball	72	3	15-20	10 sec
Plank	61	3	Static hold	10 sec
Bird dog	56	3	Static hold	10 sec

WEEK 1   Day 2

Exercise	Page	Sets	Reps	Rest interval
Upright row with resistance band	24	3	15-20	10 sec
One-arm row with dumbbells	139	3	15-20	10 sec
Standing chest press with resistance band	48	3	15-20	10 sec
Lunge with dumbbells	156	3	15-20	10 sec
Rotating crunch with stability ball	70	3	15-20	10 sec
Side jackknife	59	3	15-20	10 sec
Hyperextension with stability ball	68	3	15-20	10 sec
Side bridge	62	3	Static hold	10 sec
Plank	61	3	Static hold	10 sec

WEEK 1   Day 3

Exercise	Page	Sets	Reps	Rest interval
Standing shoulder press with dumbbells	113	3	15-20	10 sec
Lat pull-down with resistance band	44	3	15-20	10 sec
Flat fly with dumbbells and stability ball	143	3	15-20	10 sec
Sumo squat with dumbbells	154	3	15-20	10 sec
Toe touch	52	3	15-20	10 sec
Side crunch with stability ball	67	3	15-20	10 sec
Superwoman	55	3	15-20	10 sec
Bird dog	56	3	Static hold	10 sec
Side bridge	62	3	Static hold	10 sec

Core Stability Routine, $500 Budget

WEEK 2 Day 1

Exercise	Page	Sets	Reps	Rest interval
Upright row with dumbbells	115	3	15-20	10 sec
Prone lat pull with stability ball	41	3	15-20	10 sec
Push-up	36	3	15-20	10 sec
Split squat lunge with resistance band	96	3	15-20	10 sec
Reverse crunch	58	3	15-20	10 sec
Helicopter with stability ball	69	3	15-20	10 sec
Horizontal woodchop with resistance band	73	3	15-20	10 sec
Plank	61	3	Static hold	10 sec
Bird dog	56	3	Static hold	10 sec

WEEK 2 Day 2

Exercise	Page	Sets	Reps	Rest interval
Shoulder press with resistance band	25	3	15-20	10 sec
Neutral-grip lat pull-down with resistance band	44	3	15-20	10 sec
Flat chest press with dumbbells and stability ball	142	3	15-20	10 sec
One-leg squat with dumbbells	153	3	15-20	10 sec
Bicycle crunch	53	3	15-20	10 sec
Bridge	63	3	15-20	10 sec
Reverse pendulum	60	3	15-20	10 sec
Side bridge	62	3	Static hold	10 sec
Plank	61	3	Static hold	10 sec

WEEK 2 Day 3

Exercise	Page	Sets	Reps	Rest interval
Standing Arnold press with dumbbells	114	3	15-20	10 sec
Seated row with resistance band	42	3	15-20	10 sec
Incline fly with dumbbells and stability ball	144	3	15-20	10 sec
Reverse lunge with dumbbells	157	3	15-20	10 sec
Twisting crunch	54	3	15-20	10 sec
Side bend with dumbbells	150	3	15-20	10 sec
Reverse hyperextension with stability ball	65	3	15-20	10 sec
Bird dog	56	3	Static hold	10 sec
Side bridge	62	3	Static hold	10 sec

Core Stability Routine, $500 Budget

WEEK 3 Day 1

Exercise	Page	Sets	Reps	Rest interval
Shoulder press with dumbbells and stability ball	113	3	15-20	10 sec
Reverse-grip lat pull-down with resistance band	44	3	15-20	10 sec
Flat fly with dumbbells and stability ball	143	3	15-20	10 sec
Step-up with dumbbells	159	3	15-20	10 sec
Kneeling crunch with resistance band	74	3	15-20	10 sec
Side jackknife	59	3	15-20	10 sec
Superwoman	55	3	15-20	10 sec
Plank	61	3	Static hold	10 sec
Bird dog	56	3	Static hold	10 sec

WEEK 3 Day 2

Exercise	Page	Sets	Reps	Rest interval
Arnold press with resistance band	26	3	15-20	10 sec
Row with resistance band and stability ball	43	3	15-20	10 sec
Reverse push-up with stability ball	40	3	15-20	10 sec
Squat with resistance band	95	3	15-20	10 sec
Crunch	57	3	15-20	10 sec
Side crunch with stability ball	67	3	15-20	10 sec
Hyperextension with stability ball	68	3	15-20	10 sec
Side bridge	62	3	Static hold	10 sec
Plank	61	3	Static hold	10 sec

WEEK 3 Day 3

Exercise	Page	Sets	Reps	Rest interval
Upright row with dumbbells	115	3	15-20	10 sec
One-arm low row with resistance band	45	3	15-20	10 sec
Standing incline chest press with resistance band	49	3	15-20	10 sec
Lunge with dumbbells	156	3	15-20	10 sec
Crunch with stability ball	66	3	15-20	10 sec
Toe touch	52	3	15-20	10 sec
Bridge with stability ball	72	3	15-20	10 sec
Bird dog	56	3	Static hold	10 sec
Side bridge	62	3	Static hold	10 sec

Core Stability Routine, $500 Budget

WEEK 4 Day 1

Exercise	Page	Sets	Reps	Rest interval
Upright row with resistance band	24	3	15-20	10 sec
One-arm row with dumbbells	139	3	15-20	10 sec
Incline chest press with dumbbells and stability ball	141	3	15-20	10 sec
Sumo squat with dumbbells	154	3	15-20	10 sec
Reverse crunch	58	3	15-20	10 sec
Rotating crunch with stability ball	70	3	15-20	10 sec
Reverse pendulum	60	3	15-20	10 sec
Plank	61	3	Static hold	10 sec
Bird dog	56	3	Static hold	10 sec

WEEK 4 Day 2

Exercise	Page	Sets	Reps	Rest interval
Arnold press with dumbbells and stability ball	114	3	15-20	10 sec
Straight-arm pull-down with resistance band	46	3	15-20	10 sec
Push-up	36	3	15-20	10 sec
Split squat lunge with dumbbells	155	3	15-20	10 sec
Bicycle crunch	53	3	15-20	10 sec
Helicopter with stability ball	69	3	15-20	10 sec
Reverse hyperextension with stability ball	65	3	15-20	10 sec
Side bridge	62	3	Static hold	10 sec
Plank	61	3	Static hold	10 sec

WEEK 4 Day 3

Exercise	Page	Sets	Reps	Rest interval
Standing shoulder press with dumbbells	113	3	15-20	10 sec
Prone lat pull with stability ball	41	3	15-20	10 sec
Flat fly with dumbbells and stability ball	143	3	15-20	10 sec
One-leg squat with dumbbells	153	3	15-20	10 sec
Twisting crunch	54	3	15-20	10 sec
Side bend with dumbbells	150	3	15-20	10 sec
Russian twist with stability ball	71	3	15-20	10 sec
Bird dog	56	3	Static hold	10 sec
Side bridge	62	3	Static hold	10 sec

Core Stability Routine, $1000 Budget

WEEK 1 Day 1

Exercise	Page	Sets	Reps	Rest interval
Shoulder press with dumbbells and stability ball	113	3	15-20	10 sec
Reverse bent row with barbell	147	3	15-20	10 sec
Incline chest press with barbell	148	3	15-20	10 sec
Squat with dumbbells	152	3	15-20	10 sec
Twisting crunch	54	3	15-20	10 sec
Side jackknife	59	3	15-20	10 sec
Hyperextension with stability ball	68	3	15-20	10 sec
Plank	61	3	Static hold	10 sec
Bird dog	56	3	Static hold	10 sec

WEEK 1 Day 2

Exercise	Page	Sets	Reps	Rest interval
Shoulder press with resistance band	25	3	15-20	10 sec
Row with resistance band and stability ball	43	3	15-20	10 sec
Incline fly with dumbbells and stability ball	144	3	15-20	10 sec
Split squat lunge with barbell	165	3	15-20	10 sec
Reverse crunch	58	3	15-20	10 sec
Helicopter with stability ball	69	3	15-20	10 sec
Bridge with stability ball	72	3	15-20	10 sec
Side bridge	62	3	Static hold	10 sec
Plank	61	3	Static hold	10 sec

WEEK 1 Day 3

Exercise	Page	Sets	Reps	Rest interval
Upright row with barbell	130	3	15-20	10 sec
One-arm row with dumbbells	139	3	15-20	10 sec
Flat chest press with dumbbells and stability ball	142	3	15-20	10 sec
Reverse lunge with dumbbells	157	3	15-20	10 sec
Kneeling crunch with resistance band	74	3	15-20	10 sec
Side crunch with stability ball	67	3	15-20	10 sec
Reverse pendulum	60	3	15-20	10 sec
Bird dog	56	3	Static hold	10 sec
Side bridge	62	3	Static hold	10 sec

Core Stability Routine, $1000 Budget

Exercise	Page	Sets	Reps	Rest interval
Arnold press with dumbbells and stability ball	114	3	15-20	10 sec
Lat pull-down with resistance band	44	3	15-20	10 sec
Push-up	36	3	15-20	10 sec
Lunge with dumbbells	156	3	15-20	10 sec
Superwoman	55	3	15-20	10 sec
Roll-out with barbell	151	3	15-20	10 sec
Side bend with dumbbells	150	3	15-20	10 sec
Plank	61	3	Static hold	10 sec
Bird dog	56	3	Static hold	10 sec

Exercise	Page	Sets	Reps	Rest interval
Standing shoulder press with dumbbells	113	3	15-20	10 sec
Seated row with resistance band	42	3	15-20	10 sec
Incline fly with dumbbells and stability ball	144	3	15-20	10 sec
Back squat with barbell	162	3	15-20	10 sec
Toe touch	52	3	15-20	10 sec
Rotating crunch with stability ball	70	3	15-20	10 sec
Bridge	63	3	15-20	10 sec
Side bridge	62	3	Static hold	10 sec
Plank	61	3	Static hold	10 sec

Exercise	Page	Sets	Reps	Rest interval
Upright row with dumbbells	115	3	15-20	10 sec
T-bar row with barbell	145	3	15-20	10 sec
Standing chest press with resistance band	48	3	15-20	10 sec
Sumo squat with dumbbells	154	3	15-20	10 sec
Bicycle crunch	53	3	15-20	10 sec
Horizontal woodchop with resistance band	73	3	15-20	10 sec
Reverse hyperextension with stability ball	65	3	15-20	10 sec
Bird dog	56	3	Static hold	10 sec
Side bridge	62	3	Static hold	10 sec

Core Stability Routine, $1000 Budget

Exercise	Page	Sets	Reps	Rest interval
Upright row with resistance band	24	3	15-20	10 sec
Prone lat pull with stability ball	41	3	15-20	10 sec
Flat fly with dumbbells and stability ball	143	3	15-20	10 sec
Reverse lunge with barbell	167	3	15-20	10 sec
Crunch with stability ball	66	3	15-20	10 sec
Russian twist with stability ball	71	3	15-20	10 sec
Bridge with stability ball	72	3	15-20	10 sec
Plank	61	3	Static hold	10 sec
Bird dog	56	3	Static hold	10 sec

Exercise	Page	Sets	Reps	Rest interval
Arnold press with resistance band	26	3	15-20	10 sec
Neutral-grip lat pull-down with resistance band	44	3	15-20	10 sec
Reverse push-up with stability ball	40	3	15-20	10 sec
Step-up with dumbbells	159	3	15-20	10 sec
Crunch	57	3	15-20	10 sec
Side jackknife	59	3	15-20	10 sec
Reverse pendulum	60	3	15-20	10 sec
Side bridge	62	3	Static hold	10 sec
Plank	61	3	Static hold	10 sec

Exercise	Page	Sets	Reps	Rest interval
Shoulder press with dumbbells and stability ball	113	3	15-20	10 sec
Row with resistance band and stability ball	43	3	15-20	10 sec
Standing incline chest press with resistance band	49	3	15-20	10 sec
Hack squat with barbell	164	3	15-20	10 sec
Reverse crunch	58	3	15-20	10 sec
Twisting crunch	54	3	15-20	10 sec
Hyperextension with stability ball	68	3	15-20	10 sec
Bird dog	56	3	Static hold	10 sec
Side bridge	62	3	Static hold	10 sec

Core Stability Routine, $1000 Budget

Exercise	Page	Sets	Reps	Rest interval
Shoulder press with resistance band	25	3	15-20	10 sec
Straight-arm pull-down with resistance band	46	3	15-20	10 sec
Incline chest press with dumbbells and stability ball	141	3	15-20	10 sec
Lunge with barbell	166	3	15-20	10 sec
Kneeling crunch with resistance band	74	3	15-20	10 sec
Bicycle crunch	53	3	15-20	10 sec
Side bend with dumbbells	150	3	15-20	10 sec
Plank	61	3	Static hold	10 sec
Bird dog	56	3	Static hold	10 sec

Exercise	Page	Sets	Reps	Rest interval
Standing Arnold press with dumbbells	114	3	15-20	10 sec
Reverse bent row with barbell	147	3	15-20	10 sec
Standing low fly with resistance band	51	3	15-20	10 sec
One-leg squat with dumbbells	153	3	15-20	10 sec
Crunch with stability ball	66	3	15-20	10 sec
Side crunch with stability ball	67	3	15-20	10 sec
Superwoman	55	3	15-20	10 sec
Side bridge	62	3	Static hold	10 sec
Plank	61	3	Static hold	10 sec

Exercise	Page	Sets	Reps	Rest interval
Military press with barbell	129	3	15-20	10 sec
Reverse-grip lat pull-down with resistance band	44	3	15-20	10 sec
Push-up	36	3	15-20	10 sec
Front squat with barbell	163	3	15-20	10 sec
Roll-out with barbell	151	3	15-20	10 sec
Rotating crunch with stability ball	70	3	15-20	10 sec
Reverse hyperextension with stability ball	65	3	15-20	10 sec
Bird dog	56	3	Static hold	10 sec
Side bridge	62	3	Static hold	10 sec

Core Stability Routine, $2500 Budget

WEEK 1 Day 1

Exercise	Page	Sets	Reps	Rest interval
Arnold press with dumbbells and stability ball	114	3	15-20	10 sec
Reverse low row with cable	193	3	15-20	10 sec
Flat chest press with dumbbells and stability ball	142	3	15-20	10 sec
Step-up with dumbbells	159	3	15-20	10 sec
Crunch with stability ball	66	3	15-20	10 sec
Side jackknife	59	3	15-20	10 sec
Horizontal woodchop with resistance band	73	3	15-20	10 sec
Plank	61	3	Static hold	10 sec
Bird dog	56	3	Static hold	10 sec

WEEK 1 Day 2

Exercise	Page	Sets	Reps	Rest interval
Upright row with cable	179	3	15-20	10 sec
Reverse bent row with barbell	147	3	15-20	10 sec
Standing incline chest press with resistance band	49	3	15-20	10 sec
One-leg squat with dumbbells	153	3	15-20	10 sec
Reverse crunch	58	3	15-20	10 sec
Rotating crunch with stability ball	70	3	15-20	10 sec
Bridge with stability ball	72	3	15-20	10 sec
Side bridge	62	3	Static hold	10 sec
Plank	61	3	Static hold	10 sec

WEEK 1 Day 3

Exercise	Page	Sets	Reps	Rest interval
Standing shoulder press with dumbbells	113	3	15-20	10 sec
Front lat pull-down with machine	190	3	15-20	10 sec
Push-up	36	3	15-20	10 sec
Front squat with barbell	163	3	15-20	10 sec
Kneeling crunch with cable	195	3	15-20	10 sec
Side bend with dumbbells	150	3	15-20	10 sec
Russian twist with stability ball	71	3	15-20	10 sec
Bird dog	56	3	Static hold	10 sec
Side bridge	62	3	Static hold	10 sec

Core Stability Routine, $2500 Budget

WEEK 2 Day 1

Exercise	Page	Sets	Reps	Rest interval
Arnold press with resistance band	26	3	15-20	10 sec
Neutral-grip lat pull-down with machine	190	3	15-20	10 sec
Incline chest press with dumbbells and stability ball	141	3	15-20	10 sec
Sumo squat with dumbbells	154	3	15-20	10 sec
Roll-out with barbell	151	3	15-20	10 sec
Reverse pendulum	60	3	15-20	10 sec
Superwoman	55	3	15-20	10 sec
Plank	61	3	Static hold	10 sec
Bird dog	56	3	Static hold	10 sec

WEEK 2 Day 2

Exercise	Page	Sets	Reps	Rest interval
Upright row with barbell	130	3	15-20	10 sec
Straight-arm pull-down with cable	194	3	15-20	10 sec
Incline fly with dumbbells and stability ball	144	3	15-20	10 sec
Reverse lunge with barbell	167	3	15-20	10 sec
Toe touch	52	3	15-20	10 sec
Kneeling and twisting crunch with cable	196	3	15-20	10 sec
Side crunch with stability ball	67	3	15-20	10 sec
Side bridge	62	3	Static hold	10 sec
Plank	61	3	Static hold	10 sec

WEEK 2 Day 3

Exercise	Page	Sets	Reps	Rest interval
Shoulder press with dumbbells and stability ball	113	3	15-20	10 sec
Prone lat pull with stability ball	41	3	15-20	10 sec
Standing chest press with resistance band	48	3	15-20	10 sec
Hack squat with barbell	164	3	15-20	10 sec
Bicycle crunch	53	3	15-20	10 sec
Kneeling crunch with resistance band	74	3	15-20	10 sec
Hyperextension with stability ball	68	3	15-20	10 sec
Bird dog	56	3	Static hold	10 sec
Side bridge	62	3	Static hold	10 sec

Core Stability Routine, $2500 Budget

WEEK 3   Day 1

Exercise	Page	Sets	Reps	Rest interval
Shoulder press with cable	178	3	15-20	10 sec
T-bar row with barbell	145	3	15-20	10 sec
Crossover fly with cable	189	3	15-20	10 sec
Split squat lunge with dumbbells	155	3	15-20	10 sec
Crunch	57	3	15-20	10 sec
Side bend with cable	197	3	15-20	10 sec
Helicopter with stability ball	69	3	15-20	10 sec
Plank	61	3	Static hold	10 sec
Bird dog	56	3	Static hold	10 sec

WEEK 3   Day 2

Exercise	Page	Sets	Reps	Rest interval
Upright row with dumbbells	115	3	15-20	10 sec
Reverse-grip lat pull-down with machine	190	3	15-20	10 sec
Flat fly with dumbbells and stability ball	143	3	15-20	10 sec
Lunge with barbell	166	3	15-20	10 sec
Rotating crunch with stability ball	70	3	15-20	10 sec
Reverse crunch	58	3	15-20	10 sec
Reverse hyperextension with stability ball	65	3	15-20	10 sec
Side bridge	62	3	Static hold	10 sec
Plank	61	3	Static hold	10 sec

WEEK 3   Day 3

Exercise	Page	Sets	Reps	Rest interval
Shoulder press with resistance band	25	3	15-20	10 sec
Row with resistance band and stability ball	43	3	15-20	10 sec
Flat chest press with dumbbells and stability ball	142	3	15-20	10 sec
Squat with dumbbells	152	3	15-20	10 sec
Crunch with stability ball	66	3	15-20	10 sec
Low-to-high woodchop with cable	198	3	15-20	10 sec
Bridge	63	3	15-20	10 sec
Bird dog	56	3	Static hold	10 sec
Side bridge	62	3	Static hold	10 sec

Core Stability Routine, $2500 Budget

WEEK 4   Day 1

Exercise	Page	Sets	Reps	Rest interval
Upright row with resistance band	24	3	15-20	10 sec
Seated row with cable	191	3	15-20	10 sec
Reverse push-up with stability ball	40	3	15-20	10 sec
Reverse lunge with dumbbells	157	3	15-20	10 sec
Kneeling crunch with cable	195	3	15-20	10 sec
Side jackknife	59	3	15-20	10 sec
Bridge with stability ball	72	3	15-20	10 sec
Plank	61	3	Static hold	10 sec
Bird dog	56	3	Static hold	10 sec

WEEK 4   Day 2

Exercise	Page	Sets	Reps	Rest interval
Lateral raise with dumbbells and stability ball	117	3	15-20	10 sec
One-arm row with dumbbells	139	3	15-20	10 sec
Chest press with cable	188	3	15-20	10 sec
Squat with resistance band	95	3	15-20	10 sec
Bicycle crunch	53	3	15-20	10 sec
Side bend with dumbbells	150	3	15-20	10 sec
Reverse pendulum	60	3	15-20	10 sec
Side bridge	62	3	Static hold	10 sec
Plank	61	3	Static hold	10 sec

WEEK 4   Day 3

Exercise	Page	Sets	Reps	Rest interval
Standing Arnold press with dumbbells	114	3	15-20	10 sec
One-arm low row with resistance band	45	3	15-20	10 sec
Incline fly with dumbbells and stability ball	144	3	15-20	10 sec
Split squat lunge with dumbbells	155	3	15-20	10 sec
Roll-out with barbell	151	3	15-20	10 sec
Side bend with cable	197	3	15-20	10 sec
Hyperextension with stability ball	68	3	15-20	10 sec
Bird dog	56	3	Static hold	10 sec
Side bridge	62	3	Static hold	10 sec

12

Ultimate Fat Loss

Have a few extra pounds to lose? Perhaps more than a few? If so, the ultimate home routine for fat loss is for you. It's a high-energy cardio regimen designed to melt away excess fat without sacrificing the lean muscle you've worked so hard to develop. The exercise variables are structured to avoid redundancy by varying intensity, duration, and mode. You'll be continually challenged, never bored.

> ▶ **Use this routine if . . . you want to expedite the loss of body fat and improve your cardiorespiratory fitness.**

You're probably expecting me to dish out the standard advice, telling you to hop on a treadmill or bike and exercise in your fat-burning zone for an hour at a clip, right? Not a chance! In reality, the fat-burning zone doesn't exist. The myth is based on a misperception of research that shows that the body prefers to use fat for fuel during low-intensity exercise. Unfortunately, the selective use of fat for fuel doesn't translate into burning more total fat calories. It's the total number of calories burned—not the percentage of calories that come from fat—that sheds the pounds. And in terms of burning maximal calories, high-intensity exercise always comes out on top.

Don't get me wrong, there's nothing inherently wrong with steady-state, low-intensity aerobic exercise. It most definitely helps you lose fat and improve your general cardiorespiratory health. Exercising at a leisurely pace is a fine way to derive aerobic benefits without expending significant physical effort. Adherence is the most important aspect of exercise. If you dislike high-intensity activity or have a medical condition that precludes you from vigorous training, then by all means, opt for steady-state cardio.

For optimal fat burning, however, intense aerobic exercise is clearly your best bet. Therefore, the ultimate home routine for fat loss employs a specific type of cardio known as *interval training*. Interval training combines high-intensity and low-intensity bouts of exercise to stimulate the sympathetic nervous system to burn more fat in less time. Both research and personal experience have proven it to be the most effective type of cardio for fat loss. Better yet, it's been shown to be superior to steady-state aerobics in terms of reducing cardiorespiratory risk factors and improving blood pressure, insulin sensitivity, and heart function.

The secret of interval training with respect to fat loss is its effects on EPOC (excess postexercise oxygen consumption)—sometimes called the *afterburn.* Simply stated, EPOC is a measure of the number of calories burned after a workout is finished. A high EPOC level is associated with elevated metabolism and increased secretion of growth hormone and noradrenaline. These hormones help break down stores of fat and increase their use as a fuel source. The net effect lasts as long as 36 hours after exercise, burning as many as 150 calories a day beyond resting levels.

In addition to its direct influence on fat loss, interval training also helps supercharge metabolism. You'll turn your body into a fat-burning furnace that works 'round the clock to keep you lean. Here's how:

▪ *Increased capillarization.* You'll expand your network of capillaries—the tiny blood vessels that allow nutrients such as protein and carbohydrate to be absorbed into body tissue. The more capillaries you have, the more efficiently your body can liberate and utilize fat, particularly from stubborn areas like the thighs and love handles. Blood flow tends to be poor in these areas, which inhibits the mobilization of fat.

▪ *Increased cellular sensitivity.* You'll improve the sensitivity of your muscle and fat cells to fat-fighting hormones such as adrenaline, which helps move fatty acids from their stored form into the bloodstream, where they can be burned for fuel. Another example is insulin, which allows sugars to be stored in muscle tissues as glycogen rather than shuttled into fat cells as a lipid.

▪ *Increased mitochondrial density.* You'll increase the size and number of your mitochondria, the power plants of your cells that burn fat. This means that your body can rely more on fat—rather than glycogen (carbohydrate)—for fuel, helping to sustain long-term weight management.

▪ *Increased enzyme activity.* You'll boost the number of enzymes available for catalyzing metabolism. These specialized bodily proteins speed up cellular processes, accelerating the rate at which your body burns fat. And the faster you burn it, the more you can burn!

While all these things add up to ultimate fat burning, there is one catch. Like any cardiorespiratory routine, this one must be combined with one of the targeted resistance-training routines (body conditioning, body sculpting, or core stability) in order to sustain results over time. Here's the skinny: Although cardio is great at creating a caloric deficit, it does virtually nothing to preserve muscle mass. In fact, some studies show it actually accelerates the loss of muscle when accompanied by a strict diet.

Why is muscle so important for weight maintenance? Because it's by far the most metabolically active tissue in your body. Even while resting, you can burn as many as 50 calories a day for each pound of muscle you carry. Read: You'll burn more calories even when you're lazing on the couch, watching your favorite TV show. Therefore, when you lose muscle, your metabolism is suppressed. This makes it increasingly difficult to shed unwanted pounds over time, inevitably leading to a weight-loss plateau. Frustration sets in, the weight creeps back on, and you end up even heavier than you started.

The only way to prevent muscle catabolism (the breakdown of muscle tissue) while losing fat is to add resistance training into the mix. Not only does lifting weights attenuate the loss of muscle, but it can actually increase muscle mass. Metabolism stays elevated, the pounds come off faster, and, most importantly, you keep them off—permanently.

Perform the fat-burning workout either on the same day as your resistance routine or on alternating days. The choice is yours. Both workouts are very time-efficient, so you won't need to exercise for hours to get results.

If you choose to perform both routines in the same session, do the resistance workout first. Interval training saps vital energy reserves, diminishing your ability to lift weights with adequate intensity. It is much easier to push through the cardio component after an intense lifting session than to attempt the reverse.

A better option is to split things up, performing one component in the morning and the other one later in the day. With this plan, the order of routines is irrelevant, since the several hours of inactivity help your body replenish its resources.

Program Protocol

Although resistance exercise is all about sets and reps, cardio training boils down to two basic factors: duration (how long you train) and intensity (how hard you train). Follow this protocol for the best results.

Exercises

Physiology dictates that no single cardiorespiratory activity can maximize your ability to burn fat. I've mentioned this before, but it bears repeating: Over time, the human body adapts to any repeated stimulus by becoming more proficient at dealing with that particular stimulus. The more often the stimulus is applied, the more proficient your body becomes at dealing with it. So it is with cardio. If you use the same form of exercise over and over, your body will adapt, which ultimately leads to diminished returns for your efforts.

With respect to cardiorespiratory exercise, variety is referred to as *cross-training.* The best way to cross-train is to alternate between two or more different activities for your workouts. As a general rule, the more variation, the better. This practice keeps your body off guard and reduces wear and tear on your joints. Changing your movement patterns spares your bones and connective tissue from continual impact, which helps prevent injuries related to overuse.

You can use virtually any activity with interval training. I've successfully employed outdoor running, jumping rope, rowing, elliptical training, and a host of other modalities with my private clients. Ideally, you should choose exercises that you enjoy. Enjoyment encourages adherence; the more you like an activity, the greater the chances are that you'll keep doing it over time. That said, keep an open mind and try out as many different activities as possible. Sometimes you learn to enjoy an exercise more with time. Remember, variety is the spice of fitness.

Duration

Time efficiency is yet another attribute that makes interval training so appealing. Forget about marathon cardio sessions where you labor away for an hour or more. These workouts last a mere 30 minutes, with high-intensity intervals of 1 minute and low-intensity intervals of 1 to 4 minutes. In fact, given the high-energy nature of the routine, exceeding the 30-minute limit can rapidly lead to overtraining, which diminishes results. The routines map out the time intervals in exact detail.

If you are strapped for time, you can break the routine into smaller chunks. Research has shown that multiple short bouts of activity are just as effective for burning fat as one longer session. You could opt for two 15-minute sessions or three 10-minute spells. You'll derive excellent results, just as long as you do it.

Better Lifting Through Cardio

Want to improve your resistance-training performance? Supplement it with cardio interval training! When you lift weights, your body uses a process called glycolysis to convert glucose into a high-energy compound called ATP (adenosine triphosphate) that fuels your performance. During this conversion process, lactic acid is produced, and it rapidly accumulates in your muscles as you train. The point at which the level of lactic acid surpasses your body's rate of metabolism is called your lactate threshold. When you reach that threshold, you experience an intense burning sensation in your muscles. Ultimately, the burn becomes so strong that you are unable to continue training. However, by increasing aerobic capacity, your cardiorespiratory system becomes more efficient at delivering oxygen to your working muscles. This helps to raise your lactate threshold and delay the buildup of lactic acid. The end result is a greater capacity to train at a high level of intensity.

Intensity

In this routine, intensity alternates between high-intensity intervals and low-intensity intervals. Each workout begins with a 3-minute warm-up, progresses to the target intervals, and then finishes with a cool-down.

During high-intensity intervals, you will train at a level that exceeds your lactate threshold—the point at which lactic acid begins to accumulate in your muscles. You'll feel a burn in your exercising muscles that makes it increasingly difficult to maintain your pace. Don't succumb. You'll soon shift to a lower-intensity interval that gives your body a chance to clear lactic acid from the blood and replenish oxygen. You'll repeat this cycle multiple times over the course of the cardio workout, burning hundreds upon hundreds of calories.

You'll monitor your intensity with a concept called a *rating of perceived exertion* (RPE). Simply stated, the RPE measures how hard you feel you are exercising. It takes into account the physical sensations you experience during exercise, including increases in heart rate and breathing rate, as well as sweating and muscle fatigue. The RPE scale ranges from 1 to 10, with 1 being the lowest and 10 the highest. Table 12.1 provides a framework for estimating your RPE; use it in conjunction with the protocol.

The talk test is a good way to measure whether you're training hard enough. The concept is simple: During high-intensity intervals, you should be sufficiently winded and unable to carry on a conversation. During low-intensity intervals, you should be able to speak easily.

TABLE 12.1

RPE Scale

RPE	Intensity
1	No exertion at all
2	Extremely light
3	Very light
4	Somewhat light
5	Light
6	Somewhat hard
7	Hard
8	Very hard
9	Extremely hard
10	Maximal exertion

Going Forward

To prevent your workout from growing stale and hitting a plateau, you should strive to change exercise variables on an ongoing basis. Here are some suggestions for sustaining progress in the ultimate home routine for fat loss. Consider implementing some or all of these concepts going forward:

- *Shorten low-intensity intervals.* I mentioned earlier that cardio is all about duration and intensity. Since too much interval work can lead to overtraining, you don't want to mess around with increasing the duration of the routine. This leaves intensity as the primary modifiable factor for sustaining results over time. As your lactate threshold increases with persistent training, aim to shorten the time you spend on low-intensity intervals. Your total workout time won't change, but you will spend more time exercising at a high intensity, resulting in more fat burned. Just be careful you don't overdo it. As always, stay in tune with your body. If you're feeling worn out, cut back on the intensity of your training.

- *Take it down a notch.* Interval training is very intense. That's what makes it so effective. But high-intensity training has a downside: Fatigue eventually sets in. Although I've programmed the intervals to minimize the potential for overtraining, you can still get run-down with consistent performance. The solution: Implement a brief transition period of long, slow distance exercise. A few weeks spent exercising at low to moderate intensity (between 6 and 7 on the RPE scale) for 30 to 40 minutes is usually sufficient to regenerate your energy levels, allowing you to come back strong and renewed.

Ultimate Home Routine for Fat Loss

Beginner Cardio Interval Routine

Minutes	RPE
3	3
4	5
1	7
3	5
1	8
2	5
1	9
2	5
1	9
3	5
1	8
4	5
1	7
3	3

Intermediate Cardio Interval Routine

Minutes	RPE
3	3
3	5
1	7
2	5
1	8
2	5
1	9
2	5
1	9
2	5
1	9
2	5
1	9
2	5
1	8
2	5
3	3

Advanced Cardio Interval Routine

Minutes	RPE
3	3
2	5
1	7
1	5
1	8
1	5
1	9
1	5
1	9
1	5
1	9
1	5
1	9
1	5
1	9
1	5
1	9
1	5
1	8
1	5
2	7
3	3

Index

Note: The italicized *f* and *t* following page numbers refer to figures and tables, respectively.

About the Author

Brad Schoenfeld, CSCS, CPT is widely regarded as one of America's leading fitness experts. He is the owner of the exclusive Personal Training Center for Women in Scarsdale, New York. Schoenfeld is a lifetime drug-free bodybuilder who has won numerous natural bodybuilding titles, including the All Natural Physique and Power Conference (ANPPC) Tri-State Naturals and USA Mixed Pairs crowns.

Schoenfeld is the author of seven fitness books, including *Sculpting Her Body Perfect, 28-Day Body Shapeover,* and the best-seller *Look Great Naked* (Prentice Hall Press, 2001). He is a columnist for *FitnessRX for Women* magazine, has been published or featured in virtually every major women's and fitness magazine (including *Cosmopolitan, Self, Marie Claire, Fitness,* and *Shape*), and has appeared on hundreds of television shows and radio programs across the United States. He also serves as the fitness expert contributor on diet.com and diet-to-go.com.

Certified as a strength and conditioning specialist by the National Strength and Conditioning Association and as a personal trainer by both the American Council on Exercise and the Aerobics and Fitness Association of America, Schoenfeld was awarded the distinction of master trainer by the International Association of Fitness Professionals. He is also a frequent lecturer on both the professional and consumer levels.

Check out Brad's Web site at www.lookgreatnaked.com.